THE
INVISIBLE CHOIR

THE
INVISIBLE
CHOIR

a true story of soul mates & angels

Tessa Lynne

Lifepath Press
Spearfish, South Dakota

The Invisible Choir: A True Story of Soul Mates & Angels / Tessa Lynne.
—1st ed.

Copyright © 2016 by Tessa Lynne

Lifepath Press, Spearfish, South Dakota

Cover image by CanStock Photos, rolffimages

ISBN-13: 978-1-945333-10-1
Library of Congress Control Number: 2017954120

Published in the United States of America

*Dedicated, with love,
to our children and grandchildren*

Contents

Part III A Search for Truth

Preface

It was September 1995. I was catching my breath. A turbulent few years had turned to relative calm—it ended when my intuitive self collided with its rational counterpart. In the year that followed, one surreal event after another left me questioning my professional judgment and my personal beliefs.

At the time, I had been a psychotherapist for ten years. My strong sense of inner truth influenced my work sessions and existed in close harmony with my analytical, logical mind—until the day I was confronted with something from outside the physical realm.

My dilemma—could I accept the truth of my encounter? Could I trust my initial, intuitive belief? My logical mind clamored for undeniable proof. Which would prevail, logic or intuition? It was to be an extended battle.

This is a story in three parts.

First, the prologue will introduce you to Sally. This is not her story, but some knowledge of hers will help you to understand my inner conflict.

Part I begins with what was revealed to me: details of the spirit world, our purpose in taking physical lives, and predictions of future events. It ends with how I learned of a long-lost destiny, Michael, and then that he was near death.

Part II is excerpts from our letters—the power and possibilities of a spiritual connection and our heart-wrenching discoveries of a lost life. You will learn if Michael recovered and if our destinies were restored.

Part III reveals more information about spiritual life and details of the extraordinary events that propelled me further on my journey to know truth.

Finally, the epilogue summarizes subsequent events, from 1996 to the present.

I was told that I was meant to share the information I was given, but I can no longer limit the telling of my story to family, friends, and interested others whose paths have crossed with mine. The events foretold twenty years ago have come to pass; we live with their repercussions. It is for this reason that I want to reach a larger audience.

My hope, for every reader, is that you will open your heart and mind and consider the story of your own life path as you reflect on my experience and the message I was given.

Tessa Lynne
September 2016

Note: To protect confidentiality, some nonessential details have been altered, a number of pseudonyms have been used, and the exact location of the setting has been kept vague.

Prologue

1990

Excerpts from Case Notes

March

Sally has come to the mental health center at the urging of a friend. She is 40 years old, married, with a son in college and a daughter in high school. She trained in laboratory science and now manages a private lab. Physically, Sally is broad-shouldered, above average in height, and overweight, but with a muscular appearance that is healthy and fit. She wears her long, auburn hair in a loose bun and often props her glasses on top of her head. Today Sally seldom makes eye contact and is agitated, her voice weak and hesitant. Among her interests are: music, she plays guitar and sings in a church choir; art, she draws caricatures at art fairs; and softball, she is an avid player. She states she has no prior history of a mental health diagnosis or treatment.

Presenting complaint for Sally is the experience of extreme anxiety for the last two months, with frequent nightmares and episodes she describes as "losing time." She says the only stressful event in her life is that her daughter has started to babysit. Sally feels a sense of terror and she fears for her daughter's safety, even though she knows and trusts the family. I ask Sally if she feels comfortable talking with me and if she wants to begin regular sessions. She replies that she would and adds, "I want to get my life back."

April

Sally is more comfortable now with the process of therapy and speaks easily and openly about her adult life, often with insight. Her general competence and abilities, her high standards at work, and her devotion to her family are apparent. She speaks warmly of her close circle of supportive friends. Her sense of humor is evident, her full face breaking easily into a smile when a subject is not threatening.

Sally reports she experienced a loss of time while writing in her journal. She returned to find an entry in childlike printing. Several more entries gave increasing hints of trauma and abuse. They refer to a man for whom Sally would frequently babysit, friends of her parents. She denies any memory of mistreatment by him, but her voice loses conviction and she shakes her head and pauses, as if listening to someone. She admits she hears a voice, which she tries to ignore, but she has been hearing it more frequently and more insistently, saying, "It did happen."

May

A few memories have become clearer to Sally; she can no longer deny they are of real events. She has been aware of what she calls "warring forces" within her. Today she found it difficult to focus and shook her head as if to clear it. Then, with a deep intake of breath, she closed her eyes for a moment. When they opened, it was not the Sally I have known. Her demeanor was one of single-minded intent, her voice stronger. "I am The Protector. I am doing everything in my power to hold back the memories. That has been my role since the earliest abuse, by the grandfather, when Sally was very young. That was when I first helped her to leave her body. It was the only way to protect her. She cannot handle the return of the memories. I will fight to keep them away; that is my function."

Sally often stayed with her grandfather and older male cousins while her parents took her grandmother out of state for medical appointments. She recalls little of that time and says her entire childhood is a blur, with few distinct memories. She several times found herself in the principal's office at school, was told she had been in a fight, but had no memory of it.

June

The Protector appeared again today. She said she is battling an entity she calls "The Destroyer." She claims it is "he" who insists that more memories surface. The Protector believes as strongly that the memories will destroy Sally. The Destroyer then came forward to say, "Sally cannot be whole if the memories are not returned—it is essential to her eventual well-being."

The Protector and The Destroyer sometimes engage in battle in their attempts to assert dominance and come forward to plead their case. It is draining for Sally, and, with the toll of anxiety and lost time, she has taken a leave of absence from work. The Destroyer remains adamant that the memories must be returned.

July

The Protector and The Destroyer have reached a truce; he has agreed to return the memories at a gradual pace. I assured them that I will help Sally to process and assimilate the memories. Now that they are in agreement, she feels rested and refreshed after they appear.

As I began this session with Sally, she lost focus and concentration and then closed her eyes. A minute later, when her eyes opened, it was not the Sally I am used to. She was timid and spoke in a soft, hesitant voice. Her name is also Sally, but she is fourteen. She said that she and several others exist in an old dilapidated house where they each inhabit a small room. Their efforts to communicate are brief and disjointed, each existing in solitary isolation. She occasionally hears the voices of others at some distance from the house.

August

The teenage Sally is gradually sharing her memories of abuse and torture. When she told the abuser she wouldn't accept requests to babysit, he named friends of hers he would ask instead. When she threatened to tell the police, he convinced her that his friends on the police force would protect him and that her parents would also believe him.

The young Sally said today that there was someone else who needed my help. She retreated, and I could hear her coaxing someone to come forward, explaining how to make the transition as if there was a special passage to traverse. A minute later, I saw the innocent face of a child. She spoke in a whisper, with a lisp, and frequently reached down to pull up her (invisible) knee socks. Her name is Molly; she is four years old. In bits and pieces, she told how her grandfather had hurt her. Molly told her mother she didn't want to go back there, but she couldn't convincingly explain why. The adult Sally pieced together her own memories of going to her grandparents' house with Molly's account; they form a cohesive, but devastating, history, and she is realizing how the early abuse led to her later vulnerability.

September

Today only The Destroyer came forward. "The Protector has withdrawn, but she intends to remain vigilant. She trusts you, with my assistance, to help Sally." When I said it no longer makes sense to refer to him by that name, he replied, "You may call me Reality. It was my task to return Sally to the reality of her everyday life after she escaped the abuse by leaving her body, what you call dissociating. I knew she needed to experience her life; she could not disengage from it. You have shown a high level of commitment and that you are capable of the task before you. It will not be an easy one. You have been tested. The memories will be returned gradually, but they *will* be returned. Sally will never be whole if they are not. That is my concern: that she becomes whole."

I consider Reality to be an Internal Self Helper, a common factor in the treatment of those with Dissociative Identity Disorder (Diagnostic & Statistical Manual, DSM IV-R). Of my many clients with histories of trauma and abuse, Sally is the only one who has met the key criterion: one or more alternate personalities assume executive control—they make decisions, and act in the world, independently of their host.

Case Summary through September, 1995

During the first year of Sally's therapy, the eight primary alter personalities came forward, urged and supported by those who had come before them. Then came their eight counterparts, who held the most negative emotions of the alters. They had split off when the abuse ended and were relegated to a primitive existence on "the other side."

Nine months into therapy, Sally was able to return to work, but the first three years were intense. The teenage personalities were tempted to experience the world and often took control, creating havoc in Sally's life. Through therapy, each gave voice to the reality of her past and learned to accept the limitations of the present. Reality took control on a few occasions to prevent serious harm coming to Sally, but he said he could not intervene every time an alter took over. When I suggested that a change in their internal environment would be therapeutic, he somehow provided building materials for them to replace the dilapidated old house. In their internal, psychic world the alters constructed and furnished a beautiful home. In the process, they began to interact with each other, establish individual roles, and become a functional family.

Now, after five years of therapy, the eight primary alters are ready to integrate with their counterparts. The five older ones appear to each other to have aged to their early thirties. Most of our work now revolves around how the alters will be a part of Sally's current life and on her acceptance of them as essential to her identity and her wholeness.

Early in her therapy, Sally said, "I feel like a shattered vase. Pieces of myself are scattered all over the floor. I don't see how they can ever be put back together." Recently, she said, "The pieces of the vase have been gathered up and are roughly in place. I think they need only a few, small adjustments before they mesh as one."

PART 1

A Spiritual Journey
1995

1. Outside the Realm

SALLY HAS JUST LEFT. I need to make a record of this encounter with Reality, but it does not belong in a case note; it is outside the realm of my therapeutic work. In fact, it is far removed from any part of the physical realm—it is a journey to the realm of spirit.

How can I explain this encounter to others? How can I even explain it to myself? I need to first put it in context.

Reality has always presented as both more and less than the alter personalities: less, in that he has no personal history and does not interact as one of them; more, in that he has demonstrated powers they do not have and he is wiser. In their internal world, he is perceived as a father-like figure who appears among them only when he is needed.

Sally has been aware, since childhood, of a source that brings her peace and comfort. More recently she has been aware of Reality's soothing presence to the alters. She has come to realize that it is the same force; he has always been close to her. "I am surrounded by a strong, calming energy field. I can't explain it, but Reality can be present to the others, somewhere inside of my mind, and I can also experience him as a spiritual presence."

After the first crisis-filled year of Sally's therapy, Reality has sometimes been unavailable. He has talked vaguely of a need to be elsewhere, has said he must replenish his energy, and has referred to a superior entity that guides him. In recent weeks, he has implied that he is more than the role he has assumed with Sally. I wish now that I had made notes of his brief, elliptical comments that hinted of knowledge beyond her conscious, or even her unconscious, mind. He has turned our brief exchanges away from Sally's needs; his usual terse manner of speaking has changed to one that is more conversational.

Reality is in no hurry to leave today. I start to say my usual goodbye, but he interrupts me, looks at me intently.

"Tessa, Sally can spare a few minutes. I wish to speak with you."

There is a subtle change in his tone, but his appearance is much the same as usual. It is still Sally, in a typical outfit of neat slacks and blazer, but when he inhabits her body it is with less animation and facial expression, and the voice is slightly deeper, with little inflection. Sally wears her long hair pulled back and never wears makeup, so the differences suggest a gender-neutral mien. The one change Reality always makes is to take off her glasses; he says he doesn't need them.

Here, in my private practice office, we remain in the same comfortable chairs Sally and I always take, sharing a corner table. The large window lets in filtered light and a glimpse of the Missouri river through half-closed blinds. A fig tree and two philodendrons bring a touch of green indoors; an area rug adds rich but muted colors. The pictures on the walls depict scenes from nature, except for one, a portrait of three Native American elder women—weathered, dignified, filled with spirit—their long black hair flowing in the wind.

I wait for Reality to continue.

"Have my recent comments led you to question my role in Sally's life?"

When I answer that they have, he does not keep me in suspense.

"I am Sally's spiritual guardian. It has been necessary for me to play a much larger role in her life than what is common for guardians. As you know, my efforts on her behalf are now less in demand, leaving me free to pursue other objectives related to my purpose in the spirit world."

I have raised an internal eyebrow in skepticism but my interest is stronger, as is a sense of the truth of what Reality is telling me. I suspend any disbelief and ask him if a guardian is the same as a guardian angel.

"Guardian angel is not a term used in the spirit world, and it is not an accurate one. A spirit does not take the role of guardian from the angel realm."

My tendency to be flippant comes into play, and Reality confirms my light-hearted assumption that he does not have wings, even shows a glimmer of a smile, and then I hear a more serious tone.

"Angels carry messages from one spirit to another and to spiritual human beings with the ability to receive such messages. They also watch over situations on behalf of the Creator. Most angels are in that realm as a learning experience and will eventually return to the realm of spirits who take physical lives. Archangels remain in a permanent position of nurturing and teaching; it is the manner in which they have chosen to serve the Creator."

I listen, still trying to take in the idea that Reality is a spirit.

"It is to the spirit world that I sometimes return—to replenish my strength and to seek the guidance of my superior. Permission was recently granted for me to reveal my identity to you. This was after close scrutiny of you in the years you have worked with Sally, and even before then. The final decision was not mine; it was made by those I answer to."

Reality cuts off my next question and tells me that Sally's schedule requires him to leave.

"I hope we can soon have a longer conversation. I will be alert for opportunities. Sally is to know of my identity, and all that I tell you, but not until she has made further progress toward full integration."

In the moment it takes Sally to return, I consider the ethics of speaking to an entity who is not my client, but it would be useless to search the guidelines; they contain no reference to speaking to a client's guardian. I would not have entertained the possibility early in her treatment. Now I need to give it further thought.

Sally is my last client of the day. As soon as the door closes behind her, I look for a notebook to record this encounter. So far, it is a matter-of-fact account, a reflection of my twenty years of experience writing reports and assessments. I start with known facts and observations and then add my professional analysis and conclusions, keeping my personal opinions and feelings at a far remove. I cannot do that with this development.

I would write of this encounter in my journal if I kept one current. Every few years I am hit with an urge to start one, and I carefully select the perfect notebook and pen. I compare cover designs—which one says me at that point in time? I touch the paper to find just the right feel, the subtle texture I like. Is the weight of the pen balanced, does it fit the contours of my hand? Does the ink glide on smoothly? And then the few sporadic entries I make in each one take less time than the selection process. I often recommend to clients that they journal, but it is not how I process my own life.

If I continue this conversation with Reality, I will want to record it, but not as case notes, and it does not precisely fit in a personal journal. It will require a recording of facts and a certain distance, my usual writing style, with the addition of personal reflections and opinions. I will use this ordinary spiral notebook, bought two for a dollar when my daughters were in junior high.

Rational vs. Intuitive

I stop at home for a quick bite to eat and to trade my dress for a tank top and shorts, all I need on this first day of September. Charkey comes running and meows for his supper and a little attention. I remember to turn on the sprinklers in the back yard, then drive a mile out of town and over the causeway to the island.

I have kept at bay my reaction to this encounter with a new reality (the pun is noticed, if not intended). I do not want to err on either side of this—by dismissing Reality's claims outright or by blind acceptance of them. This is the place for me to consider them, but not quite yet.

I walk here on the island several times a week, making it a more intentional act when I need to reflect deeply or to center myself in meditation within the solitude and sustenance of nature. It is where I review my therapeutic work and my role as a single parent, where I release the tensions of the day or week. Less frequently, I give vent here to feelings of anger and frustration, a clearing of negative emotions as I walk. Always, I am replenished by the simple act of connecting with the earth. A fast walk over gently sloping natural trails puts me in touch with my body; a slower, meditative, walk connects me to myself.

This is where I reflect on and process the passages of my life. It is where I grieved for my father twelve years ago and where, a year before that, I made the anguished decision to divorce. More recently, it is here that I faced frustration and loss when my ability to walk for hours was reduced to five minutes or less. Now, three years later, I can manage an hour on my best days.

This ground has known my tears; the trees have absorbed my pain. I have picked up sizable rocks, transferred to them the weight of the past, and heaved them into the river—letting go. I have felt here the sheer joy of being alive and have merged with the sights, sounds, and textures of the natural world: a newborn fawn curled in a nest of grass; skunks scratching in the dirt for insects; minks playing tag among the ruins of an old stone cabin. I lean against the largest trees and feel their energy; the wind carries my prayers. This is my living journal: an organic, visceral process of reflection and renewal. I need no pen or paper—it is written directly on my soul.

Now, alternating fast and slow walking for thirty minutes, I make my way to the shelter on the bank of the river. The open, wooden structure, set among tall pines and cottonwoods, is a natural fit. I sit in a lotus position and admire the dusty-blue seed clusters of a dark green juniper, appreciate their contrast with the narrow, silver-green leaves of a nearby Russian olive tree. I listen to a squirrel's angry chatter at my intrusion. While he makes his peace with me, I look out at the gently flowing water and up to the bluffs rising opposite. I settle into myself, take some deep, calming breaths, and consider the question I have come here seeking to answer.

I am aware first of an inner energy rising up within me in confirmation: some part of me knows Reality's truth. I rest in that for a minute, until my rational mind asserts itself and asks if I am not being too quick—it is a familiar pattern.

When my more spiritual, intuitive self conflicts with my more practical, rational side, I have learned to seek inner guidance. More accurately, I have learned that it would be wise for me to do so, but I do not consistently follow the path of wisdom. Like a whining child, my rational mind has learned that persistence often prevails. It is louder and more insistent, convinced of its superiority and its ability to wear me down with repetition.

In contrast, when I work with clients on an intuitive level my rational self is blocked to some extent. At the close of a session, I often find myself incapable of writing a client's name on a form, even one I have known for years. I need to pause, and I can almost feel the neural pathways of my brain shifting to the areas that deal more easily with memory and writing. Now I want input from both intuition and logic.

I will need to remain somewhat detached, as I do with my clients. It may prevent me from entering fully into this experience, but it will keep me grounded in my professional role and I can use my analytical skills to assess the credibility of what I have been told. Some part of me wants to cast aside rational thought and simply believe; my training and experience urge me to be more cautious.

Seeking inner resources and spiritual direction, I sit in meditation.

I let my mind be clear and place my attention on my breath. After a time, I say a prayer for guidance and wisdom and then sit in reflection. I stay alert to messages from spirit while my rational mind, which never needs to be asked, frequently interrupts. Almost an hour goes by before I reach a tentative conclusion: Reality is who and what he says he is.

I base my belief, in part, on the history of our relationship and the role he has played in Sally's life and throughout her healing journey. He has always represented truth, and he has supported Sally's growth and independence. He has said there are strict limits on the degree to which he can interfere, and he has done so only a few times.

I cannot ignore the possibility that Reality is a part of Sally, that he is manipulating me, has a hidden agenda. I counter it with the fact that he has maintained complete consistency over the years— internally, as to who he is, and externally, in his interactions with me. Part of my work with the alters has been to help each develop a sense of self-worth and to recognize her gifts. Reality supports me in that effort but maintains his distance and a low profile, allowing the alters to grow through the choices they make and through their relationships—with me, and with each other in their inner world. The totality of my experience of him fits better with his being Sally's guardian than with his being a part of her.

I consider Sally's experience of Reality as a presence, one she feels as external to both her mind and her body. I have been aware of at least one similar presence, throughout my life, that I have come to realize is of a spiritual nature. I believe that each of us has a spirit and a guardian. It is an intuitive belief but, once accepted, logic would dictate that a guardian must play a more prominent role in the life of someone with Sally's history.

As I lean toward acceptance, my rational mind interjects: what if you are wrong? It is a fair question: if Reality is not who he claims to be, it would be detrimental to Sally for me to listen to him. It would also be a strong blow to my sense of professional integrity and to my trust in my own judgment. How far could I go down a false path before it would become self-perpetuating and leave me mired in the mud of my misconceptions? I turn the question around: what if I were to discount what Reality said, but he spoke the truth? It is not something I can accept on an outside chance it might be so, but do I need to have absolute proof?

There are no reference books for me to consult, nothing with which I can compare this experience. I must trust my instincts and intuition as much as the logic I apply here. All that exists in me, outside of rational thought, believes; my logical self demands evidence. My belief outweighs any skepticism, and I can make it a working assumption that Reality is who and what he says. My logical argument carries weight, but my belief is more a matter of trusting in my ability to know truth. Reality's words come back to me. "I have been authorized to reveal certain information to you, but I cannot tell you all that I know of the spirit world." Though tentative, my acceptance of Reality's truth is strong enough that I am eager to hear more.

Should I tell anyone? He said it is at my discretion to disclose as I see fit. My daughters have expressed an interest in spirituality and the supernatural, but I will wait and see how things develop before telling them. What about friends and colleagues? This community is small enough that I cannot afford to be known as a therapist outside of the mainstream. I know some, perhaps most, would question my conclusions. Could I convince them that my belief is based, not on what I was told, but on my inner, confirming experience of it?

It is not until I am walking back that I think to ask: why me? I am in close proximity to Reality on a regular basis, but that cannot be the only reason, which begs the question: why reveal himself at all? Have others been approached in this way? It is nearly dark, a few stars are visible as I make my way back to the trailhead. I have found the answer I came for. I leave full of questions.

2. The World of Spirit

I HAVE AN OUTDOOR SESSION WITH Sally. We cross the street and walk along the river path, then stop at a picnic table that gives us some privacy. Near the end of the hour, Reality appears and says he wants to meet with me in a natural setting. He adds that Sally has no other plans for this time and then he reminds me of his references to his superior in the spirit world. His next words take me by surprise.

"Eli wishes to speak to you. He desires direct contact to confirm that a wise choice has been made."

Reality walks the short distance to the river's edge and stands with his back to me as he faces the water. He seems to intensify his connection with the earth as he slowly raises his arms over his head and then lowers them. I observe a slight stiffening of the body and then a brief, mild tremor before he turns around.

It is Eli who walks slowly over and sits down across from me. I notice that he inhabits the physical body more fluidly and that his demeanor is softer; he carries with him a strong presence and emanates an aura of kindness and acceptance. Throughout our brief conversation, Eli's voice is resonant, his eyes gently expressive. He speaks with quiet authority, his attention taking in the totality of my being. I am honored by his parting words.

"Zachary has chosen well."

Eli's presence is such that it is a confirmation in itself. All of who

I am that has known the depths of despair, the heights of joy, has experienced the pain of another, has known love and laughter—from deep within my being, his truth is revealed.

Zachary returns seconds later, and I wait for him to speak.

"Eli is a strong spirit. Throughout his many lifetimes, his faith never wavered in his belief in, and service to, the Creator. He advanced steadily to a high Master level and now gives direction and guidance to a large group of spirits."

I am not surprised at the change of name. When Zachary said, years ago, to call him Reality, he defined himself in terms of his function in Sally's life. Now he explains that Eli's assessment had more to do with what he could sense and observe about me than with what I said. I think of how the reverse is often true among us in the physical world. We grow attached to our thoughts and opinions and believe they are what define us, at the expense of learning to trust our senses and our intuition.

The World of Spirit

Zachary proceeds to tell me more about the spirit world. Influenced by the change of scene and the significance of Eli's appearance, I want to know everything. I press him for specifics until he establishes parameters.

"Child, it is in your nature to want to know, and you do insist on details, which can sometimes get in the way of what simply is. It is beyond the scope of my current mission to fully describe the spirit world or even begin to do it justice. It is a place of acceptance and love, and it is a place of rules and consequences. It is vast, intricate, and purposeful—it is eternal."

His voice is gentle, but I feel a bit chastened and wait for him to continue.

"It is my mission, at this critical time, to seek those in a position to reach out to others. My purpose is to share vital information. These approaches are being made to many, in every corner of the earth. Each of you will find your own way to tell the story. My approach to you is in line with your intended lessons for this lifetime. It is also a result of you having opened your mind and your heart to the world of spirit. You have been tested, faced with challenges, and we are pleased with how you have responded."

We sit in silence for a moment as twilight descends. It may be that singular quality of the atmosphere that prompts Zachary to further describe the spirit world. His usual sedate manner conveys a timeless endeavor. I am left with sensory impressions: a great expanse, subtle movements and gentle currents, diffused light and muted colors. It is not so much a place as it is an ambiance—a deep resonance within which purpose is contained. Overlaying it all is a pure white light that illuminates everything and infuses it with love.

I am aware of images as much as I am of the words he uses. Perhaps the images come from my spirit or from Eli's lingering presence; they surround me, inhabit me. I am aware of a subtle quality to Zachary's tone. It is that of a distant traveler, speaking with longing of the place where he is grounded in connection and love—his mission takes him far from home.

The Creator

A longer silence … I notice our time is almost up, but I am determined to make use of every minute, and I ask Zachary about some popular conceptions of the spirit world.

"The spirit world is not a formless void in which all spirits merge as energy, and it is not a state of perpetual bliss. It provides opportunities for, and it nurtures the continued growth and education of, every individual spirit. It is the goal of each spirit to grow to be more like the Creator through the opportunities He has provided in the creation of this, and other, physical universes."

I note his use of a masculine pronoun and ask if the Creator is male.

"Within the Creator is encompassed all; sometimes His appearance is that of a male; other times, it is that of a female. It was necessary, for the purpose of procreation, that there be two genders, but it was never the intention that one be elevated over the other."

I ask if Creator is the preferred or correct name.

"It is the closest equivalent, in the English language, to the spiritual concept. I could just as easily say God and will use that designation if you prefer."

I tell him that Creator resonates with me, as does Great Spirit, in a way that childhood Sunday school images of either a wise or judgmental old man, sitting on a throne, did not. Reminded of childhood images, others come back to me. I questioned everything from harp-playing angels sitting on clouds, to streets paved with gold, to a fiery hell—the one I ask Zachary about.

"As it has generally been depicted, hell does not exist. There is what is called the wandering plane, distant from the Creator, where a spirit spends time for certain choices made, appropriate to the amount of reflection that is required. Indeed, there are consequences to human behavior, but the intent is to assist in learning, not to punish. There is always a path back to the presence of the Creator."

We are out of time. I am aware of feeling a greater sense of awe than after my last meeting with Zachary, when it was difficult to view him as other than an earthbound entity called Reality. Eli's presence tonight was such that it transcended human qualities, the physical body immaterial to his identity—he made use of it as a formality, not from necessity.

3. Creation

WE ARE BACK IN OUR usual office setting. At the end of an hour with Sally, Zachary appears and says we can take one more. I always set aside two hours, but we seldom need the second one now. (I will not bill for this time that does not directly involve her.)

Zachary tells me that he wants to start at the beginning, with the creation of this physical world.

"The Creator set in motion the forces that resulted in this world, and He touches every living thing—but creation is not without its flaws. This planet took eons to develop to the point where several human-like species emerged with the necessary potential. Of them, Homo sapiens was the most suited, but it was a long time before they were fully capable of supporting spiritual life. That was only possible after the Creator intervened and made several adjustments in their development."

I ask him why our species took so long to develop.

"The family unit, with the relationships it supports, was slow to evolve, and this world was a harsh one. The time and energy of its inhabitants were devoted strictly to survival needs, and their life spans were short."

What is required for a spirit to make constructive use of a life?

"Eventually, Homo sapiens came to be capable of advanced cognition, the ability to reason, and complex communication skills—the qualities necessary to the freedom of thought and action that spirits require. That was when more advanced spirits first took lifetimes on this planet, inhabiting the physical lives of the entire species at approximately the same time."

In my view, the creation story of the Old Testament (and those of other belief systems) has meaning, but I do not take it literally. It makes sense to me that an entire species, capable of functioning as individuals and in groups, was the beginning of spiritual life on earth. I want to know how long ago it was.

"Given the age of this planet, it is a relatively recent event, almost 9,000 years ago."

I am surprised that it was so recently, then recollect my knowledge of history and share my assumption with Zachary.

"You assume correctly. The presence of the intelligence and skills needed to support a full spiritual life would also predict a population on the verge of developing a written language."

I recall Carl Sagan's chart compressing our planet's history to a twenty-four hour timeline, with humans arriving less than two minutes before midnight. Our spiritual history would have us arriving in the last few seconds. I ask Zachary how the Creator assisted in the evolution of our species.

"One intervention was to aid in the development of the larynx to make speech possible; the ability to communicate is essential for spiritual learning. (Strictly speaking, speech is not a requirement; some worlds have what you call extra-sensory perception.) The other major adjustments were to assist in the complex development of the higher functions of the human brain."

My next question is about the process and necessity of evolution. Couldn't the Creator have simply brought this world into being?

"The Creator could have fashioned a world ready made, but He was aware that a perfectly created world would have led to weaknesses over time. He deemed it necessary—to the inter-relatedness, both of and within ecosystems—that it evolve naturally. This built support for their interdependence on each other and also for their individual strengths."

I have more questions, but Zachary wants to move on.

"Sally will not always be this available. Her husband has had to work evenings lately, leaving her with time to fill, but he will soon return to his regular schedule. It is important that any disruptions to her life be kept to a minimum. Let us proceed."

Multiple Lifetimes

Zachary states his understanding that I believe in multiple lifetimes. I nod in agreement as he emphasizes his first point.

"It is not the individual person who reincarnates; it is the spirit who attaches to a succession of human lives. As each lifetime is completed, the spirit integrates significant experience into their spiritual identity."

I ask if, when spirits choose a lifetime, it is with the knowledge of others who will share it with them.

"Spirits are aware of who the parents will be and of any prior spiritual connection with them. They sometimes are aware of siblings and other key figures expected to be present in that lifetime."

If it is the spirit who reincarnates, what explains those who claim to remember a previous life?

"A spirit will retain relevant details from several past lives, those most pertinent to their current lifetime. It is possible for a mortal to have glimpses of those past lives, and it is natural that they would want to claim them as their own."

Do humans return as animals? (I have never thought it plausible.)

"Animals do not have the necessary cognitive and language abilities, and they are largely incapable of making free choices. Their spirits are simply animating spirits, with the purpose of protecting and propagating each species. Their kingdom is vastly different from the one designed for human spirits, and it is completely separate."

What of those who have had near-death experiences and report seeing loved ones, including animals?

"In the initial plane of transition, an animal spirit may be present briefly if there had been a close bond. It will assume the same appearance it had in life."

Purpose

I pick up on Zachary's mention of spiritual purpose and ask what more he can tell me about it.

"The spirit world has been structured to provide opportunities for growth, so that all spirits might approach that which exists within the Creator—an immense, benevolent power that emanates only outward, that diminishes no one. The Creator welcomes all who approach the same status. As the Creator also continues to evolve, there are few who come close and none who are, or who will ever be, equal."

Is there a clear, well-defined path that all spirits follow?

"It is essential that the individual spirit be free to choose whether to follow the path of opportunity. This path diverges into many as each spirit designs and follows their own agenda."

So each spirit goes their own way?

"The Creator is generous. Assistance is offered at every turn to help guide a spirit, but, ultimately, they make their own choices. A spirit must contend with its own unique personality and with those of the spirits to whom it is accountable. In this regard, it is similar to individual goals and relationships as they exist in the physical world."

Do spiritual goals change over time?

"The purpose of spirits who attain a certain status is to assist other spirits and to contribute to an environment that sustains and perpetuates the growth of *all* spirits. It is necessary to maintain an awareness of one's own status and purpose while focusing always on the greater design, purpose, and being of the Creator."

Whose Life is it?

Listening to Zachary, I begin to question: is it my life or my spirit's life?

"It is both—more so yours throughout your lifetime and more that of your spirit after it. Primarily, it is the spirit that serves the human rather than the human that serves the spirit, which hesitates to impose its will too much."

Does my spirit know the direction my life will take?

"Your spirit is aware of the lessons to be learned but is not aware of the specific situations that will bring them about. For instance, a spirit will not know if what seems to be a bad choice might lead to an intended lesson, as is often the case."

I question if this contradicts what is taught about following a straight and narrow path.

"Your spirit knows that you must learn from the consequences of your decisions. Like a good parent, your spirit will be there to help you process the results of your actions and, usually, to provide guidance before you act. You will aid that process if you spend time in reflection and in making considered choices."

I am still not clear on the extent to which a spirit will join with the desires of a human life versus us responding to theirs.

"There is a balance that will meet both of your needs, conditions that nourish your spirit and conditions that nourish you as a human entity. Most of these will be the same or will grow to be so."

What role does a spirit play when we humans are behaving badly?

"What I have just said applies mainly to constructive pursuits. A young spirit, or one slow to make progress, may become caught up in destructive behaviors or unable to dissuade a mortal from them. Their intent on taking that life would have been to deal effectively with the challenges presented, learn from them, and then return to a path of growth , but, as is the case with humans, a spirit's best intentions are not always realized."

If a spirit's intent is always positive, how do you explain some of the worst examples of human behavior?

"A long-term, viciously destructive life would not be part of an intended lesson, or of a destiny, but it is not uncommon for a spirit to lose control of the direction a life is taking. I expect you are aware of some notorious examples. A spirit will continue to make attempts to direct a wayward life and will be alert for opportunities to resume their guidance."

My confusion must be evident; Zachary enlightens me.

"Some intended lessons might lead to years of following a destructive path, seeking to learn the lessons thoroughly, but the spirit's intent would be to return to a more positive life path. One example would be to follow, and then turn away from, the path of addiction; however, an intended lesson would not involve the taking of a life or other egregious acts."

Our time is up and Sally returns. I once asked her what she experiences while Zachary is talking to me. She replied that she is in a place of rest and calming energy that she welcomes as a respite; her appearance reflects a rejuvenating experience.

As I drive across town to a meeting of mental health professionals, I think of how my spirit knew who my parents would be and where they lived. Can I make any assumptions about why she chose this life over others? Have I had past lives with either of my parents? Did my spirit seek my somewhat isolated childhood in the country? Is it she who was first drawn to nature? Did she know the type of person I would be, or was it her influence that forged me? My first impulse is to give her credit for my better qualities and blame myself for my lesser ones. What I've learned about the interplay between mortal and spirit suggests I am, perhaps, being too hard on myself.

I feel that I have a more complete answer in what Zachary said about the purpose of the spirit world. (I see an image of millions of spirits who have achieved Eli's strong presence, the immensity of their combined power and influence.) Of the various descriptions I have heard, Zachary's, brief as it was, leaves me the most satisfied: within the benevolent presence of the Creator, there exist opportunities, growth, and purpose.

4. Lessons

IN TODAY'S SESSION WITH SALLY, I work with her and two of the alters. For her to move closer to integration, they need to come close enough to observe her life, but she doesn't yet trust them to not take control. When Zachary comes, he tells me he will encourage her in that direction, and then he briskly says we must take advantage of the available time.

"The essential purpose of a spirit taking a physical lifetime is for the lessons it offers. There are many of them, presented at various degrees of difficulty over a number of lifetimes. Each repetition leads to an increase in understanding through a greater depth of experience."

Zachary explains that many lessons are learned in incremental steps. For instance, a lesson first presented in a lifetime that is relatively uncomplicated will later be presented in a more difficult context. Or, the circumstances may escalate, e.g., a younger spirit will learn to forgive minor offenses, an older one what we would consider an unforgivable act.

I ask if every lesson requires multiple exposures.

"Many do not, but you should never underestimate the value of a lesson, even one to be gleaned from an event that appears to be insignificant."

I do not expect Zachary to provide me with a complete list of lessons in order of importance, and he does not.

"There is no order, as such; it is a series of opportunities to acquire knowledge. A spirit is guided to build and expand on the lessons of previous lifetimes, but they are free to ignore what has been recommended."

I share what I think could be lessons, and Zachary adds a few to my list.

Lessons — A Partial List
Love, in its many forms
Awareness of one's spirit
Self-awareness
Self-discipline
Self-integrity
Faith in one's convictions
Honesty
Generosity
Humility
Faith and Trust
Respect for all humans
Appropriate use of power
Forgiveness
Knowledge of human societies
The psychology of the individual
Awareness of the Creator
The laws of physics and other scientific knowledge
Awareness of the inter-relatedness of all races
Awareness of the inter-relatedness of ecological systems

"What you have here is enough to give a general idea. Lessons are often intricate and they overlap, with layers of meaning from accumulated lifetimes. An extensive review is required, at the end of each lifetime, to grasp their full impact."

Some people attribute life's hardest lessons to our past actions, either in this lifetime or in a previous one. I ask Zachary if that is the case.

"Do not assume that any one challenge is due to your actions in a previous life—most often they are not—and they are rarely based on actions from your current lifetime. And, do not think that lessons are always presented in a negative fashion; the circumstances may as often be positive, or neutral. There is one common factor: lessons require that you make choices."

What about those situations not under our control? Do we not learn from them as well?

"You are correct. Much can be learned from situations that are not of your choosing; however, you do have some choice in how you respond to them."

I ask if he can give me an example of a lesson that would be common to most lives.

"In almost every lifetime, there are debts to be paid from a previous lifetime. You have harmed others, to some degree and in some fashion, and you must make amends in this lifetime. Humans have a tendency to become mired in the past as they seek a reason for the bad things that happen, and they tend to view them as punishment. They would be better served to put their focus on their present life and on how they might increase their understanding and acceptance of others—and then choose to act accordingly."

Zachary has paused, but not as if he is finished. I wait for him to continue.

"Keep in mind: most of the events in your life are either chance occurrences or arise out of choices you have made that are not related to your intended lessons."

I've never accepted the common saying that "everything happens for a reason." If interpreted to mean that all was meant to happen, it leaves little room for free choice. Zachary has confirmed my viewpoint. (Cause and effect are a different matter.)

I ask if it is helpful to uncover past-life experiences.

"It is not necessary, and it may even be detrimental, as few practitioners are capable of eliciting accurate accounts. There is a strong tendency for the human mind to find what it expects to find. Rest assured: if a past life issue needs to be addressed, it will be presented to you in some manner. Upon your return to the spirit world, you will know of any connection to a past lifetime. That will be soon enough."

Are we likely to have some sense of those past-life issues?

"You have, located within your subconscious, the elements of certain events from past lives that may contribute to your reaction when you confront a similar situation in this lifetime. It is not necessary that you know the details."

I have long thought there is too much to learn for any one lifetime to be adequate to the task. As Zachary has been talking about lessons, I have flashed on scenes from the movie *Groundhog Day*. It is accurate in concept, if not in particulars. We do not go through multiple repetitions of one day, as in the plot of the movie, but if some lessons are not learned a spirit will be guided to choose a next lifetime that offers opportunities for them.

Zachary next tells me that sometimes a spirit will step back, relinquish their efforts, and observe how we manage on our own. I am puzzled and ask if this doesn't conflict with the idea of us following our spirit's guidance.

"It is a mixture. Sometimes the balance shifts one way and sometimes the other. Your spirit is here to guide you but also to learn from observing the course of your life and from you as an individual. Giving you free rein is an opportunity for both of you to learn."

An image comes to me of two paths intertwining, but not without some tension. I see those lives most in tune with spirit as two paths almost indistinguishable, so closely are they aligned. I see the least harmonic relationships as two paths that meet only occasionally, out of alignment but irrevocably linked. I see my own path as one that is generally aligned with that of my spirit, mostly in harmony, often overlapping.

Zachary begins to change the subject, but I interrupt to ask if he can tell me what lessons my spirit was to have learned in this lifetime. I wait while he pauses, eyes closed, and seems to search a file of some sort.

"I can tell you of two. First, it was known that you would face chronic health issues. The second is associated with your career. You have had past lifetimes of doing similar work among the more privileged classes. In this one, you were to choose to work with the less fortunate, as you have mostly done. I can also inform you that you have learned all of the lessons intended to this point in your life. If you had not, you would not have been approached, which requires a certain status. That is my next topic."

I excuse myself to get a glass of water, and I ask Zachary if I can bring one for him.

"Yes. The body requires fluid."

I walk out of the room, flexing my fingers, cramped from note taking. In a few minutes we are ready to continue.

Status

Putting aside curiosity about my own status, I listen to Zachary.

"A spirit gains in status primarily through the successful learning of lessons. Upon physical death, and return to the spirit world, the intended lessons are compared to what was learned. Upon completion of the full review, any increase in status is awarded."

What happens if an intended lesson does not present itself?

"Attempts are made to substitute others; the Creator does not intend for any lifetime to be wasted. In recent decades, though, many spirits have returned disappointed. The pace of modern life, and its emphasis on the material, has made it difficult for them to accomplish their planned lessons. With so many options for superficial success and enjoyment, they can easily lose sight of their spiritual journey."

What distinguishes one status from another?

"There are seven levels of status before the Master level. Those at the first two levels are considered junior spirits; five more levels reflect increases in knowledge and ability. Each level requires proficiency in a number of competencies."

Do all spirits make progress at the same rate?

"No. Most spirits do not proceed on a steady climb up the ladder; status can be lost as well as gained. It is usually not a great amount, but it is possible to lose all status and have to start over. Failure to learn a planned lesson does not, in itself, lead to a loss of status."

As Zachary talks, I mentally compare the gaining of status in the spirit world to how we are promoted in school, the next level not reached without passing grades. The standards in the spirit world are high, at times requiring the equivalent of going back to first grade; it is not a pass/fail course.

It occurs to me that I tend to think of spirits as being fairly uniform in their nature and abilities. I ask why learning is more difficult for some.

"It varies. A spirit might be less than diligent in their guidance of a human life due to their inexperience, to not paying attention, or to a lack of skill. One spirit might fail to make a wise choice in selecting a lifetime, another may not be strongly motivated to achieve a higher status, and yet another may not realize how or when to exert influence."

Zachary pauses, then tells me there is just enough time left to explain what he had meant, five years ago, when he said it was essential that Sally's memories be returned to her.

"If Sally were to complete her life without integration, her spirit would lose all status; the fragmentation of her mind would prevent any of the necessary learning. Because her spirit is of quite high status, it would be a great loss to the spirit world if she were to have to start over. As her guardian, I knew it was imperative that she seek help and achieve integration."

Our time is up.

I have an hour before an evening client is due. I visit with a colleague as she is leaving for the day and wonder if I should confide in her. What would she think if I told her I was just talking to a spirit? Could she understand? Could I convey to her the basis of my belief? This is not the time.

I cross the street to the river, walk a short distance to a bench, and consider Zachary's last comment. I have wondered why, years ago, he used the word "essential" when he said Sally's memories had to be returned. It was a clue to his identity, and I did pick up on it. I asked myself how, if he was a part of her, he could make such a strong statement, with all the authority of an expert consultant. I did not take that thought to its logical conclusion—he is not a part of her.

I am not surprised that my health issues were a known lesson. They have been an immense challenge, one I first failed as I wallowed in self-pity, envied active friends, compensated with food and gained fifty pounds. I flash back three years: I get up from a week in bed with the flu and find that my life has changed. Walking is as easy as moving through quicksand; my body pushes against an unrelenting force. My right leg drags, I frequently fall down, and I can't hold a ten-pound baby. I don't have the muscle control to skip a small stone across the water. My dreams are filled with detailed scenes of my daughters in danger. I struggle to reach them but I can't move. My doctors have no answers.

By the end of the first year, I could often walk for twenty minutes.

I took control of my own recovery: cut out processed foods, lifted weights when able, lost thirty pounds and then ten more. I returned to meditation, abandoned when I had needed it most, and added healing practices. My progress has been uneven—for every few steps forward, I take one back—but I no longer let myself be defeated by a bad day. I have learned, each to some extent, lessons in acceptance, determination, perseverance, and hope. To reflect on it now calls back feelings of helplessness and despair. I need to shake them off.

I have time for a brisk walk along the river, ten minutes one way, enough to clear my head and to feel my strength. I slow down on the walk back, crouch at the water's edge, and search out a small, flat stone. I hold it firmly horizontal between my thumb and middle finger. Then, in a precise move perfected as a child, I swing my arm back just above the surface and, with intention and purpose, release the stone. It skips … then once more … and then a third and final skip before gently sinking beneath the still water. I am ready for my client.

Masters

9/14

I see Sally in the waiting room and wonder if, when Zachary comes, he will appear to be in drag. Sally has plans for a night out with friends and is dressed in a flowing pants and tunic outfit, wearing heels. She has makeup on—eyeshadow, mascara, deep red lipstick—and contact lenses. Her long, auburn hair falls in gentle waves to her shoulders. This is the first I have seen her dressed to go out. When I compliment her, she says, "I feel like my old self again. I am ready to reclaim my life."

By the time Zachary appears, I have grown used to Sally's look, and it is only slightly disconcerting as he returns to the subject of status. I have come to recognize a deliberate pattern: he gives me a minimum of information and then expects me to question him.

"The number of lifetimes needed to reach the status of Master is not a set amount."

I ask him for examples of how and why it might vary.

"Some spirits are quicker to learn, just as some people are, and some are more ambitious and focused on a quick rise in status. Some spirits feel at home in the physical world, return often, and thrive here; others are reluctant to return and do so less frequently."

What is required to achieve the Master level?

"It is attained when a spirit has learned all of the lessons of this world. At that point, they are no longer required to return to a physical lifetime."

Thoughts of my own status and lifetimes intrude. I can't ignore them. I ask Zachary if he can tell me how many lifetimes my spirit has completed. He doesn't answer me immediately but pauses, his eyes closed.

"The total is eighty-seven, including this one."

I don't know what to make of that number and ask him what more he can tell me.

"Your spirit is close to the end of her physical lifetimes. The exact number will depend on the outcomes of those yet to come."

I put my personal thoughts aside. Zachary said a Master is not required to take another physical life, but I assume it is possible.

"Yes, they do return. At any one time, there will be many Masters among you. They take a physical lifetime for a specific purpose: to impart wisdom to a group, to provide guidance at a turning point in history, or to bring a message from the Creator. Many well-known figures, throughout the course of your world history, have been returning Masters."

I have to ask Zachary to name names: who would I recognize as a returning Master?

"First, I must mention the next level, that of Sages, the highest level of status. Masters and Sages you would recognize include the great religious teachers Jesus, Mohammed, and Buddha; great philosophers, including Confucius and several from early Greece; artists, including Michelangelo; great scientific thinkers, including Einstein; and many others from all walks of life."

It comes as no surprise to me that our greatest spiritual teachers have been Masters or Sages. I think of the Renaissance, that rebirth following the Dark Ages, and assume that a number of Masters, besides Michelangelo, returned at that time. Did their number include Da Vinci, Mozart, Shakespeare, and Galileo? I wonder: who are the Masters among us now?

I think of the many lifetimes needed to rise to the level of Master and remind myself that progress in the spirit world takes place within the context of eternity. Time, as we know it, does not exist. I have read variations on a description of eternity similar to this: imagine a granite mountain, impervious to the elements; then imagine that a bird flies by once every one hundred years, brushing the tip of a feather against the rock; and now imagine the time it would take for the mountain to be thus worn away. That length of time is the beginning of eternity—there is no end.

Parallel Spirits

Zachary firmly suggests that we move on, to the topic of parallel spirits—those who often take a physical life within the same time-frame and geographic area. I still my wandering mind and listen.

"You and Sally are such parallel spirits. Among your shared lives are those as siblings, as student and teacher, and as a tribal leader and his shaman among an island people in the Pacific. Sally's spirit has most often sought leadership roles in physical lifetimes; the role of shaman fits with the preferences of your spirit."

Several months ago, Sally told me of a dream in which she and I were brother and sister, playing outdoors and wearing rough-hewn snowshoes. I did not dismiss her interpretation, or immediately accept it, but I did consider the possibility that she was right. My only confirmation is a childhood fascination with snowshoes and that I retain a clear image of a storybook illustration of a Native American boy using them.

Zachary now tells me it was a lifetime in the early 1700's, near the Northern Great Lakes with the Blackfeet, and we did use snowshoes. I once worked with a man who had grown up on a reservation. On one of our road trips, always good for deeper conversations, he turned to me and said, "Are you sure you're not Native?" He was referring, not to my looks, but to my nature and my view of the world. Now Zachary tells me more about our parallel lives.

"It was determined more than twenty years ago, before you entered college, that you would be the one to someday help Sally. It was known that your prior spiritual connection would assist in the process, and perhaps be essential, given the extent of her needs."

I have a vivid memory of the first time I held my high school psychology book. It was small for a textbook, a rich deep red, the simple title, *Psychology*, embossed in gold. I can still almost hear what seemed to be an alert signal as I looked at it, but when I started college the next year I was intent on a major in foreign languages. Zachary now confirms that I was guided to switch my major to psychology and later in my choice of graduate study.

"A great deal of influence was used to help your spirit guide you to your destined career."

I am not surprised. When asked why I chose this field, I have always replied that it was not a considered choice, that I was somehow led to it. I think back to Sally's first appointment, made for her by a friend who Sally insisted come with her to my office. Her friend mentioned that, when she called the mental health center and was given the names of three therapists, a strong feeling came over her to select me. Now Zachary tells me that she was guided to make that choice.

When we did a detailed history, Sally told me how she came to live here ten years ago. She and her husband had been building a house in a small community near her parents, five hours from here. They considered it an excellent place to raise their preschool children and planned to stay at least fifteen years. Their house was half finished when her husband got a letter from his company offering him a management position here. He had not sought promotion, there were several qualified people in line ahead of him, and the position had not been advertised. Sally said they had never understood why that offer came so unexpectedly. I ask Zachary if that move had been arranged.

"Yes, it was. Circumstances sometimes *are* orchestrated, but only when strictly necessary. It might be to direct a life away from an unproductive path, toward an imperative lesson, or to obtain needed assistance. A person may even be deliberately led down an unsavory path for the lessons to be found there. Do not conclude that your entire life is orchestrated, but most lives will contain one such life-altering event and some may have several."

His words prompt another memory. When I moved here, eighteen years ago, there were no openings in my field, so I found related work with a large organization. Eight years later, I was managing a program, enjoying my work, expanding the services, and raising revenues. Then, without warning, I was told that management of the program would be transferred up a level. Shocked, unwilling to accept it, I called the mental health center, found they had an opening, and started there three weeks later. I ask Zachary about it.

"It was important to arrange something dramatic to get you to change direction, not solely for Sally's sake but for that of other clients and to fulfill your career destiny. Your employer was urged to restructure that office and the director of the mental health agency was convinced to open a new position."

I now see the sudden changes made in my previous job from a new perspective. It had bothered me for some time that work I loved, and a program I had helped develop and grow, was arbitrarily taken from me.

Our time is almost up. I ask Zachary if, when taking a lifetime, a spirit knows which parallel spirits will be near.

"It is sometimes known but as often it is not, and it is not always predestined that your paths will cross. For instance, you and Sally were not expected to interact in this lifetime. When her need became apparent, as a young teen, a search was made for a parallel spirit destined to pursue your line of work."

I say it sounds as if a large group of parallel spirits is like money in the bank, there to be drawn upon if needed. Zachary says that is an apt comparison, and then he says goodbye.

I walk on the island in the late afternoon. Before long, I fall into a meandering stream of consciousness, my mind full of thoughts about lessons, status, and the many lifetimes of my spirit.

Where does this lifetime of mine fit? It is not, I think, either the most exciting of them or the most difficult, and it is not one of high status or financial gain, apparently was never meant to be. It has been a rich mixture of challenges and intrinsic rewards.

Lessons are associated with making choices, with being free to act. How might I determine the lessons meant for this lifetime? A first step would to be to consider those times when I have been faced with a choice, when my life could have taken one direction or another based on my decision—but how do I know if I made the right choice?

Were there more lessons in my marriage or in my divorce? I felt more strongly guided to the latter. Years ago, making plans for my wedding, I realized I was not a starry-eyed bride, but I did not stop to reconsider. The marriage brought lessons of love and loss, of finding my own voice, knowing that I had to leave, and acting on my decision. Were any of these what I was meant to learn?

An ordinary day is filled with choices: to offer a helping hand, or not; to be open or closed to the opinions of others; to overlook or confront what offends or upsets us; to see those who differ from us as other or to see our common origin; to act on our impulses, or not. Could these be as important as our major life decisions?

Some lessons are about self-discovery. Was it Socrates who said, "To thine own self be true"? No, that was Shakespeare, I think in Hamlet, which I fell asleep to at the Guthrie. Socrates said, "Know thyself," and "An unexamined life is not worth living." I have been reading a lot of Emerson lately. He would reflect on a routine set of questions at the end of each day. I am less structured and consistent in my approach.

How do I apply self-knowledge to my life? Are my choices in line with my purpose in life? What is my purpose? If that question can be answered with a simple statement, I would say it is to align myself with spirit, to enter into a relationship in which I make choices arising out of that alignment.

My awareness of my spirit is, in part, a retrospective one. In the last ten years I have recognized certain energies and messages that I have had some awareness of since childhood. They have had a consistency of feeling and a sense of immediacy that I have acted upon—they are the markers of my life path. But how many times have I not listened or not acted?

My walk almost over, my final thoughts are of how it is one thing to meditate, reflect, develop self-awareness, and renew intentions. It is another matter to act on our insights when we return to the daily routines and rhythms of our life.

5. Catastrophe

ZACHARY ONCE REFERRED TO VITAL information he would share with me. He reminds me of that now.

"I want to more fully explain why you, and others, have been approached at this time in history. It is known that a catastrophe will occur in this country in the not-too-distant future. I have not been told the exact details. What I do know is that this catastrophe will be the first in a series of events that will cause disruption, upheaval, and a period of unrest in the world for many years afterward."

Struck by the gravity of his tone, and the implications of what he has said, I ask if he can tell me more.

"I will tell you what I can. Some of these events will be political, conflicts between countries and cultures, and some will be physical, natural disasters. The cumulative effects in the decades following the initial catastrophe will lead many to question the meaning of life and the continued existence of this world."

This is a sudden turn in what I have thought to be my education in what *is*, the nature of the spirit world. Now a disturbing picture emerges of what *will be*, in this physical world. Zachary notes my reaction and calmly continues, with emphasis.

"This will not be *the end of life as you know it*. In the distant future, as more drastic effects are experienced, that will, indeed, be the case."

My immediate feeling is one of relief: we have been given a reprieve. Then I realize I am being selfish and shortsighted. I think of future generations and ask if he can be more specific.

"I cannot give you an exact date, but it will be after your present lifetime and also those of your daughters (and perhaps their children too) that life will be quite changed on this planet."

I quickly calculate that the more drastic changes would be near the end of the twenty-first century or early in the next one, about one hundred years from now. As I do the math in my head, he adds a clarification.

"It is not that I refuse to tell you; it is simply that I do not know. I am, in this regard, a messenger. I do not have access to all that is known at higher levels in the spirit world."

Opportunities

Zachary goes on to present an outlook that is not entirely gloom and doom.

"As one crisis after another develops, and your way of life changes in response, it will become necessary for human beings to work together—to an extent they often seem incapable of—at a local level, as a nation, and with global efforts. There will be many opportunities for spiritual growth as this world turns away from its current focus, on the material, to one that is of service to others and to the planet."

Zachary conveys a sense of the spiritual force of those he answers to and of their compassion and support for us and for future generations. Then it dawns on me that—not only will our descendants be affected—our spirits will be returning to this same world and to the legacy we leave. I check that assumption.

"You are correct. A spirit will return most often to the same physical world, with a few lifetimes in others to observe and learn from them. It is easier for spirits to learn lessons in a familiar place. By returning again and again, they become more engaged in, and responsible for, the direction taken by the inhabitants of that world."

I think of our tendency to act selfishly rather than for the greater good. I see it now in a context that extends far into the future. It is we who will inherit this earth; we cannot predict where, or in which one of many cultures, our spirit will return.

Held within the Eternal

It is unsettling, yet believable, as Zachary conveys that this is the way it is—the die has been cast. However, he says there are steps we can take to minimize effects and to extend timelines. Most importantly, he conveys that, as the inhabitants of this earth respond to the dilemmas and demands of our physical world, we will be held within the eternal.

He said he doesn't know the exact timing of the more imminent event, the catastrophe, but I ask if he can give me an educated guess.

"All I can tell you is what I know. It would be pointless for me to speculate."

I cannot help but make an attempt, and I arrive at five to ten years from now, around the turn of the century, the year 2000. Logic suggests that contacts with me and others would not be left to the last minute.

When I say that it seems a daunting task, Zachary's response is reassuring.

"Efforts on a small scale may have far-reaching ripple effects; few of those approached will have widespread recognition. Some of you will be planting seeds that will grow to greater action over time, as events unfold and momentum grows. Some of you will reach a few key people who will then go on to have a great impact."

As I wonder which of these outcomes might be true for me, I see that Zachary has paused and appears to be listening to someone.

"I am told our time is up. Sally's spirit is always near when we talk and keeps me informed of her schedule."

As I drive home, I consider possibilities. Zachary said the Creator was dismayed that Homo sapiens evolved with both the capacity and the will to destroy each other. He said we are possibly the most aggressive inhabitants of all worlds, though we do not need to act on those inclinations. There are myriad ways in which we humans could bring about a catastrophe. Natural disasters are nothing new, but I recently read a prediction of worse to come. The greenhouse effect is often in the news; its potential impact on our climate is being debated in Congress. Devastating earthquakes have been predicted, and there is the possibility of a major volcanic eruption. It is easy to imagine that a combination of manmade and natural events could lead to disillusionment and high anxiety about our future.

There was nothing specific in what Zachary said, no simple way to warn everyone. It is not something to be shouted from the rooftops. (Perhaps it is, but that would do little to establish my credibility.) He said it isn't necessarily an immediate task, that a lesser number of approaches related to the current purpose have been made for much of the last century, with mixed results.

My initial feeling, of dismay verging on dread, has been replaced by a sense of inevitability and acceptance. As I consider the weight of Zachary's message, and the significance of having been approached, I know that I must accept my part in this mission.

6. Core Beliefs

I AM DOING RESEARCH AT THE library this morning, absorbed in my reading, when I have a strong urge to get up and walk over to the section on religion and spirituality, a collection that fills both sides of two long aisles. I have neither title nor author in mind, but I am immediately drawn to one shelf and then to a particular book—a slim paperback wedged between tightly packed, hard cover books. I hardly register the title on the narrow spine, but I reach and gently tug it from the space. Paging quickly through it, I find it is an account of an experience similar to mine: *Many Lives, Many Masters* by Dr. Brian Weiss.

This afternoon, it is disconcerting when Zachary begins by asking me a question.

"Did you find some interesting reading when you were at the library this morning?"

Keeping my surprise (that he knew where I had been) to myself, I describe the book and its similarities to my experience.

"Eli and I have been aware of this book; you were guided to reach for it."

I am relieved to know that others have been approached in this way, through a client. I can now place this experience, not in the category of *commonplace*, but at least in that of *an occurrence that is not unheard of.*

Zachary says our time is short, but he wants to tell me more about the decision to approach me.

"It had been considered for some time, due in part to your status, and because we knew that your spirit had groomed you since childhood to be accepting and open minded. I was on the scene, so to speak, and Sally is what we term a receptor. She has the requisite personal qualities, and her spirit has chosen the role of receptor in most of her lifetimes, making Sally's capacity better than most. This makes it possible for me to speak to you in this conversational manner."

I ask why he could not have always spoken as he does now.

"That requires me to tell you about councils. A spirit world council must be consulted whenever a mortal is approached, and they are also involved when a guardian plays a prominent role in a lifetime. Five years ago, I needed permission from a particular Council to reveal myself to you as Sally's internal helper, and they instructed me to speak to you in a stilted, abrupt manner. When they gave me the go ahead to approach you, that was changed."

So the decision to approach me was made recently?

"No. It was made some time ago, but it was known that Sally's treatment was the first priority. You needed to give considerable attention and energy to her needs, your other clients, your children, and your health issues. And now, I must go."

9/22

This morning, after an hour with a client, the receptionist gives me an envelope she says Sally left for me. Inside is a single sheet of notebook paper with several paragraphs of neat printing, the name Zachary at the bottom. "Tessa, I have been recalled to the spirit world for a brief time." He reminds me of our conversation about my being destined to help Sally. "I want to clarify what I said about destiny. Not every aspect of a life is destined before birth, and many life events are not a part of one's destiny."

Zachary then turns from the general to specifics of my personal life. "It had not, for example, been your destiny to marry who you did, but you had been destined to give birth to your twin daughters. It was always the destinies of their spirits to share this lifetime with you." I smile and feel a warm glow in my heart. I am pleased with this information and then with his final words. "You are an adept student. I look forward to our conversations and will appear to you upon my return."

It is still early when I leave the office. I stop at home for a quick snack and to exchange my skirt for my favorite pair of old jeans and my heels for hiking shoes. I feed Charkey, chat with him for a minute, and then drive out to the island.

As I walk to the shelter, I breathe deeply of the fall air. The sharp, scorched, scent of high summer has given way to the first tinges of rich autumn decay, mixed with the faint aroma of wood smoke from a distant campfire. I sit in a half-lotus position against one of the large, upright support logs, facing the river, and close my eyes. I place my awareness on my breath and on my senses: the marine scents of the river now blend with those of the earth; the poignant, two-tone call of a black-capped chickadee mixes intermittently with the tap-tap-tap of a red-headed woodpecker; the sun warms my left knee; and I feel the soft caress of a gentle breeze as I let go into a deep relaxation.

Imagining myself a small owl, I repeat a mantra of "one" as I melt into the woods—just another creature aware only of the moment. This is one of my favorite meditations, bringing to me a sense of oneness with all creation. I picture the owl, six inches tall, that I came face to face with a few months ago. It calmly stared at me, for a long moment, and then closed its eyes, at peace on the inner branch of a juniper tree.

Now centered and at peace myself, I consider whether to tell my daughters of our shared destiny. I think back to when I was pregnant with them. Three doctors, at different stages, in that pre-ultrasound world, gave no credence to my strong feeling that I was carrying twins. At my first appointment it was quickly dismissed with, "There is no reason to believe that you are." In my seventh month the most arrogant of them leaned back in his chair, steepled his fingers, and smugly said, "If there was any chance of it, we would have x-rayed before now." I decided to believe the experts, but I was hardly surprised when, five minutes after Kenna arrived, she was joined by Callie. I believe it was my spirit who knew of their impending arrival and prompted my strong conviction. I am going to tell them.

I hear laughter as I walk in the door, music to my ears. The girls are both home and welcome an excuse to put off their homework. Through the window, the sun catches the natural highlights of their long wavy hair, streaked every shade of blonde by summer days on the beach. At sixteen, they are old enough to form their own opinions and to draw their own conclusions. It has been some time since they took my word as final authority.

I have recently broached the topics of guardian angels and past lives. Now they are open and accepting when I tell them of my meetings with Zachary and of how I have been approached. Then I tell them it was their destiny to spend this lifetime with me. That they are pleased is reflected in their smiles, in their deep blue eyes, and in their teen argot of "That is so cool!" and "How awesome!" Our hugs are an affirmation of the meaning this news holds for us.

Core Beliefs

9/25

There is time for a longer discussion with Zachary today. I expect him to tell me more about destiny, but he introduces a new topic: the importance of certain basic beliefs. Speaking at a measured pace, and with authority, he tells me these beliefs are not unique to any one religion or creed. "As civilizations were established and various cultures developed, each was given an awe-inspiring experience that gave rise to their belief in a Creator and an afterlife. Rituals and tenets then evolved in support of these beliefs. Throughout subsequent human history, many individuals have been given extraordinary experiences to reinforce them."

What has been the role of organized religion?

"Over the course of centuries, the differences in interpretation multiplied. Established religions were formalized and then became complicated with personal and political agendas. They have largely promoted the core beliefs, but their codified structures and dogmas have sometimes been a detriment to spiritual growth. This is most often the case when the focus is on arbitrary rules."

What encourages spiritual growth?

"It is often one's own sense of the spiritual—and the confronting of ambiguities and contradictions—that acts as a catalyst for spiritual growth as mortals search for truth, either within or outside of traditional belief systems."

What are the basic beliefs?

"Of primary importance are four core beliefs. These are a lesson in every lifetime:

1. There is a Creator.
2. Each of us has a spirit.
3. One's spirit returns to the Creator.
4. There is an afterlife, both spiritual and physical.

"The precise nature of these beliefs differs widely. In some cultures they are difficult to put into words, held at a feeling level as much as at a cognitive one. In other cultures they are held in myth and ritual, and for yet others they exist within a professed creed or a well-defined theology. It is the core beliefs that are essential, not the specific organization or structure that surrounds them."

Are these beliefs strictly defined?

"They are not: there are some who believe in a higher power that they do not name as the Creator; some individuals or groups are devoted to the ideals of the Creator; and some belief systems venerate a particular spiritual teacher. All of these examples, and others, might be accepted as adhering to the core beliefs."

Are there other important beliefs?

"There are four key supporting beliefs:

     1. Each life has a purpose or destiny.

     2. One's spirit has chosen this particular lifetime.

     3. A spirit takes a number of physical lifetimes.

     4. Guidance and support are always available."

What can you tell me about those who have conveyed these beliefs to us?

"Throughout your history, there have been great teachers of spiritual truths. Among them, the one you know as Jesus is the best exemplar of a life lived in touch with spirit, of his spirit speaking through him and accessing and expressing the will of the Creator. He is the most advanced of spirits and is referred to by other spirits as "The Son.""

How might we gain some degree of similar access?

"Prayer, whatever its form, across all religious and spiritual traditions, is the most effective means of communicating with the spirit world and thus with the Creator."

Which spiritual teachers are of a similar high status?

"In the highest circle, nearest the Creator, besides the spirit of Jesus you would recognize the spirits of Buddha, Mohammed, and Gandhi."

Are the major religions of the world equally valid?

"The seven major belief systems all have the Creator as their source. I speak of Judaism, Shintoism, Jainism, Buddhism, Hinduism, Christianity, and Islam. The original teacher of each of these brought people together into a community of believers. They each took a lifetime, in a particular time and place, for the express purpose of bringing the truth of the Creator. The same is true of those Masters who influenced the belief systems of many of your indigenous cultures."

I assume that all spirits, over their many lifetimes, will experience most or all of the major belief systems, and Zachary confirms it. Then I ask what he meant by a physical afterlife.

"Each spirit has an observable essence, vaguely human in form, and each is an individual. Spirits who are of greater status appear more substantial and are surrounded by a greater energy."

What do you mean that each is an individual?

"The individuality of a spirit is in their form and is also made evident in that each has their own, independently held, agenda. As they gain status and have a greater sense of purpose, along with the determination to achieve it, their appearance is enhanced. As is true in the physical world, the freedom to make choices is essential to the growth of the spirit."

Guardians

Our time is almost up. Zachary changes the subject and tells me he has been requested to go before a Council for a review of his guardianship of Sally.

"It is an educational process, not a punitive one, and it is routine. I have been expecting it."

His absence could extend to several weeks, so he has requested that a temporary guardian be assigned to Sally. Like most of us, she would not be directly aware of the absence of her guardian, but the alters are likely to become anxious and fear Zachary has deserted them. I ask what more he can tell me about guardians.

"When a guardian is assigned to you, there is a bonding process in which the guardian spirit pledges to abide by certain responsibilities and rules. That spirit is made aware of your needs, the lessons you are to learn in this lifetime, and relevant background information. Your guardian is also given the ability to foresee certain aspects of your future, more than what your spirit knows. Like your spirit, your guardian is limited to subtle guidance."

Can you tell me in more detail how a guardian will influence a human life?

"Your guardian will celebrate your accomplishments and calm your fears, will lift you up, give you strength, and enhance your sense of well-being. When you take time to contemplate choices, your guardian is often close to reinforce those that are in your best interests."

That a guardian is "often close" leads to my next question.

"Your guardian is with you in your greatest need, at times of peak experiences, and at pivotal times in your life to signal the need to take a new direction. Strong emotions, both negative and positive ones, alert guardians, who are generally not present to the degree I have been with Sally. They often are guardian to more than one person and will attend to the one in greatest need. If your guardian cannot be with you, then your spirit will guide you, sometimes calling on other spirits for assistance."

Zachary says a guardian is often, but not always, a spirit who has had some prior connection with our spirit. He adds that the process is referred to as a guardian being "bound" to their "charge." Our time is up.

It is late when I leave the office. I change to the hiking shoes I keep in the car and drive straight to the island. It is cloudy, no moon to light my way, so this will be a short walk.

I consider my beliefs. Yesterday, if asked to list them, I might not have included all that Zachary just told me. However, if handed his list, I would have agreed that each item has a place in my own informal belief system.

I look back to my mid-twenties, when I questioned whether this life is all there is. My rational mind pointed to the lack of proof of an afterlife. I did not experience a dark night of the soul, did not abandon my beliefs so much as hold them in one hand as I considered their antithesis in the other. I was reading a lot of philosophy then, including Pascal's wager: you have everything to win if you believe and nothing to lose if, at death, you are proved wrong. I couldn't take that position. I wanted to find my own way to a definitive acceptance.

Throughout my life, I had been aware of an energy that transcended my physical self. I knew it did not arise out of my mind; its presence was simply made known to me. I made an effort to be more aware of it and after several months I knew with certainty—that presence would continue after I took my last breath.

My conscious awareness of my spirit, and of being in relationship with her, is often obvious when I work with clients. Sometimes it is something more. When I first met one of Sally's alters, relegated to a deprived life on what they called "the other side," she didn't believe herself worthy to speak to me. When I tentatively reached out to touch her hand, she recoiled in horror. She silently indicated her forearms and hands and was finally able to say, in a hoarse whisper, "Can't you see it? Can't you smell it? I am covered in excrement."

She spoke her truth, and she couldn't understand why I didn't see and smell the filth as she did. I went to the waiting room and returned with paper towels and a container of water, then gently washed her hands and arms. It is the moment in my life in which I have been most definitely and undeniably touched by grace. A soft, beneficent version of a bolt of lightning entered into me and radiated from my heart to every cell of my body. I felt blessed, and I felt humbled—and envy for those in a position to routinely offer such assistance to others.

It is growing dark and I turn back. As my reflections turn to a walking meditation, I am aware of a distinct presence that I recognize as a spiritual energy, stronger than any I have felt before. I realize it is Zachary—walking with me. It is a knowledge that, like his presence, is suddenly there, fully formed, existing outside of thought.

Are You Content?

9/28

Just a minute or two with Zachary, and I am quick to ask if he was present with me a few nights ago on the trail. He confirms it and gives me an explanation.

"You are now in a period of greater awareness, due partly to your own efforts and partly to your having been approached."

He says he must go, but he wants to leave me with a question.

"Tessa, we do not have time to discuss it today, but my question is this: would you say that you are content with your life?"

Zachary's question echoes one I have been asking myself in recent weeks, as I look back on my life in light of what I have learned. This evening, an almost full moon rising, I walk on the island and sit in further reflection at the shelter on the bank of the river. It is cooler; night is settling more decisively. Summer has packed its bags and is deciding whether to linger yet awhile.

Synergy—the whole being greater than the sum of its parts—a concept I use in my work with organizations. Now I see its application to my life. Situations or events I have viewed as negative or insignificant assume, in retrospect, an importance roughly equivalent to the highlights. Together they form a synergistic whole, interwoven as the fabric of my life.

In a high-school writing assignment, an autobiography, I described my childhood as idyllic. The teacher gave me a grade of A, but he noted my use of hyperbole. I admit that I put on rose-colored glasses. For one thing, I said nothing of my persistent feeling of loneliness that was more piercing as a teen. A middle child among five brothers, and with no near neighbors, I was often excluded by circumstances. Attending a one-room country school for five years, the only one in my grade, continued a pattern of being more observer than participant.

I found companionship in nature, feeling the pull of the rolling hills merging with wetlands, compelling and sustaining me. I wandered when I could, on foot or on horseback, feeling a combined sense of freedom and connection. Though I lacked self-confidence and was painfully shy, I felt an inherent sense of self-worth, instilled during my solitary pursuits—it seemed by the process of osmosis—the influence of my spirit.

At age thirteen, I felt a growing spiritual awareness. In school, it was in a familiar sense of connection and discovery when I was drawn to books on world religions and easily accepted that there is more than one path. In church, it was in the loss of ritual and meaning when the service was changed and elements that had been, for me, a meditation, gave way to ones that did not engage my spirit. At home, I had a pre-cognition, a dream in which I saw details of several unusual events of the following day. I became more open to and curious about the nonrational and the mystical.

I look back on my adult life with a general sense of contentment, with a few exceptions: my marriage was not a true partnership, I could not give my children the home life I had wished for them, and my health issues have changed the rhythms of every day of my life. On the plus side have been a variety of challenging and fulfilling career experiences. I have had the pleasure of working with small and large groups in the areas of management and personal growth. My work with clients is equally rewarding, using a different level of energy that is quieter but often intense. I know I have made a difference in the lives of others. For some it is an almost immediate change that is life altering. For others it is assisting with the unfolding of a series of self-discoveries. I have come to realize that I am as much the beneficiary of our contacts as are my clients.

Callie and Kenna have been the great joys of my life. I can't imagine it without them. In childhood, they were absolute delights and I was privileged to watch them delight in each other, a unit of two. Then I watched them grow into distinct individuals as their personalities surpassed their oneness. In the midst of their teenage angst, we remain essentially close, a small family unit, enhanced now by knowledge of our destinies.

For the last fifteen years, I have lived near the Missouri river. Beyond the river breaks, the prairie extends for two hundred miles. I respond to the expansiveness and treasure the landscape that some call bleak. Then mountains rise up as counterpoint and offer a frequent change of scenery and climate. I am fortunate to be able to immerse myself in nature on almost a daily basis.

I anticipate a future of better health, giving me the energy to pursue neglected aspects of my life. Two years from now, at age forty-five, my daughters in college, I expect to be more physically active, expand my professional networking and social life, and be open to a serious relationship.

My answer to Zachary will be: "Yes, I am content with my life, but I am not resting in that contentment."

I have been gazing at the reflection of the moon across the rippled surface of the silvery-blue water, a path of light as I reflect on the course of my life. I take another few minutes in a gazing meditation and then, unaware of the chill until now, I need to walk fast to warm up. When I slow down, it occurs to me: was there a correct answer? can we be too content? or for too long? does being content deprive us of the desire to change and grow? I think the answer is in the quality of our contentment. It can be static or it can be dynamic and flowing. I see an image of a stream cut off from its source— stagnating, dying a slow death. I compare it to one that is connected to its source—alive and changing, contained within purpose.

7. This Earth of Yours

THE ENTITY BEFORE ME TODAY is obviously not Zachary but a more feminine presence—softer features, a lightness in the body. She maintains eye contact with a look that is as much an assessment of me as it is a greeting. Her first words confirm my assumption.

"Hello, Child. I am Amelia. Zachary has left to meet with the Council. They summoned him abruptly, so there was no opportunity for him to introduce us."

I say hello and look at her expectantly.

"It has been a long while since my last physical life, but I am often a guardian and have thus maintained a strong connection to this world. For most of this century, I was guardian to a woman well-known in this country. My charge recently returned to the spirit world, and now I have been assigned to assist Zachary."

I can't restrain my impulse to ask her the identity of the famous woman. I find it fascinating, yet disconcerting, to learn who it was. I am reminded of those who claim to remember past lives as Cleopatra, Napoleon, or someone of equal renown, and I have a fleeting moment of doubt as I consider the implications.

More differences between Amelia and Zachary have become apparent. Her voice is quieter, well-modulated, and she sometimes smiles; her speech is more natural and reflects emotional content. I share my thoughts with her.

"Zachary's recent contacts with this world have been less frequent than mine and of a different quality. It was necessary for me to be quite close to my last charge. Her public life demanded more, at times, than she was equipped to handle."

We move on to a review of Sally's current needs and those of each alter. Then Amelia appears to receive a signal.

"I must leave you now, but I am looking forward to continuing our discussion."

I walk on the island at twilight. The mild evening is an echo of summer, with an occasional slice of autumnal contrast as a cold current cuts through the warm air. I recall the atavistic pleasure I have found here foraging for asparagus and morel mushrooms, imagining a distant hunter/gatherer existence. Have I had past lives in a similar setting? Is it the memories of my spirit that prompt my sense of repeating a timeless endeavor?

I sit on a bench at the edge of the meadow and look up at the cottonwood trees, thinking how very tall these are; their leaves are a golden yellow that will soon light my path in the moonlight. As I merge with the night, I am aware of a strong energy surrounding me. I feel as much a part of the past as of the present and a strong connection to my spirit—and to the presence that is here with us. It is not the same energy I recognized last week. It is Amelia.

This Earth of Yours

10/5

My second meeting with Amelia. I start to tell her of my walk, to explain the presence I felt a few nights ago, but she interrupts me with an enigmatic smile.

"Yes, those trees are very tall."

I had not yet mentioned the trees. Before I can say more, she firmly changes the subject, intent on her purpose for being here.

"Let us continue with your education."

Amelia expands on a topic Zachary has covered—the impact of human actions on the environment. I hear in her somber tone a reflection of the gravity of the subject.

"Mankind has done a great disservice to this earth. There are three broad categories: the toxicity and large quantities of chemicals being released into the ground and atmosphere, the proliferation of products detrimental to living beings, and the sheer bulk of waste products of one kind or another."

I nod in agreement, aware of and concerned about these issues.

"It is known in the spirit world that disastrous effects will ensue from what has been done. It is still possible for some reversal of current trends, but self-interest and goals focused on profit making are preventing sufficient action."

Was the current state of affairs destined for this planet?

"It is part of the Creator's plan that all worlds will continue to evolve and change over time, in accordance with the actions of their inhabitants. The Creator provided each population with the information and tools necessary to turn the world given them to their benefit, but these were not intended to be put to use in a destructive manner."

As Amelia continues, I hear a change in her tone, to one of subtle chastisement with an underlay of sadness.

"Humans do not realize how fortunate they are that their physical existence is here, on this earth of yours. It is perhaps the most beautiful of all universes. It was not made for humans in particular, but it evolved in such a way that great beauty resulted from the forces set in motion by the Creator. Other universes have tended to be less beautiful and some of them are rather desolate, though not purposely so."

A deep sadness comes over me and I blink away a tear. I think of my frustration with those who speak of us having been given the beauty of this country as if we were specially chosen, somehow deserve it. I feel a collective guilt and shame for what we have done to destroy it. Amelia's expression indicates she is aware of my reaction, and then she speaks with certain knowledge of the future.

"If this world knew what it was facing in the years ahead, you would change your focus now—from military spending to using those resources to promote peace. The time will come when you will have to operate as one body in order to feed the population. You will be forced to shift from war efforts to a survival mode of life. The more affluent nations will have to accept the contributions of developing ones and integrate your efforts with theirs. You will come to recognize the inadequacy of the attention now given to the guidance of the spirit world."

Amelia's words are stronger than Zachary's, and I feel their greater weight. She counters them with a series of statements that brighten our outlook.

"Some who were approached earlier have made connections with world leaders, with positive results. There will continue to be growth in many fields of endeavor. The answers to many problems will come from the oceans, including cures for several diseases; one ocean species holds the answer to regenerating tissue. As the future reveals itself, there will be many opportunities for spiritual growth, including the capacity to love others, on a broad scale, and a greater intent to protect Mother Earth.

Amelia has paused, but while I am considering my next question, she speaks first.

"And now Child, I must go."

I leave my office in a quiet mood. Why do Amelia's claims about the future resonate more intensely than Zachary's did? Is it that she has recently had a closer association with this world? Is it because she has more explicitly implicated us in creating the conditions that will lead to our destruction? I think it is both, and I think she intentionally chose stronger words to convey her message of grave consequences.

Should I tell others now? I am not in a position to have a major impact. Am I to inform a select few? How do I convey what I have learned? I have been given no guidelines.

The girls are home. How much do I tell them? I do not want them to be weighed down by the prospect of what is to come. The need for an immediate decision is lifted from me by the routines of our daily lives. I am soon caught up in listening to the events of their day, preparing a meal, and making a grocery list so I can do the modern, detached from nature, version of hunting and gathering. Throughout the evening, the theme song from a recent television series recurs in my head—*Life Goes On.*

The Role of Your Spirit

10/9

Amelia begins today by asking if I have any questions. I recall Zachary's mention of a spirit's personality and ask her if theirs mesh with ours.

"It is reflected in the human to the extent the human allows it to be—a spirit does not impose its personality on the mortal life. They will try to impact the life, but they hesitate to influence too much as they are not aware of the future events tied to each choice."

Are all human personality traits represented in the spirit world?

"In general, spirits (especially younger ones) have the same assortment of traits as do humans. The same is true of emotions, but in the spirit world you will not find anger, hatred, or jealousy—which is not to say there are no rivalries, for there is a certain amount of competition. Also, there is no deceit, for honesty is inherent to our lives. There is one exception: when spirits first return to our world, still caught up in human tendencies, these negative emotions can prevail."

Human personality traits remain fairly consistent over time. I ask if a spirit is aware beforehand of what those traits will be.

"A spirit, especially one who is more mature, will be aware of what traits the genetic history might produce and of the general circumstances of childhood that will influence certain traits. Ideally, the spirit will work with and shape those traits to meet their needs."

I ask question after question of Amelia, wanting to understand more fully our spirit's relationship to us and to our daily lives. Her answers form a list, some items new and some reinforcing what Zachary has told me.

The Role of Your Spirit

A spirit decides which lessons to pursue, makes a careful study of several available lifetimes, and then selects the one most likely to assist in learning those lessons.

Your spirit will attempt to influence you, to lead you to necessary or desired outcomes, and is often the instigator of your routine decisions and actions.

With a few exceptions, a spirit is always attempting to influence the human life in ways that will help to fulfill their purpose. With more experience they are better able to recognize opportunities that will fulfill their intended lessons.

Your spirit will often lead you into difficult situations for the lessons to be learned. Some examples are: the challenge of resolving conflicts, both personal and interpersonal; realizing the negative effects of a situation and changing course; and opportunities to assist others.

A spirit, especially a young one, may get caught up in destructive pursuits. A wiser spirit will not get involved in them but will stay close, to learn from that path and to protect the human life.

Most spirits are drawn to certain aspects of the material world—nature, music, a particular field of knowledge, people, etc. It is not just your own interest that gives you that feeling of engagement, peace, or fulfillment; it may be as much theirs.

Your spirit may choose to be distant from some aspects of your life, e.g., around certain people or activities that do not appeal to them. They may also become distant if you show no recognition of them or if you are pursuing a life that does not offer fulfillment of their purpose.

Your spirit will join you in deliberate thought that leads to making decisions. Such thought is often instigated by your spirit for a particular purpose.

Those who maintain contact with their spirit through a combination of prayer, meditation, and reflection are more likely to respond to their influence.

It is a lesson of every lifetime that a spirit love the life that has been made available to them and given to their keeping.

I remember Zachary said spirits are accountable to others, and I ask Amelia to elaborate.

"There are two main categories. First, those in leadership positions who supervise a spirit's progress. Second, what you would call a council—a group of spirits, usually twelve in number, who are brought together to decide certain matters of destiny. And, there is a third category: all spirits are accountable to the Creator. It is not a one-way street: the Creator is accountable to all spirits and is available to assist them."

Amelia's tone changes to one of deep reverence as she speaks of the Creator. Then she pauses and says she is being told by Sally's spirit that our time is up.

8. Destiny

Amelia tells me there is not much time today, but enough to begin a new topic.

"I want to speak to you about destiny, which provides a pathway for your life. Some elements, but not all of them, are ordained by the Creator. The spirit world is anything but whimsical, but neither is your destiny set in concrete. Your path will be swayed by your spirit and altered by the choices you make."

I ask her if lessons and destiny are one and the same.

"Your destiny includes the lessons to be learned, and more, but not every circumstance of your life. Your life intersects with others, and the result is many more events in a life than those that are destined. Even so, it is likely that the major events of your life were meant to be a part of your destiny."

Destiny is often spoken of in romantic terms, so I ask if marriages, or committed relationships, are always destined.

"Most people will have a destined relationship. Currently, less than half are to that intended person, but do not assume that every break up is because the relationship was not destined. It is not that simple. Relationships are destined for reasons other than a great love affair. For instance, there are usually one or more intersecting lessons to be realized."

Is your destiny determined before your life begins?

"Only partially—many aspects will not be set until events transpire throughout your life. The Creator has an intimate knowledge of every life and holds each one to be precious and of great importance. He is vigilant to assist every spirit to learn their intended lessons, and He will open up pathways and opportunities for them."

A Missed Opportunity

The mention of relationships reminds me that Zachary said I wasn't destined to marry who I did. I didn't think to ask him if I had been destined to be with someone else. When I ask Amelia, her eyes close for a minute, then open.

"You were destined to marry a man named Michael, with whom you spoke on one occasion. I saw an office at the end of a long hallway. You were sitting at a desk and he approached you. There was a calendar on the wall showing that the year was 1973."

Given that place and time, I have immediate recall of an incident etched in my memory. I was in graduate school and worked in the university administration office. I do not share that with Amelia but ask her what more she can tell me.

"Michael was a graduate assistant who had noticed you on an earlier visit. A friend of his worked in that office and he asked her if you were involved with anyone."

I ask Amelia if she can describe the friend. She does—age, body type, raven black hair, green eyes. Only one woman comes even close to her detailed description. When I mention Pearl by name, Amelia confirms it was she.

"Pearl replied to him that, not only were you involved, you were married. She knew both Michael and his wife, and she reminded him that he was also married. It was on his next visit to the office that you were at the front desk."

In my three years in that office, I had thousands of encounters with students and staff. One memory stands out as singular—all others are a composite blend. A man, about my age, came to the front desk with a large envelope in his hand. I routinely asked how I could help him. Pearl was standing at the mailboxes a short distance back. Before he could answer me, she stepped forward and loudly and firmly said, "*I'll* take that." She reached out her hand for the envelope, the man turned to her, and they exchanged a few words. I watched him as he walked out the door and down the long hallway.

I retain a strong sense of that moment. I could not understand the tone Pearl used, her emphasis that *she* would help him, not me. It seemed that she had intervened in some way. If I said I felt a loss, it would come from what I have just learned. Then, it was … a sinking feeling. I was aware of a slight pressure from my chest to the pit of my stomach, a mix of a physical response and an emotion I could not name. Shock or dismay come close but made no sense to me then. The memory of that incident comes back to me every year or two, leaving me as puzzled the last time as the first.

I do not want to invent a memory that the man in that vivid, enduring scene was Michael, but there is a consistency between what I felt then and what Amelia now tells me of our destiny. I share my memory and my thoughts with her, and she confirms that the man I remember was Michael. What I experienced as a sinking feeling was my spirit's reaction of dismay. She was trying to alert me that my destiny was standing there in front of me, was walking away from me.

Amelia looks kindly at me and speaks with empathy.

"Humans often do miss their destinies—even when they are staring you in the face."

I tell her I want to know more about Michael.

"All I could glimpse of his current life is that he is divorced, is a college professor, and that he lives in this general region of the country."

Unable to drop the subject, I ask her if it is still possible that we might meet.

"I believe there is nothing to prevent you from contacting him. I will attempt to get more specific and current information before we meet again."

My first impulse, to wait until my health improves, quickly passes. I picture a college calendar—Thanksgiving vacation, about a month from now—enough time to exchange a letter or two. I ask Amelia why I was not as firmly guided in this choice as Zachry said I was in my career.

"Your guardian could have been more diligent in guiding you to Michael but considered your career to be paramount. It was known that you would have a positive impact on a number of people."

Amelia goes on to tell me that the man I married was one possible choice for me. I was to have met both him and Michael and then choose between them.

"It is common in matters of destiny to have two clear options. It is the task, and the challenge, of your guardian and spirit to guide you to the right one."

Our time is up. I put my swirling thoughts aside and speak with Sally, relieved that she is my last client of the day. Now that she has left, I feel a surging of strong emotion, a combination of loss and anticipation.

I can't stop thinking about Michael. I try to picture the man I remember—fairly tall, slim, brown hair and eyes—but the image I have of him is vague. I was not looking for a man or in the habit of rating one on a scale of attractiveness. (I might have flirted a bit, if he had started it, but not with the intention of taking it further.)

In 1973, I had been married for less than two years. If asked, I would have said happily so, but our goals and interests were beginning to diverge. I can imagine being drawn to Michael, but would I have agreed for us to meet away from my work?

Further reflection gives me my answer: graduate school, a mutual attraction in a group process class … sitting together on an outdoor step … regret in the air as he tells me of a brief affair with a married woman, says he can't do it again. We hadn't discussed it, but the possibility must have been floating in the air between us. Two other classmates—temptations, soul-searching conversations—left me aware of needs not met. I know I would have agreed to meet Michael. In my naivety, I would have convinced myself it was an innocent coffee date, and I expect it would have been. It is the second or third meeting that I cannot vouch for.

My marriage continued for ten more years, until I lost all hope for what we had never quite had. I have a clear memory of meditating then and seeking guidance. As I contemplated staying in the marriage, an image came to me of being chained to a rock, the impossibility of any movement or growth. When I thought of leaving, that image changed to one of butterflies set free.

My reflections take me further back in time, to the night I met the man I married. It was the end of our freshman year, a blind date, and he said he would call me over the summer. I showed no enthusiasm, silently wished he would not call, and experienced a similar sinking feeling to the one I would have a few years later. He did not call, but our paths crossed again in the fall and he asked me out. I responded to his enthusiasm and said yes, but my feelings for him were initially lukewarm. I didn't stop to question why. My spirit was urging me away from him, knew he was not the one, but I did not heed her guidance. I did not listen to my heart.

Anticipation

I decide to write a letter to Michael, hoping that Amelia can provide a clue to his address. It is true that I had been in our college town in August. I make up the part that I had lunch with a former colleague. I imagine Pearl, telling me she now regrets her intervention. I write that she had known us both, knew he was now divorced, and, when she learned I was too, said we had to meet. I go on to tell him a little about myself and end by saying I can't pass up this opportunity.

Excited about the possibility of us meeting, I think ahead a few weeks and imagine it. Knowing we were destined to be together, will I project more intensity than he would expect? Do I tell him about Zachary and Amelia? How do I not? When do I tell him? If immediately, I might frighten him away. If I wait too long, he might think I had deceived him. But I am getting ahead of myself; he might not respond.

My letter is finished, written from my heart, and now my rational mind takes over. Were the details Amelia gave me lucky guesses? Did I tailor my memories to fit what she told me? Have I imagined the strong connection I feel? Am I capable of that degree of self-delusion? I try to sort it out. I tend to be more skeptical than credulous, more pragmatic than fanciful. If someone told me a similar story, I would be intrigued but reluctant to accept it as truth. I seldom daydream, even less often do I fantasize about men, and never about celebrities. Dream about men, I do, but only when there has been an obvious, mutual attraction.

I need a break and drive out to the island, reminded on the way of a perennial dilemma. Every year, as I enjoy the fall colors, I ask myself if it is legitimate to enhance the sight with sunglasses, if I am not thus distorting reality. I then give reality its due by observing both ways. Another example of my bent toward the rational is that I frustrate joke tellers when I fail to respond as they expect, prone to pointing out elements that are unlikely or impossible. On the other hand, I am quick to see humor in an unexpected comic twist and in real-life anecdotes that reveal our humanity and are as endearing as they are amusing.

Can I make an objective assessment of myself? I will attempt it. Relaxing with friends and colleagues, I am usually spontaneous and engaged. I am equally at ease with a room full of strangers but less so when joining an established group. I relish my time alone but thoroughly enjoy being with others, almost as much an extrovert as an introvert. I have dated frequently enough and have turned down more than one prospect for a long-term relationship. I feel no sense of desperation.

I begin a slow walk as I complete my thought process. My self-assessment is that I am a rational person, not given to fantasy, and that I am well-adjusted socially. I am not so open to suggestion that I can be persuaded a long-ago encounter was the love of my life. In fact, initially Amelia said very little. She merely mentioned a time and a place. She went on to describe specific scenes that fit my life of twenty years ago— *before* I gave her any details.

Despite Amelia's unexplained knowledge, it is my own enduring memory that informs me, and my strong inner sense of what could have been, of what has been—in past lives—of what Michael has meant to me. Amelia said nothing about past lives, yet I know we have been together before this lifetime. It is this inner sense that I rely on. It joins me in a reasoned approach to life but is capable of overriding reason.

I haven't come to the island to reflect. I want to walk fast, get in touch with my body, get out of my head. I push myself to my limits for almost an hour, do some stretches, and then sit in meditation for ten minutes before a slow walking meditation back to my car. My mind is clear now, free of excitement about unknown possibilities and of any fear that I am wrong. I am left with what I know to be true—and a peaceful anticipation of meeting Michael.

9. Destiny Undone

SALLY CATCHES ME BETWEEN MORNING clients, says she had an urge to call and confirm her appointment, but it is Amelia who wants to talk to me. I hear regret in her voice.

"I have just been informed. I thought you would want to know."

She sounds like someone who has just received shocking news, but there is no time to consider the implications before she explains.

"You and Michael cannot meet, for two reasons. One is that your destinies were changed after several missed opportunities to meet. The other is that Michael is quite ill and is in a hospice. I do not want you to get your hopes up any further. I will tell you more later—until then, Child."

Amelia speaks with sadness, with empathy, and with utter finality. She has quashed any hope that we might reclaim our destinies. I hang up and realize I have been holding my breath. I breathe deeply now and try—without success—to integrate this new information with the undercurrent of anticipation I've been feeling.

I go to the kitchen nook for a second cup of coffee. My usual black won't do. I add a spoonful of sugar and filch some cream from the fridge, using the diversion, and the sweet brew, to push aside my feelings and erect a wall between them and my clients, the last one Sally. When Amelia comes, she tells me about Michael.

"He became ill with leukemia three years ago and had a quick remission, but the disease made an aggressive return several months ago and he has been steadily losing ground."

Hearing details, I feel a resurgence of the feelings I have had to keep tamped down since this morning—grief, despair, incomprehension. When she asks me if I want to know more, I cannot tell her no.

"Twelve years ago, you missed a third and final opportunity to meet. Michael lived in this state and had signed up for one of the classes you taught then. It was canceled and your destiny was changed—there is to be someone else."

I take little comfort in that thought now, but I need the distraction of a change of subject. I ask Amelia if she can tell me the name of my new destiny.

"I have been cautioned. I am not to give you any additional information that could affect how you choose to conduct your life. I have already stepped over the line."

Her answer does not disappoint me. What I feel for Michael leaves no room in my heart for anyone else.

At home now, I read and reread my letter to Michael. My mind, my body, my heart—none are prepared to absorb this sudden change. I feel the loss of a dear friend. No, it is much more than that. A few days ago, I coolly told Amelia I wanted to wait awhile to contact Michael. In the hours since then, I have felt a strong connection. How can I say goodbye when we have not met? Yet, we have met ... somewhere. I do know him. I will have to try, in my desolation, to get some sleep.

10/17

I've been busy today, distracted by the routine demands of work and children. This evening I am home alone, a steady rain keeping me indoors. Michael is back on my mind, thoughts of what might have been. I read my letter to him again, then see myself endlessly reading it until the ink has faded away and the paper has disintegrated. I read it once more—then force myself to throw it in the trash. I convince myself there is little point in trying to hang on to a dream, but if I hadn't ripped the pages into tiny pieces I would retrieve them now and read it again. I can't make myself stop thinking about Michael, and I don't want to, but my thoughts are interrupted by a memory from twelve years ago, 1983.

Looking through the yellow pages, a name caught my eye, and I felt compelled to make an appointment with a man whose services I didn't need. I will call him John, a man I had never met or seen. I was baffled—it made no sense for me to contact him, but I did—and then felt the nth degree of foolish as I walked back to his office. I could hardly look him in the eye as I mentioned a minor concern, one I had already addressed. I got his take on my options and made a quick exit.

There is a similarity to my one contact with Michael. When I first arrived at John's office complex, I experienced a heightened level of awareness. I have a vivid memory of exactly where I parked, the brilliant June sunshine, the pink seersucker dress I was wearing, the white sandals with three inch heels. And a tiny bell sounding in my head, a "ding, ding, ding" to signal a momentous event. It was all in stark contrast to the embarrassment I felt when I left.

This was about the time Amelia said my destiny with Michael was changed. Is John my new destiny? He is an attractive man, but I felt no connection when we met. Besides that, he was married then, and he still is. I know his wife. I easily push thoughts of him aside.

I want to take action. I want to find Michael and go to him, but I have agreed to not search for his home address, and besides, Amelia said the hospice is in a city even more distant.

There is another possibility. I have reached out spiritually to a few clients who were in extreme distress, attempting support beyond what is possible in a therapy session. I did not tell them what I had done, but each of them mentioned having had a sudden feeling of lightness and hope at the same time that I reached out to them.

I spend some time in meditation and then reach out to Michael. My heart and mind come together to send a message to him, though I do not know, in any ordinary sense, who he is, or where. I believe I have reached him, more deeply and more personally than I have the others. I feel a strong connection. I know that Michael has a son. I have known him before—in a past life.

Soul Mates

10/19

I have been impatient, eager to tell Amelia of my attempt to reach Michael. She offers to communicate with his guardian, closes her eyes, and withdraws. When she returns, I see a look of intrigue on her face, hear a hint of wonder in her voice.

"You did reach him. He had a dream in which he saw a woman— he believes her to have been an angel. It has given him comfort. He will know, upon his return to the spirit world, who you are."

To know that Michael experienced my presence helps to ease the tremendous loss I feel. I ask Amelia if she can tell me more of what might have been.

"In 1973, if the two of you had met more decisively, you would have left your marriages to be together."

I know with certainty that Michael has a son, but I ask her to confirm it.

"He does have a son, who was two years old at the time. Together, you would have had a second son. Then the spirits of your daughters would have been born to you. That was to be their destiny."

I feel a shooting stab of pain in my chest and know the origin of the term *broken heart*. My abs clench in a reflex to ward off another blow. My right hand clutches repeatedly at the pleats of my linen skirt. The pain envelops me, dulls my senses. As if from a great distance, I hear Amelia's voice.

"You have had a number of previous lives together. You are significant others in the spirit world—eternal spirits. You were granted permission by the Creator to be together for eternity."

A few moments pass. I start to breathe again. Here in my office, I cannot abandon myself to my feelings. I need to talk to regain my equilibrium. I ask Amelia if we are soul mates.

"That would be an equivalent term, but it is not the one used in the spirit world. Eternal spirits do not share every lifetime, or even most of them. Many lessons are meant to be learned with others. In the lifetimes you have had together, there has always been a known alternative, another man—you have always chosen Michael."

Our time is up. I need to put a damper on my emotions as I visit with Sally for ten minutes.

When I leave my office, I open the floodgates to feelings that are a mix of discovery and loss, joy and sadness, gratitude for what I have learned, and deep remorse for what we have lost. We are soul mates—it is impossible now for me to forget about Michael.

If I could reach him once, I can do it again. Exactly how it is possible is not clear to me. I first connect with my spirit through meditation, and then I envision the one I am reaching out to and their spirit. I engage with my spirit, from my core to my heart, and generate an energy that I bring somewhat to my mind and transmit to that person through their spirit.

I meditate for twenty minutes and then concentrate my thoughts on Michael, but I do not feel as close to him as I did two nights ago. I let go of trying and relax into being. Time passes. I feel a surge of concentrated energy from deep within my body, my soul. I make a conscious effort to channel that energy through my spirit, through Michael's spirit, to him—a combination of effort and no effort.

A moment later, I have an overwhelming sense of having connected with Michael. To say my heart is filled would be far from adequate to describe it. I experience a welling up from within, a warmth emanating from my heart, and the deepest feelings of love, connection, and contentment. It is not that I *want* to connect and then wonder if I succeeded. I *know* that I am with him. It is a process—external as much as internal—not wishful thinking. The strongest feelings last for about five minutes and then gradually diminish; they have not yet left me an hour later.

I feel stronger. My wish for Michael is that he, too, will gain strength. There may be a chance for another remission. I sit here, still in awe of what is possible. My sense of having known Michael has been replaced by certain knowledge—we are everything to each other.

Mahalia

10/22

I wake up to find that the feelings of last night have not yet left me. I was there with Michael, and I am still in awe of the depth of our contact. I think of telling the girls, but it is too private and too strange. These last few days have been so utterly surreal that I keep listening for the theme song from *The Twilight Zone* to be playing in the background.

On this mild Sunday afternoon, I have to be out on the island. I take a path, little more than a deer trail, through faded, rustling rushes, remnants of cattails floating in the air. The scent of autumn is at its most intense, redolent of entropy, yet holds some promise, a single note, of spring. A hard frost in the night, the morning crisp, now brilliant sunshine brings hints of summer.

The enormity of the loss I have felt has been eased by my connection with Michael last night. I feel his presence as I walk in reverie, warmed by the sun.

Then, shattering the stillness, I hear a voice. It is distinct from my thoughts, and clear.

"I am Mahalia."

A few beats of silence.

"I return often, for the elements to be found here and for the children."

The words come from my right, as if someone is walking beside me in conversation.

"I feel a deep grief that we cannot be together. His name was also Michael in an earlier life, Philip in another. Amelia is new, but Zachary is an old friend who has been with us in the past."

The voice speaks to me of Michael.

"His spirit is kind and giving and full of love. He does not seek to control, as did the other—who had never been my choice—but you did not follow my guidance. I knew Michael was waiting, but I did not know where to find him."

A longer silence and I think that is all. It is not.

"There has been much joy for me in watching your twins grow. I knew they were to arrive, but I could not fully convince you. They too have been with us before."

The voice continues, at a diminished volume, with long pauses.

"We do not easily suffer fools ... I am well pleased with the conduct of your life ... I will always be with you ... we will walk together."

I am again in awe of my experience. Mahalia must be my spirit, the one who has been present in my other lifetimes and holds those memories. More accurately, it is I who play a part in this lifetime she has chosen. I think of how I heard her name, Mah-huh-lee-uh, the accent on the first syllable, the second one very short, the last two soft and musical.

The girls are both home tonight and want to watch a video of *Ghosts,* which I haven't seen. I am surprised to hear an old song playing: "Unchained Melody," by The Righteous Brothers. I watch the movie but my mind is more on Michael. The song reflects the torment in my soul. It is Mahalia who has yearned for his touch, and now I join her in that desire.

The movie is over and the girls have gone to bed. The song continues to play in my mind. I reach out to Michael again, singing the song to him, willing him to hear me. I feel a strong connection—achieved more easily—there is now an open conduit from my soul to his.

10. Odyssey of the Spirit

MONDAY MORNING—MY CONNECTION WITH MICHAEL has not been severed. I need to make a conscious effort to cut that tie and turn my attention to clients. I see Sally last and Amelia appears. I tell her I reached out to Michael again, ask if she can verify it, and she withdraws for a minute.

"You did make contact with Michael. He was aware of what he considers to be some outside source—you have touched him deeply. He told his son that he had a dream that has brought him serenity and fulfillment."

I ask her if there is any hope that Michael will recover.

"There may be a chance of another remission. Even so, it would not be possible for you to be together."

Her voice is deeply empathetic, but I hear the certainty of a final answer. She responds to the disappointment that must be written on my face.

"Child, destinies are not easily altered. There is much that has to be considered."

I am glad to have made a difference, but also sad and full of regret. I need to do something, take action. I tell Amelia that I would like to explain it to Michael—who I am, what he has been experiencing—express it in a letter. She will ask Eli. It is he who must grant me permission.

I sit here in my wing chair in the corner of the ell-shaped living room, with a view of the spacious yard that reaches back to the ridge of the hill. The round table beside the chair is stacked with books, an exotically scented candle tucked among them, a cup of oolong tea resting on the highest one. Charkey has jumped up and purrs in my lap as I rub his ears with one hand, hold my pen in the other.

I have been writing a letter to Michael, and rewriting it, trying to convey what is in my heart and the extraordinary circumstances that have brought us together. I flash on an image of him here with me, but there is no point now in thinking of what might have been—or so I try to tell myself.

10/26

I take a final look at my letter, make a few changes, but no words I put on paper can express what is in my heart. If Michael has felt the same deep connection, he will be reading the pages of my soul; the exact words will not matter. I finish it in time to leave for a late morning appointment and then three more this afternoon, the last one Sally.

To my surprise, Zachary is back. He tells me his meeting with the Council went well; they are pleased with his guardianship of Sally. He has been informed of recent events in my life, and he has just paid a visit to Michael.

"He has been quite unwell in recent weeks and has been asleep much of the time, almost comatose. The vision and dreams have affected him profoundly, and he has been writing of his experience in his journal."

Zachary says he has told Eli of my desire to write to Michael.

"Eli is not in favor of it, but I reminded him that your spirits are of equal stature and that you have often been paired in past lives."

I show Zachary the letter. He reads it, an intent look on his face, then says that he is touched by it. And then he departs even more from his usual reserve.

"You are not an easy one to be a type of guardian to. You tug at my emotions."

Amelia also wishes to speak to me, and I read the letter to her.

"I can see why Zachary is touched. I will share it with Eli and suggest that he pay a visit to Michael. I have spent some time with him today. He has been more alert; thoughts of you consume much of his waking hours. He is a very determined man."

Last week, Amelia expressed some remorse that she had told me about Michael, that she hadn't checked more thoroughly when I asked about my destiny. Tonight, she shows no regret.

"Do not tell Zachary, but I would not do it any differently if I had the chance to do it over again."

I do not have to think twice before replying, "Neither would I."

Odyssey of the Spirit

10/30

I have reached out to Michael every night and when I have had time during the day. I am eager to hear word of him. Today it is Zachary who comes first. He has visited Michael again and thought I would be interested in reading some of his journal entries, shared by his guardian. It seems an invasion of Michael's privacy, but that doesn't stop me. Amelia comes while I am reading. I glance up at her.

"Eli has consented to your letter being delivered. He knows that you and Michael will find each other in a future lifetime, but his heart is not unaffected by your plight. He wishes to bring Michael some comfort in the time he has left on this earth, and he believes your letter will ease his mind."

While I feel a quiet pleasure at her news, I am intent on reading Michael's journal entries. Zachary takes her place, waits for me to finish, then changes the subject and forces me to return—from a far off hospice bed and the man who occupies it.

"You may be asking yourself why we are willing to assist you in this unusual endeavor. It is, in part, because you have been approached and also due to the status of your spirit. Beyond that, it is because of your acceptance of what you have been told. It was not immediate, but we had expected to have to fight for every small increment of your belief. With others, it has often been a long process. It is to your credit, and to that of your spirit in guiding you, that you have been an adept student. You have searched your previous knowledge and beliefs and have asked pertinent questions that have led us to reveal as much to you as we have, and to now support you in your desire to communicate with Michael."

Zachary says that, not only may I write to Michael, but he will be allowed to reply. Amelia will be our courier, by some method beyond my comprehension and at odds with my rational mind. She will take my letter and place it inside the cover of Michael's journal. I am to tell him to leave his answer there. She will retrieve it and give it to me at Sally's next appointment. My acceptance of all that has happened thus far leads me to now accept, on faith, that Amelia can transport our letters without the use of physical means.

I ask Amelia if, now that Zachary has returned, she will be leaving, this temporary assignment completed.

"There has been a conference, of sorts. As you and I have discussed, my appearing to the alters as a strong female figure is assisting them in their healing process. I will remain as Sally's guardian. Zachary will now be a less constant presence as he continues with his mission of approaching others."

Amelia pauses, then looks at me intently.

"That is one reason. The other reason I requested to stay is that I want to remain a part of what you have started here. You have astounded many in the spirit world with your success in reaching Michael and with the depth of your connection to him. Your efforts are being followed with great interest, and I want to continue my involvement."

Amelia says goodbye and Zachary returns.

"I have just come from a visit to Michael. He was awake and listening to music."

I can't resist. I have to ask him to describe the music. From his reluctant, rather awkward, attempt, I am able to recognize the song as "Unchained Melody." (I have not mentioned it, either to him or to Amelia.)

Now I wait. It will be several days before I might expect a letter. Like Amelia, I want to pursue this. I pause to consider what "this" is. I pick up and read again the entries from Michael's journal—it is a spiritual journey in the most literal sense. I have traveled with my spirit to his dreams and to his side.

I get an image of my spirit looking for Michael over the years, and it comes to me: this has been an odyssey of the spirit—years of wandering and searching by Mahalia—with a final, valiant effort to reach him, assisted not by Greek gods but by angels. Did she ever think that her search would culminate in a spiritual connection and not a physical one?

Odyssey triggers an image of another echo of Greek mythology, with its mix of gods and mortals, hero journeys, and destinies lost and found. In telling me of my destiny, Amelia unleashed a reverse-themed Pandora's Box. In the myth, it was filled with unknown evils; this is a golden treasure chest. It is filled with goodness, joy, love, and light—released and set free as possibilities. I have to follow them. I must listen to my heart.

Michael's Journal Entries

10/20

To the lady in my vision—if you hear me, come again. I know you, but I don't know who you are. If we never walk together down the twisting roads of time, I will hold you always with me in my heart.

I have tried to explain to Vince what the dream meant to me. He thinks I'm delusional due to the pain killers. Maybe I am, but it seemed so real. Who can she be? I feel that I should know her.

10/21

I can't get her out of my mind. No pain killers last night, I want to have a clear head. Someone was here—it was not a dream. She touched my hand. Has the leukemia affected my brain? Sometimes I feel as if I am traveling down a deserted road all alone, but now I don't feel so alone. Who is she?

I am surrounded by a presence. I know it is her. How can I explain it to Vince when I can't even explain it to myself? I know it's not the pain killers. I haven't had any since yesterday. She haunts all my waking thoughts and disturbs my sleep—a disruption I welcome.

10/22

Vince has another date with Tara. I think he is serious about her. Oh, to be young again. He was upset with me because J.T. told him I've been refusing my medication. I practically had to do handstands to prove to him I didn't need any.

I don't understand what is happening to me, but maybe it's another remission. Physically, I know that I am feeling better. Mentally, I am probably off my rocker. They finally quit pushing their pain pills at me. I long for the night, when I know she will come again. I know that she is with me—she touches my soul.

Am I being visited by an angel? It is sensual, and even almost sexual, an overwhelming feeling of love, peace, and serenity. If I told Vince that, he would think his dad is getting senile.

Who is she? Why does she haunt my dreams? How is this happening? She knows things about me—my name, that I am sick, that I have a son. How does she know? Maybe I shouldn't ask, only accept. She breathes life into me.

10/23

I have felt her again, and last night I heard the lyrics from an old song—the one about being lonely, hungry, something about touch. How can I be feeling like this now? It has been so long since I held a woman in my arms.

I've sure given everyone here something to talk about. They can't figure out what is going on with me. I only take the pain pills occasionally, and then it is more to make them happy than that I need them. I go to the hospital today for more tests. I hate them. Please, God, let it be good news.

A long day, but I feel great considering I can't have much blood left for the undertakers. Her essence was by my side. She comforts me as nothing else can. I know she is out there. I just know it. Maybe there's a chance for us to meet. I suppose that's a stupid thing to wish for. What do I have to offer anyone?

10/24

No word yet from J.T. If it is bad news, I hope he keeps it to himself. That song keeps playing in my head, but I can't remember who did it ... Mary was here with her damn pills again and I asked her. She thinks it is "Unchained Melody." I spit her pills out after she left. I don't want to be groggy tonight.

I can't believe it! What a night! I want to remember every detail. I almost made love to my angel. She is soft and gentle, with small hands that fit perfectly in mine. Her forehead comes almost to my chin. Her hair is a soft brown, her eyes are two blue sapphires—they say so much without a word being spoken. Damn! I hate these interruptions.

PART II

A Love Story

11. Body and Soul

10/26 - 11/01

Dearest Michael, I write to give you some explanation of these last few days and nights. I picture you having just opened your journal and discovered this letter inside the front cover. I see the puzzled look on your face, then one of curiosity. Do you immediately connect it to your dreams? I will tell you what I know.

Last week, I was reminded of a brief contact we had more than twenty years ago, and I was told we had been destined to be together. In the hours that followed, I felt a connection to you far beyond that of a chance acquaintance. A few days later, my source told me of your illness and that our destinies had been changed after three missed opportunities to meet. They cannot be restored. I was devastated, sat numbly for hours, then finally gained some degree of acceptance. My grief was not for a stranger. I know you—your essence, your nature, what we would have been to each other.

I could not forget you and go blithely on with my life. I reached out to you on a spiritual level, from the depths of my being, and felt a profound connection. I saw glimpses of the life we might have had together and knew—had we come face to face for any length of time—we could not have denied ourselves to each other.

My source confirmed that I had reached you. So intensely had I felt it that I was not surprised but filled with awe at the possibilities of a spiritual connection. Michael, I long to be with you for whatever time is possible. I deeply regret that our paths did not cross in a more obvious and sustained manner many years ago.

A few days ago, I heard an old song, "Unchained Melody." Do you remember those words that speak of hunger? We have touched so deeply that physical contact would hardly be more than what we share now, but I want to explore your face, look into your eyes and see there a reflection of my love for you. I want to feel your lips on mine, my hand in yours, the beating of your heart.

As much as I long for it, a physical relationship seems almost irrelevant, or at least separate from what we have shared on a spiritual plane. The depth of our experience leads me to accept that we will never meet. It is a fragile acceptance, one filled with longing, but, in this moment, possible. I cannot answer for the moments to come.

The second time I reached out to you, we connected so intensely that I wondered if we should end on that glorious high note. You already know that I could not restrain my heart from reaching out again ... and again .... I will continue for as long as it gives you comfort and strength, serenity and fulfillment. Know that it gives the same to me. What we have shared has meant more to me than ... I expect for both of us the closest experience has been our love for our children.

As I write, I feel the intensity of our connection and desire. Our brief experience, made possible by the assistance of angels, is more than what some have in a lifetime spent together. Believe me when I say we will be together in lives to come. You will have realized by now that I am no angel, but—filled with love and longing—the woman in your dreams.

Dearest Michael, I have had the best news. Permission has been granted for us to write, not only this one time but twice a week. Our angels have smiled upon us—they are our messengers.

We must agree to some restrictions. I am not to reveal my full name and neither of us is to refer to our location. I have promised not to search for you. If you were only an hour or two, or three or four, away, I don't know how I could restrain myself. I believe it is farther than that. Can we be content with the limits imposed on us? Can we explore completely all that is possible and not waste our time on frustrated attempts to achieve what is not?

I long to feel your touch, to be with you in every way. It is almost frightening to imagine what we could have been to each other. Our experience thus far suggests that, if we were to meet, it would overwhelm our senses. Someday, somewhere, we will find each other, in the fullness of youth, and we will recognize the old souls within— they will not let us miss our chance.

You are to place your reply in your journal. I long to hold in my hands the paper that has been touched by yours, to see the writing of your hand, to have some sense of the physical dimension of your being. I am told that you may know my first name. It is Teresa, but I am called Tessa, or Tessa Lynne. Or, you may continue to call me your angel. Whichever name you choose, I am yours.

Dearest Teresa, I can't believe this is happening to me. I knew you were real. Oh God, there is so much I want to ask you and so much I am afraid to ask. You said we are being assisted by angels. (Please— don't tell me you are an angel too.) If we are truly being helped by angels, nothing should be impossible, but there obviously can be no future for us.

You must already know that I am dying. I was diagnosed with leukemia three years ago, had a quick remission, and then it came back a few months ago. I was started on a new drug, had a severe reaction, and was in a coma for five days. I haven't told anyone this, but I had what is called a near-death experience and was given the opportunity to return to my life. It was not an easy decision, but

my son will graduate medical school in two years and I want to be there. Now I have even more reason to live.

Teresa. That name sounds so good on my lips and the taste on my tongue is like honey. I say it with soft vowel sounds—Teh-rey-zuh. I feel that I have known you all of my life. I, too, know that there are other lifetimes and believe we have been together in the past.

Our song—it has to be our song. I hunger for you in every way a man can want a woman. I want to hold your hand in mine, touch your face, and look into your eyes to see all the love and longing I feel reflected back at me. You speak of physical love as secondary to our spiritual love. I agree it must be so, but how can I feel this depth of love and not want to hold you in my arms, kiss your sweet lips, explore every inch of your body.

I mourn our loss, but I must keep alive in my heart a hope that the angels who have smiled upon us will relent and allow us to meet—face to face, heart to heart. As you are mine, I am yours.

Michael, are you familiar with the poetry of Kahlil Gibran? He is most widely known for *The Prophet*. Our experience prompted me to search for a small book of his work that I have had for years, since the time our paths so briefly crossed. It was not on any of my bookshelves or among the stacks of books scattered about the house. I finally found it, helping to prop up a three-legged couch downstairs. I am sending you one of his poems, torn from the book with care, the pages yellowed with time. "Tears and Laughter" reflects much of what I have felt these last several days. He speaks the language of the soul.

A moment ago, I felt you close and then, without intention, my fingers were touching my face, gently exploring its contours. Was it me touching you? Or was it you touching me? I could not tell. I know now why we cannot meet—it is because I could never leave you—too large a part of me would be left behind. If you sense the torment in my soul, that is why. I must try to sleep.

You are still here with me. I have wiped the tears from my eyes, or was that you? I could not sleep, kept reaching for you. My soul was not to be satisfied until we had finished what was started earlier in the night. I am reminded of a time when my marriage still seemed viable. We had made love that left me satisfied, physically. Then I collapsed onto him sobbing, heaving, deep passionate tears of longing and loss, not knowing why, only that something essential was missing. After last night, I know what it was—the full union of body and soul. Do you believe now that I am as much flesh and blood as you?

I cannot hide my pain from you. As I held you close, I knew in every fiber of my being what it would have been to have borne your child. I mourn the loss of what we might have had; you reach out to comfort me. The pain lessens—joy remains. You are still near, but I must begin my day.

My love, you are never far from my thoughts, but others take me away from you. I am home for lunch. Have you read my letter? I sense that you are deep in thought. Has it been too much? I long to be there to tell you in person, to remove some of the mystery.

Sometime in the night, I felt my soul reach out to yours. In return, I felt a touch so soft and gentle I knew it was not of this world. I thought I heard my name. Is it you who said it? I do not want to imagine anything, only to know what is real between us. I must somehow get through the afternoon.

My dear Teresa, such sweet words fill my heart and soul that surely I will die from their magnitude. Every word of your letter is imprinted on my heart. I long to hear your voice—one I have surely heard a thousand times before.

Were you with me early this morning? I felt your presence and held you in my arms. So strongly did I feel your touch ignite my soul that our coming together was love in its purest form. Oh my love, my sweet love, you have given my heart wings. Can anything in life

equal this rapture, this passion I feel for you?

I am tormented. My tears fall freely, born of anger and helplessness. Why has God, in His infinite wisdom, sought to deal us this cruel blow? Forgive me, for I do not wish to speak of anger in letters to my love. How can I waste precious time on anger when my heart is so full?

Your letter is here. I knew I wasn't alone. Yes, I believe you are as much flesh and blood as me, with all the wants and desires that are human. I wept with happiness and then with pain. I can think of no greater joy than sharing our pregnancy, watching you grow with our child in your womb, rejoicing every day that it was mine. I would not have wanted to leave your side. I fear we may have starved.

It grows late, but I do not want to quit writing—it is as if I take my leave of you. Your name is always on my lips. Do you hear my voice? Come to me, my sweet.

My dearest Michael, I have held in my hands the pages that came from yours. I have read with deep emotion your heartfelt words. They quench my thirst for you, like the first drops of water to fall on parched lips after days in the desert. My deeper thirst will be satisfied in the days ahead.

After last night, is it possible for us to know any more of each other? We were led by our spirits to a distant realm. Our experience was reflected in our physical beings but did not require our touch—two selves dissolved into one. I know pure joy, peace, and utter contentment. If we must be parted, we will yet exult in our triumph.

Like you, there is much I want to know, to tell, to explore. My daughters have been in and out as I write. Kenna and Callie are twins, sixteen going on twenty-one. The last few years have brought the usual teen dilemmas, times two, and some strong statements of independence. I had told them about the one I call my source and now a little about you. I finally convinced them our letters are too personal to let them read. As I write, the fourth member of our household is purring on my lap. Charkey is the last of a menagerie of dogs, birds, reptiles, fish, and a hamster.

I must try to sleep tonight, but I will spend the last moments of my day with you. Until now, there has been a communion of our souls. With your letters, I begin a relationship with the man, Michael. I like what I am learning about the man and want to know him better. I feel completely at one with the soul that lives within him.

Dear heart, where do I begin? Your letter asks so much and reveals so much more that I am a bit overwhelmed. I will stick to safer subjects and save my words of love for later. My days were fairly boring until you came and filled my life with such joy that I look at everything in a new light. Vince comes every day and brings my mail, reading material, etc. (The hospice is part of the same medical complex as his school.) When I am able to, I read or work at my computer. Since you entered my life, I have gained weight, have more energy, and I no longer spend most of the day in bed.

Are your daughters as beautiful and charming as their mother? Vince is all the family I have left. My younger brother, Danny, was killed in a car accident a few years ago, and my mother has been gone for almost ten years. My father lives in California. We were never close and have had no contact the last five years.

I want to know more of this woman who has captured my heart. Tell me everything—your likes and dislikes, your wants and desires. Tell me about Kenna and Callie. I always wished for daughters and maybe another son. You are so accepting of my dilemma. It fills my heart with sadness that I cannot be more of a man to you.

Yes, my love, I was safely, sensuously in your loving embrace both last night and early yesterday and then yet again this morning. Our passion was not to be denied. I longingly await your next letter.

12. The Invisible Choir

Michael, dearest of all I have known. Every word you write brings me closer to the man who conceives each thought, instructs his hand, and conveys with each sure stroke a message of such love as I have never fathomed. I do not believe the love of our souls could be any stronger. The love between man and woman has room to grow as we nourish it, cherish it, and take lessons from the lovers—many times lovers—within.

As I read your words, I cannot deny my longings for you, my ardent desire to meet. We are told they cannot be satisfied, yet I hope for a reprieve. I long for the warmth of your skin on mine; for the masculine textures of your body, in all its parts; for the scent of you, the weight of your body pressed against mine; and for the highly charged air between us as we not quite touch. I long for your greater physical strength and presence, which give pure pleasure to the very core of me.

I have my moments of despair. I walked today along a wooded river path, my steps slow and dispirited, my heart full of anguish for what we have lost. An ominous canopy of dark, brooding clouds reflected my mood—until I turned a corner and was met with the most gentle of breezes. The sun broke through at that precise moment, its golden rays penetrating the darkness, bringing back all the reasons for making the most of this hour we have been given.

I am sending you my favorite Kahlil Gibran poem, "The Playground of Life." I have read it over and over again, the depth of our experience merging with the truth of his words. He writes powerfully of the one hour in a century in which truth is revealed and a soul is rarefied by sorrow, lit by passion. His words have touched me deeply in their application writ large, but now they speak to me only of our love. Michael, this is our hour—the jewel we have been granted.

Vince is coming soon to take me for some tests, but I would much rather stay here with you. I pray you just experienced the power of our union as I did. Yes, my love, my soul, my reason for living, I was with you spiritually, physically, and so emotionally at the times you mention. How can I continue to question my good fortune to have found you?

Is there life after death, life after life? Yes, I believe there is, since before my near-death experience and most certainly after it. Tell me of your sources. What do they know of us? You suggest that they are not of this world; they can't be, if you have had access to my journal entries. I do know a few words of French. I want to kiss them from your lips.

Were you in the woods? Did you feel my touch as I felt yours? Your essence, your being, breathes life into me. Teresa, my love, do you feel a little frightened by the intensity of our experience? I know it is not of this earth. You wrote of my pulling away. Only one time have I done that purposely, maybe as a test to see if you would call out to me to stay—you did.

Another interruption. I have come to detest them. I am going to fall asleep tonight with your name on my lips, beseeching you to join me. Come, my sweet love, and replenish me.

What a night that was ours—a precious stone cast into the still waters of a mountain pond, resting at the center as ripples of intense, sensuous pleasure overflow the banks. I feel the ripples still. The stone rests at the center of my being, between my heart and where I draw you in.

I can give you some idea of how this is possible, so real to us. I am told that our spirits meet on some unearthly plane, attached still to our physical selves. They need that attachment to experience what is not possible on a spiritual level and to bring to us the immense power of their love and desire. I am at a loss how to describe it—dare I say holy?

I will share some of what I have been told. Our first fleeting sight of each other was in the fall of 1971. You had just become a father, and I was planning a December wedding. You glanced my way after I dropped my books in the first floor hallway of the admin building. If only I had played the helpless female looking for someone to rescue me (not my style).

Two years later, the same building, do you recall wanting to meet a young woman, asking about her, being told that she was married? Our brief exchange was interrupted at hello, but I have never forgotten the sickening, sinking feeling I experienced as you walked away from me.

Michael, what follows was agony for me to hear. I know your pain as you read this. We would have each left our spouse, married, and had another son. Vince would have lived with us from the age of eight. And then, I told you about my daughters, how dear they are to me; it was their destiny, and ours, that we share this life, what I mourn as our greatest loss.

We had a final chance in 1983 when you registered for one of my courses. In my six years there, it was the only fully enrolled class with so many last-minute cancellations that we had to drop it. I am told there was a spirit-world intervention, made to prevent several deaths as people traveled home. I was considering divorce at the time. When I thought of leaving, my inner self soared—the same part of me that now so eagerly takes flight to you.

Good morning, my love. How do I write, engage the part of my brain that knows words? I want only to savor our experience of the night. I told you of the beautiful stone anchored in the center of my being—you reached me there. I don't know what a man would experience. I think, mere man, that you must be jealous of a woman's capability. I am filled now, content. Do you see on my face the glow of our love? Leaving you, I meant to seek some distance from the intensity of last night. Foolish me. If I wanted distance, why did I return to my bed and draw you close again? It was you that I wanted, to linger with. I feel you still. Michael, I adore you.

My dearest Teresa, I have spent the last several hours attempting to fill my need for you—a bottomless pit of desire. I know it to be the complete union of our souls, our hearts, our beings. My lunch is here. I must keep up my strength.

I get annoyed now at intrusions I used to welcome. I know this will settle into less intensity; we will talk about the weather and other mundane aspects of our lives, like can we agree to put the cap back on the toothpaste. For the time being, can we not relish it and cherish the intensity and damn the intrusions? I must leave you, my love.

Your letter was here when I returned. I have sat deep in thought, trying to put on paper what is in my heart. Where was once my heart is a deep void—it has been ripped from my chest, so great is my pain. Stay by my side tonight, my love, as you have been these past few hours. Hold me, my sweet, for I will surely cry myself to sleep in your arms.

I can sense your body wracked with quiet sobs, welling up from the deepness of your soul. When I asked if you wanted to know everything, I should have warned you. I knew it was our children that would most torment you, as it does me. I have not felt you close.

Did I tell you too much? My sweet Michael, it is the part of you that feels this loss so deeply that I most love in you. I was finally able to reach you as night turned to day. Did you feel, when your pain had subsided a little, the peaceful presence that surrounded us? We are being helped to heal this sorrow.

Beloved of my soul, I am not yet ready to leave this life, this world. Will you wait for me? I am told that your illness was not destined— you have already turned the tide. If there is a chance we can yet be together, in every sense, do you want to pursue it? I will be close to you through the night. With so much in my heart, I am yours.

I couldn't write this morning, and I am still having great difficulty trying to find the words to describe how I feel, or, more accurately, how I don't feel. I am numb, void of anything but an overwhelming grief for our loss. I have not eaten today—such is the bitterness on my tongue.

Forgive me, my darling. I was deceiving myself when I said I was devoid of feeling. I am feeling so much I can't sort it all out, but I can't believe how incredibly selfish I have been to have thought only of my own pain. Sweetheart, you are my reason for waking every morning. I am so sorry that I wasn't given the opportunity to watch you grow heavy with my beautiful daughters in your womb—the pain is so intense. Last night, my anger prevented me from knowing you were near. I cursed my Lord and have since prayed for His forgiveness. I couldn't finish your letter after learning of our lost life.

Come to me tonight and lift my heart. We will weep together and find strength in each other. Let me search once more your beautiful stone, that I may find solace in the center of your being.

My love, you are still here with me. Last night, when I was free to return to you, I reached out—to absolute emptiness; you were nowhere to be found. Then, early this morning, I held you in my arms again. These past hours have been filled with a sweet love that is easing the pain, healing our sorrow.

I have referred to my sources. I call them angels but they are not from that realm. Zachary appeared to me first and is closest to me spiritually. Amelia told me of you and is our messenger; she is often close to you, as is your guardian, Bethany. One more, Eli, is kept informed of everything and gives guidance to the others. I am enclosing a poem by George Eliot—we are surrounded by "The Choir Invisible."

> *"May I reach that purest heaven, be to other souls the cup*
> *of strength in some great agony, enkindle generous ardor,*
> *feed pure love...be the sweet presence of a good diffused,*
> *and in diffusion ever more intense."*

These lines, especially, remind me of those who assist us, our invisible choir. We must open ourselves to their presence.

I can't focus on anything but my need for you. Something a little frightening occurred just before you left me, but I am not sure what it meant. A few minutes later there was another strange event, a more positive one. I will need to give it some thought.

I have been looking back twenty years to the time I was in graduate school. Don't keep me guessing. Tell me what you know. I have had some glimpses of what might have been. Are Callie and Kenna blonde? I have an urge to write in my journal.

What an idiot I am. Your letter was there. The warden, as I call the head nurse—think drill sergeant or Nurse Ratched—has poked her head in to say they are coming soon to do my IV therapy. I must leave this for now, but my mind is bursting with questions .

Can anything be more loving and tender than the hours I spend in your arms? I don't understand who has this knowledge or why we are privileged to it. Is there nothing we can do to share what is left of our lives? That is a stupid question. You have so much life ahead of you—it seems that I do not.

Yes, I have felt the Light surrounding us when we are together, the same as you describe it, a version of what I knew in my near-death experience. Is it our angels? Have they come for me? If knowing a love so beautiful is the beginning of my death, then let me die a thousand times.

Ne manqué pas de revenir me voir—do not forget to come back to see me. You are such a delight. I love the way you take me in hand so gently, but firmly. How is it possible for you to communicate both your intent and your action so unambiguously? I know exactly what you are doing and why you are doing it. You amaze me, as do the possibilities our love has shown itself capable of transforming into reality.

It was not easy for me to read the first half of your last letter, your feelings so sweet and loving. I knew they would change to heartbreak when you learned of our lost life. I have since felt some easing of your pain, a change in our time together; we now find solace more than sorrow.

Back to the past—I started university in 1968 with a major in foreign languages. I had reached the point of reading French literature (which I still enjoy) when I realized I was not likely to become a peripatetic world traveler. I switched to journalism and then to psychology, graduated early, spent two years in Colorado, and came back in time for our paths to briefly cross in 1973. If we had met in 1983, it would have required no soul searching to change our lives. I haven't had a serious relationship since then. A few men I dated talked of a future together, but I couldn't settle for an offer of security and enough attraction to kindle a small spark. I knew there was something, someone, more. I knew that you were waiting for me.

I agree that we must enjoy the intensity while we can. It would be natural for it to lessen as the days and nights go by. Were you in the woods with me today? We were laughing as we walked through the last of the falling leaves. I hear occasional words but more often have a strong sense of what you are saying, how you are feeling. Our life together would have been such a delight—we can still have that.

My darling, your words bring me both comfort and enlightenment. Our invisible choir—are they from our past, are they ghosts? I shouldn't joke about this, but it is all so incredible. No one would believe me if I told them about you.

Did we walk together hand in hand? Two young lovers full of each other's presence—laughing, talking so easily, leaves cushioning our path—how good we are together. I wanted to find a spot to lay your body down and prove my love to you.

I knew it had to be at university. I also started in 1968, after a two-year stint in the army. I was quite idealistic back then, enlisted before I could be drafted, got into communications as I had wanted to, and spent eighteen months in Vietnam. Please don't ask me about that time. I won't talk about it.

A few years later, I did notice a young woman in the admin office, through that little window where we ordered transcripts. She was working at a desk, blonde hair falling to her shoulders, and then got up to bend over a filing cabinet, wearing a short skirt (now you know what a cad I am). Do you remember Pearl? She told me you were married and warned me off. Did you ever go to the Blue Goose? I tended bar there and lived in an apartment nearby.

Sweetheart, I must say au revoir until the morning. I made a promise to a young man, Ethan, age fourteen, that I would play him a game of pool. He has been here a week and his family couldn't be here today. Come to me tonight, my love, and hold me—just hold me.

L'amour de mon coeur—you *are* the love of my heart. I have been trying to recall words and phrases in a beautiful language we have spoken as lovers long ago. Our first lifetime together was in the late 10th century in Paris. You were an artist and I was your woman.

Yes, I was with you Monday evening, and I felt the same tender closeness. Will you tell me what happened just before I took leave of you? A few hours later, I was aware of a definite presence and distinctly heard the words "personal power." Then the lyrics of an old song, "Eli's Coming," were playing in my head. Amelia confirmed my assumption. "Yes, Eli was present that night to both you and Michael, to assess the effects of the last two weeks and to leave each of you a message: you must believe in and access your personal power."

My love, when I asked if you would wait for me, I meant in this lifetime. I was told in October that our destinies could not be restored. It appears now that they might be. It would be a gift, a blessed gift—one not to be expected, much less taken for granted, but possible. When we sense the Light surrounding us, it is a special blessing, the presence of the Creator, in whose service our angels are working. It is not to do with your death; it can have everything to do with your life. You can channel their energy and use it to enhance your own healing powers.

Michael, how great is your faith in yourself and in our love, in a power and a purpose beyond our scope of understanding? You can use your faith as a guiding force. I wish this prescription came with a guarantee or a set of instructions—you are the key. Energy expended in self-blame cannot be used to heal; laughter, love, even tears, can heal; guilt, fear, and worry cannot, or hate, but I do not sense that in you. In the healing spirit of Love, I am yours.

These damn interruptions are driving me crazy. I have had more than usual today because I am running a slight fever. How can I tell them it is the afterglow of a feverish night spent in your arms? You

set my soul on fire. Describe for me what you see, feel, experience, so I can know that we are real.

I will tell you part of what happened Monday evening, the strangeness of it. I have felt it before, during my near-death experience. It was a presence that spoke to me of my personal power. I believe it was telling me that whatever I desire is within my power to achieve. How can I deny that there are other-world forces guiding, sustaining, and assisting us?

You have the fallen leaves. Can you smell the earthy fragrance of the woods? I stepped on the path and you were there with me. My love, it is all as real as the leaves you have held in your hands. When will we stop questioning? Yes, I do question, just as you do. I have known our angels longer but they speak to me, and deliver your letters to me, through a patently human form.

Our angels are not ghosts but spiritual beings who are more advanced than our spirits. Zachary and Amelia are near the Master level and Eli is at the upper reaches of it, nearly a Sage. Pascal used an analogy—of a branch that can't comprehend the tree as a whole—to express the limits of our understanding of the spirit world. What I do know is this: the depth of our love, our power to reach out to each other, and that I have experienced the presence of our angels. Michael, this is a journey we can take together—with the help of our invisible choir.

13. Encounters with the Light

Teresa, I know you are waiting for an answer to your last letter. Your handwriting tells me how strongly you feel. My darling, I have already beaten the odds once, and I am looking forward to my next remission. I almost felt I was being scolded, and then I realized you spoke out of your great love and concern for me.

Yes, the Light is a source for me. My near-death experience was one of a separation of my soul from my body. I watched the medical team as they attempted to save the life lying before them—and then I realized the body was mine. I felt an overwhelming sense of peace, love, and contentment. The Light was first a path that beckoned me, and then it surrounded me. It is the absence of color, yet it is all colors, intense and warm. I wanted to be with it, stay with it. Then I saw my mother. She said, "Michael, go back. Vince needs you—it is not yet your time."

I looked back and could see my son sitting beside my bed, overcome with grief. I nodded to my mother and said goodbye, and then it was several days before I woke up. My darling, I will do whatever is within my power to remain on this earth. I will fight for my life with you.

Michael, already I miss the comfort of your arms. My sleep last night was restless until I felt your presence. You may have gathered that I am quite independent—by necessity as well as by nature. That does not prevent my needing someone to lean on, to be lovingly taken care of, sheltered in your embrace.

Do you have a clear image of the young woman you met in 1973? Don't forget to age her twenty years. I am no great beauty, but I do have my moments. My hair is medium length, dark blonde now, and you accurately saw my dark blue eyes. I usually wear casual clothes of cotton, linen, or silk in size six or eight. No fake nails or even polish and not a lot of makeup, but always on my eyes. My lips have been called kissable, my legs have aroused comment, and, by the way, I never put the cap back on the toothpaste.

Your experience of the Light is familiar enough to me that I can understand why the choice to return wasn't an easy one for you. I mentioned the client I refer to as Sally. About three years ago, I received a strong message that I should guide her to a source of strength. I believe now that it was Eli who spoke to me then. The next day, I waited for Sally to begin our session, to set the agenda. She told me of a similar experience, puzzled at what it had meant, and said she wanted to access that source. I used guided imagery to help her, but she found it difficult, described a path filled with ob- stacles. She persisted, found faith in herself and in her worthiness, and then the path ahead was clear. I didn't suggest what she would find—I hadn't been told—and I knew it was important that she dis- cover it for herself.

Sally came to what she first described as a light, later as the Light. "It was the strongest of lights, but it was not a harsh or blinding one. It was like a cocoon that encompassed me and made me feel safe. It welcomed me and surrounded me with warmth and support. I now have the resolve to go on." She asked questions of the Light, but was frustrated with the enigmatic answers that left her to come to greater awareness through her own efforts. Michael, like you, Sally did not want to leave that loving presence. Each time, the Light would say, "You have been replenished; it is time now for you to return."

I observed Sally reach her hand outward and upward, her face uplifted. Then I saw her face suffused with awe and her physical being transformed—she was clearly in the presence of something extraordinary. I can still picture the rays of light, as visible then as if I was seeing them myself. This was long before Zachary revealed himself to me as Sally's guardian, but he recently explained it to me. "The Light is an emanation of the Creator that appears to individuals according to their need. This opportunity required that you first recognize, and then act upon, the message you were given. If you had ignored it, the message would not have been repeated."

Zachary added that "The Light provides a welcome to spirits and a pathway for them to follow on their return to the spirit world. For the living, it is a means for the Creator to communicate with your spirits. It is not usually seen but is experienced as a feeling of inner warmth, of comfort and protection." It is what I feel when we sense the Light surrounding us.

Vince and Tara were here earlier. We all went to the rec room and spent some time with Ethan. As he and Vince played pool, I pictured our two sons doing so in our home. Vince is very much his father's son, similar in looks, and he is bright and funny and handsome, of course.

I haven't described the hospice to you. It is one wing of a super hospital complex, about a hundred beds. The atmosphere is homey and I brought a few books (including my Shakespeare), some photos, and my computer—the field I teach at the college level.

Gibran's "Song of the Soul" speaks to my mine. I too have felt that our souls are of us yet apart from us, but I haven't known how to describe it until I read his words. Come to me. Speak to me our language of love that I may kiss the words from your lips.

Quel belle matin—what a beautiful morning! Tell me, my love, is it more blessed to give or to receive? What we share intensifies, deepens ... the feelings linger.

Last night, Callie and Kenna told me I am starting to look like a girl. When I questioned that, they said, "at least no more than thirty." They think it is because I have lost some weight. I am leaving for the gym for a light workout ... I couldn't help but notice the male bodies. The ones I found most attractive were, I am sure, similar to yours. They were muscular, but not too much so, with an appearance of length more than bulk.

Now that I am feeling so well, it is easier to mention that I have had some health issues the last three years. Any physical work, like cooking, pretty much anything, I could do for about ten minutes and then would have to rest for an hour or more. I couldn't go for even the shortest walk the first few months but can now manage thirty to sixty minutes. My goal is to go mountain hiking again by next summer; recent efforts have ended in defeat and a few tears shed.

Teresa, I want to cry out at the injustice of it all. I am trying hard not to make them angry, for fear I will lose you. I am flesh and blood and so are you. I want you here now—in my bed, in my life. God forgive me, but I can't help feeling this way. You are so very precious to me. Please hold me, comfort me.

How is it you know when I am hurting? Need I ask? I almost tore this up and started over, but then I realized you know my pain. I am not a sponge that can just keep absorbing everything without having to be wrung out once in awhile. I have vented my feelings here, for it does me no good to harbor them. I have just felt you near. Tell me you were here; tell me what you said. Help me to believe in us— that you are not some figment of my imagination.

I haven't been able to sleep. As always, my thoughts are of you. It is frustrating not to know when your letters will come, if I will get one or several at a time. I am going to write in my journal instead … your letters were here. When? How easily my heart takes wing.

Michael, our children have been with us before, the girls in a lifetime in Ireland in the 12ᵗʰ century. We grew old together, both past seventy, not common then. In our life together as Blackfeet, we had eleven children including Vince, the oldest, and the girls. In the moment I first reached you, I knew that your son was mine and my daughters yours.

There is more. I hesitate to tell you this, knowing it will bring heartache. About a year before the girls were born, I had a miscarriage at three months. Zachary said, "The spirit who was to take that life came close to observe you and your marriage. He then chose not to accept that lifetime without Michael as his father. It is rare for a spirit to make such a choice and it requires special permission." I was always pleased to have had daughters but can so easily imagine having had your son.

In our lifetimes together, I have always been female and you male. Most spirits have a preference that predominates, but all must experience lifetimes as both genders. It is natural and right that you are male to my female. To think of you as my husband gives that word new meaning, richer—so deeply felt it can only come from what we have shared in our past lives.

Your description of the Light appearing to Sally is incredible. It is a basic truth, one I know from my personal experience and now when the Light surrounds us. It helps me to accept what we have together and to have no doubt—in this moment—as to the truth of it.

I will tell you about my strange experience the night Eli spoke to both of us. Shortly before I heard his message, I had an awful premonition that you were in danger. I sensed that you were trying to come to me but that the journey would be treacherous. I interpreted it as you attempting to make your way here. As much as I needed and wanted you to come, I feared for your safety. I hesitated to tell you of it at the time.

It is uncanny that going to the mountains is a favorite pastime of yours. My passion is downhill skiing. Do you ski? I could show you some of the most beautiful places in the world.

Michael, I have had a message of hope—an incredible experience. Earlier today, Zachary said your letter would be here this evening, and it is four days yet until Sally's next appointment. He knew she had a meeting tonight and suggested we could meet briefly by the river, on her route home. I will tell you about it.

It is dark, a few stars visible. The full moon hides behind the clouds, softly illuminating the scene. The wind is chasing wispy drifts of snow across the ground and over the thin layer of ice near shore. I park facing the water and can see across it to a small, wooded island about the width of a football field away. Zachary joins me a few minutes later. He gives me your letter, we talk a bit, and then he pauses abruptly and says, "Do you see it?" I look in all directions but can see nothing unusual. He looks straight ahead, gives me not a clue. And then my eyes are drawn up and across the water.

I see a light above the tall cottonwood trees, now bare of leaves. It is amazing in its brilliance and in its size. The light has a core of fifteen feet, or more, and emits rays in all directions, that long and longer. It has the look of a star come to earth, of Venus, fallen from the sky. Twice, it descends into the treetops and then rises back up. It is brighter by far than any light I have ever seen. I am awe-struck, gaze in wonder, mesmerized by the sight.

A few minutes go by before Zachary says, "The light will soon begin to move off at an angle (he gestures up and to the left) and then will join with an ordinary light source." That is exactly what happens. The light begins to slowly climb at a forty-five degree angle, making steady progress on a straight diagonal path. A few stars are visible among the clouds; the light continues to outshine them. Then the lights of a large plane become visible, several miles away on its approach to the airport. The light stays on course, the two paths intersect, and the light merges with the lights of the plane.

Michael, it was extraordinary, to say the least. If I were to have only this, it would be the event of a lifetime, one to guide my every experience and perception. I can hardly believe its impact is somewhat diminished by the amazing events of the last two months.

Zachary said, "The light was made manifest through the efforts of some mischievous junior spirits—on a mission at the request of Michael's spirit." I want to believe it was a message that we will be together. Zachary said, "Hang on to your hope." That your spirit would send me such a message is totally in keeping with my experience of him.

Good morning, my love. I sit here in my corner chair, still in awe of the light. It spoke its own truth—such was the magnitude of its appearance. I have to admit, when I woke up I questioned that truth. Given the peripheral involvement of a third party, I had to run it through a logical thought process: the light appeared in an area of rough underbrush, with no access except by boat; Zachary didn't suggest what I would see or even look up; he predicted the angle the light would take and that it would merge with a more ordinary light source; and, this was no ordinary light—its brilliance alone enough to convince a hardened skeptic. One more thing: when I first looked, the plane Zachary predicted was not yet visible. My logical mind is now satisfied.

Like this light, our experience speaks its own truth. I know what I know. Yet, when I am feeling less connected with the part of myself that knows, I begin to question or to think it is all too incredible and wondrous to be true. Emerson writes, in his essay "The Over-Soul," that "Our faith comes in moments; our vice is habitual." He explains that the depth of those moments of revelation is what leads us to belief. Yet, such a moment is so brief, so outside of ordinary experience, that we soon think it has been an illusion. Exactly.

They finally came to take the IV away. It took longer today—that vein can't be much good anymore. I dread them starting another site; my left arm has already been used up.

Other than out-of-this-world and awe-inspiring, I don't know what to make of the light you described. If the soul can leave the body when we are still living, that would explain some things that have puzzled me. My spirit must have left to direct the message you received. Sometimes you are so clear to me and at other times you are not. Is it possible that our souls are apart from us for purposes of their own?

I will try to come to you tonight. I need to feel your arms around me, to hear you speak my name, to be close to the woman who has captured my heart, my soul, my very self. Love me, my sweet— slowly, gently, completely. I want to wake up in your embrace.

Michael, your letters are exquisitely expressive of your love and emotions. I treasure each one. Can you imagine our life beyond them? I will have to write of my idiosyncrasies, quirks, and imperfections so disillusionment does not mar the day we meet. Of course, you are already perfection to me, as I know I am to you, but sometimes I wonder—what if he knew this, or that, about me?

I asked Amelia to describe you. She told me of your dimples, how you tend to arch one eyebrow, giving you a quizzical look; that your brown hair is short with a little curl to it; and that your lips are firm, but I already knew that. She said your voice is medium deep and resonant, similar to that of a prominent news anchor.

I told you of the light, what I think the message was. My hope is that we will meet in the spring. Any earlier does not appear to be feasible—any later would be an eternity.

Something extraordinary just happened! My doctor, who is also now my friend, came into my room. J.T. was less talkative than usual, his voice different, softer. He said, "Please do not be afraid. I am Amelia. With your permission, I would like to examine you." Then he/she said she needed to use J.T.'s hands to touch me, and did she ever, from my head to my toes. It was different than any exam I've ever had. Her touch was warm and gentle; she applied no pressure.

Amelia explained that J.T. would have no memory of her visit or feel any ill effects. She said that I couldn't ask her any questions, that she was here for only one purpose. When she was through, J.T. started talking as though he had just arrived. I will never doubt again! I must bid you adieu. Vince is coming to take me to lunch, my first time out since I arrived here.

I have your letter in my hand. Oh, ma Cherie, you do make my blood boil. Can I ever get enough of you? I too have felt a deeper presence, a closer spiritual connection. Your explanation of our angels helps me understand them better. When Amelia was here, she was totally focused on her examination of me. Speak more to me of spring—how I cling to the thought of it.

This day has been one of sweet serenity, due in part to Amelia's visit. My doubts have fled—in their place are now certainties. Will she come again? Will she please talk to me? I don't even care if she uses the warden's body.

I now know the meaning of our simultaneous visions shortly before Eli spoke to us. I think he must have prompted them. You are a chief: your name is Bear Hunter (in translation) and mine is Morning Star. It is a time of war, and you are involved in a conflict not far from where we live. A messenger comes in the night, tells me to go to you. In my vision, I am aware of danger, of a terrible event portended. It is a precarious journey. I have to travel for a time over thin ice that is covered with snow. I vividly feel the sensation of having to tread carefully, step by step. I feel the dread of knowing that your life is in peril.

You have been mortally wounded but cling to life and wait for me. I find you lying on the ground, your strong, lean body now weak and bleeding. You die in my arms. I hear the word "noonah." It is a term of endearment that means "little one." Bear Hunter murmurs it over and over to Morning Star in their last moments together.

Michael … Michael … Michael. I say your name again and again—as a sigh, as a kiss, as deep contentment.

14. Room for Doubt

11/08 – 11/11

My beloved, I am so sorry about the miscarriage you suffered. I am truly honored that, because I was not to be the father, this soul chose to wait. I think often of us as husband and wife, but I am being premature. I wish there was a better word than wife, which can't begin to describe what you would be to me. I have to leave now for my tests.

I couldn't sit around and wait for the others and the hospice van, took a cab back from the lab wing two blocks away. I need to be alone with you, my sweet. Can I love you any more completely than I did last night and this morning? Did you cry out my name? I feel you close again as I write ... and remember.

Ethan came back from the lab in a great deal of pain. He tries to hide it, to be a tough guy, but I can see through him, have been there too often myself. I stayed with him until he fell asleep.

Michael, you would have found me on the cross-country ski trails, not the downhill slopes. Outdoors now, if not hiking, I like to garden and bird watch. I grew up ice skating and riding horses, used to skate with the girls every winter. I yearn to ride again, galloping across the prairie, that magnificent feeling of freedom to be found in synchrony with another creature.

If indoors and sitting down, I am likely to have a book in hand. If asked to name a favorite, it is a collection of twelve plays by Ibsen, each a perfect microcosm reflecting a timeless quality, the human dilemmas and motivations of today as much as those of the 19th century. In non-fiction, one favorite is Emerson. You would appreciate his beautifully expressive essay on Shakespeare. I was not surprised to learn from Zachary that Emerson was a returning Master.

My taste in music is eclectic: the nostalgia of classic rock as I drive down the highway at ninety miles an hour, cola in hand; blues or light jazz from the back of an old-fashioned night club, steeped in history; and a variety of classical, imagining that I am sitting in a stately concert hall in Vienna or Paris the first time a masterpiece is played.

I have dabbled in oil painting, start needlework projects (sometimes finish them), and play piano, though I have absolutely no sense of rhythm, except for yours. I see that I forgot to mention movies—a recent favorite of mine is *The Incredible Lightness of Being*.

My love, my *raison d'etre*, you grow more dear to me by the hour. We now have a more steady and constant connection as we walk together through our day. I will be close tomorrow as you have your tests.

Darling, I love you more with each day that passes. I am so full of thoughts this morning that I can hardly sort them out. You thrill me beyond belief, but I won't be complete until I hold you in my arms. I dream of spring. I must go.

Ethan is quite ill and they have called his parents. I haven't known him for long, but he has really touched my heart. Thank you for saying what you did about the kind of father I am. I didn't do everything right with Vince, but he always knew that I loved him. He is here.

Vince walked into my room tonight saying, *"Bonsoir, Papa."* Sometimes he can be a real smartass. I think often of telling him about us but, though he is open-minded, this news could be a real bombshell.

Michael, my heart, my soul—I have been so well taken. You could not have touched me any more deeply or completely. I feel you still. Lie to me if you must, but tell me you were just here with me. If you were not, then someone else was; perhaps your spirit was here without you. I need to change the subject so I can leave for the office with the afterglow of our love a little less visible on my face.

Amelia will request permission to answer your questions. She said, "Michael should not have to go through such anguish." Such requests are not taken lightly. Before Zachary could reveal himself to me, I had to pass a number of tests, was faced with challenges. He said about half of those selected pass the tests they are given. Of those, some can't accept the manner in which they were approached, and their memories of the contact are taken from them. Do you remember Pascal's branch that could not comprehend the tree? I sometimes feel like the smallest twig.

Your letter is here. What do you mean about me not being there? Is it possible for someone else to be there with you? Tell me it is not. I can't stand the thought of it. Teresa, listen to me carefully—the one thing that would end our relationship is infidelity. I have been through it before and will not go through it again. I was with you that night. No, I will not give you details, they may be wrong as well. Are we are having our first fight?

Before I end this letter, I must declare some basic truths: I love you, regardless of the limits set on us; I know when I am with you, feel your touch as you feel mine; I don't give a damn about the times; and I don't like being used for verification purposes. Do you love me as you say you do? Then come to me tonight, and tell me if my irritation shows when we are together.

Michael, you once wrote that you have had a good life. I have thought the same, mostly satisfied with the choices I have made. Now I know what has been missing. Your love would have enhanced every facet of my life: every contact with another, every experience in nature, every quiet moment alone. As I write these words, I do not mourn. I cannot let this knowledge flavor the entire past with bitterness.

Have you been close tonight? Earlier today, I felt you near and then, abruptly, you were gone. I reached out to find you—into a black void. Where are you? Is something wrong? I have no way of knowing. I hate this.

My God, what have I done? Please forgive me. I was going to tear up my letter, but it was gone when I woke up. I am so sorry. I had not intended for you to bear the brunt of my unwarranted outburst. I have read your letter again and can see now that I jumped to the wrong conclusion. When you wrote that someone else was with you, a red warning light flashed on—it was all I could see. If it is times and details you want, I will supply them. I will never be jealous again or take an accusing tone with you. I won't say we will never fight because I hope we do, if only so we can relish making up. I will understand if you are upset. I love you so much.

Michael, I would rather fight with you than make love to any other man. Does that reassure you? Just these few words during a short break after seeing four clients, then back to see three more this afternoon. I will write more tonight.

To feel you close again completes me. I had already read your fervent letter last night; it did not prevent my reaching out to you. In fact, I welcome seeing another side of you. Could we have sustained that initial intensity for months? Our awe and rapt acceptance have given way to questioning as our minds struggle to integrate the new with the old and achieve a state of equilibrium.

My love, it is when you have been so very real to me that I am most susceptible to the slightest indication that I could be wrong. Could I have given myself, body and soul, to a phantom lover? An out-of-sync contact puts my rational mind on high alert. If my letters were to appear from nowhere, or if Amelia spoke to me through someone I had known in a different context, it would be easier. I envy you, that you have had that validation.

About our experience—this entire situation calls for a suspension of disbelief. We have had to accept much that does not fit reality as we understood it. My acceptance, like yours, is none too constant. I turned up my furnace today and watched the indicator as it vibrated back and forth across hardly any distance. When my belief wavers, it is to that same degree. It is not a swing to disbelief, just a brief shuddering off of center—enough to believe I am feeling the first faint tremors of a major earthquake.

It is how your letters are delivered to me—I see each one withdrawn from the depths of Sally's capacious bag—and how Zachary and Amelia appear to me through her, that raises questions. Disturbing images pop up in my head of Sally writing the letters; they cannot be erased.

In addition to her alter personalities, several fantasy characters developed when Sally was a young teen, when she would so thoroughly escape into books that a part of her would take on a character from a story. Two of them came forward to speak to me about three years ago and have since faded into oblivion. They were not subversive or manipulative characters, quite the contrary, but their very existence leads me to consider whether a hidden part of her might have masterminded a complex plot. That is not a logical conclusion, for Sally has steadily moved toward integration. For a part of her to

now act out would be incongruent with that trajectory and incon-
sistent with the nature of any of the personalities. They each have,
in addition to distinctive personal traits, unique talents or skills that
they are eager to contribute to Sally's daily life.

Ethan was taken to the hospital sometime in the night. I know he
won't be coming back, and it weighs heavy on my mind. Darling,
I wish I could be bright and cheerful all of the time, be witty and
charming so you do not lose interest. I will change the subject.

I have meant to tell you more of my marriage. I was in L. A.,
fresh out of the army, young and dumb, had a pocket full of money
and the world by the tail. Two months after we met, she said she was
pregnant. I did what I thought was right and married her, and then
four days after that she claimed she had miscarried. Later, she re-
sented having to care of Vince. I stayed in the marriage for his sake,
certain there would be an ugly custody battle I might not win, and
I would not be there to protect him. This may sound terribly noble,
but I had a few affairs (not something I am proud of).

Sweetness, you are so very close this morning. I have tried to get
word of Ethan, but no one knows anything—Vince is here.

My sweet love, Amelia has told me of Ethan's death, and my heart
goes out to you in your grief. I know that he had become dear to you
and that you have been a comfort to him. I asked Amelia if Ethan's
spirit was meant to return at this time. "Yes, he was. The lessons
he had chosen for this lifetime were to be accomplished in his brief
sojourn here, including his illness. His spirit knew this, and his parents' spirits were aware that a lesson of this nature would be present
in their lifetimes."

Michael, I know these words will do little to ease your sorrow. I
want to be there with you, where I belong. Come to me, when you
are able, and I will hold you close.

My darling, I felt your comforting arms throughout the night. Ethan's death hit me hard—they called Vince to be here when they told me. I knew the minute he walked in. Your kind words, and what Amelia told me about Ethan's spirit, have helped me to a greater acceptance of his death. I love you, *ma Cherie*. Come to me, that I may be replenished.

Amelia will have brought you my letter and her own words of explanation and comfort. Writing is my way to be there at your side. I want to share some memories of my father's death. I always felt close to him—no heart-to-heart talks or obvious shows of affection, but smiles, kind words and caring looks, a helping hand. We were seldom alone together, but when he drove me to dental appointments, two hours away, I was often aware of a palpable energy between us. At age five, sitting with him in church, my mother at home with two little ones, my older brothers sitting with friends, that same energy was there. It is my earliest memory of spiritual awareness.

He had a history of heart disease, but it was unexpected when he died of a final heart attack after spending a full day on horseback. I was out of town at a conference and learned on a pay phone, my keening scream heard by everyone there. I felt the loss of more than a parent, cried all that night. Expecting a return of full grief at his funeral, I was surprised at how peaceful I felt. It was a perfect day in late May—the sun shining, birds singing, lilac blossoms scenting the air at the old country church. I was surrounded by the energies that have recently become more familiar. Though I keenly felt his loss, when aligned with those energies I understood much of what has recently been made known to me.

Kenna and Callie were five then. A few months later, they came running to tell me there was a man in a yellow raincoat standing outside. I immediately went to check but saw no one there. This was repeated several times in the next year or so. Last night, when I asked them about it, their memories matched—they saw a vaguely human form that appeared yellow to them. A raincoat was the closest image they had to describe it. My father's spirit has confirmed to Amelia that he had been watching over us.

I want to keep writing, to draw you near. The girls were very close, often holding hands. It was hard for them to see themselves as separate. I think they had just turned four when I asked them how many would be at a birthday party. One of them counted on her fingers, "Abby, Molly, Jessica, and us. Four!" Her sister arrived at the same result, both of them beaming with pride at their counting skills.

My love, someday I will show you the parks where we played, the sandy beaches; the tall slide we would pile fall leaves under and they would slide onto them again and again; the back roads we took on late summer nights when the moon would follow us home; and where we would walk in the fog along the river and they would run just far enough ahead to feel lost, then come running back to me, scared but thrilled. I picture us all sitting down together as we tell you our stories, making you a part of them. You will tell us stories of Vince and his dad—somewhere a soul will watch and know that he was right to wait.

15. What Have I Done?

11/12 – 11/14

You will not believe who was just here. I thought it was Ethan's mother until she said, "Hello Michael, I am Amelia. Please save your questions for another time. I wish to speak to you about Ethan. He, too, has a soul mate and they are now reunited."

As she was leaving, I asked if I could have just one question. I asked if you were real. "Teresa is a lovely young woman who is as much flesh and blood as you are." God, I am so happy, so blissfully happy. I must get this to you as soon as possible. I will love you tonight as I have never loved you.

Ma Cherie, I know we have not known each other for long, and the intensity of this relationship defies human understanding, but I can hold back no longer. If I can achieve remission—and the powers that be grant our wish to be together—will you do me the honor of becoming my wife? I hope I am not being premature. Please don't tell me "no" right away. I will give you all the time you need. I would much rather do this in person—properly, romantically, with all of the hearts and flowers you deserve. For all eternity, Michael

Les matins avec vous, c'est magnifique. I do love the mornings with you, Michael. We must have left some smoldering embers last night, needing only our first breath of the morning to rekindle the flames. I long for the day we can linger in each other's arms, skin against skin, until we have fully absorbed the physical essence that is now so real to us yet so tantalizingly incomplete, just beyond our grasp.

I had a glimpse in a dream of a younger you, from the time we were in college and you were tending bar at the Blue Goose. I was there about twice a month for a year or two. Can you believe our destiny depended on me going up to get my own drinks? We must have been there at the same time more than once, but I never sat at the bar. If only I had listened then, to my heart, and remained unattached long enough for our paths to cross.

The younger you in my dream had long hair, so I couldn't make out your features, but I noticed some pictures in a catalog that fit my vague memory of you. Amelia identified one as being most similar, the one I had picked myself. She said a young, handsome guy could be Vince.

My proposal is on its way to you. I will write of other things. Vince was the cutest little guy, but we had to dress him in macho boy clothes or everyone thought he was a girl. There was a park nearby where we would go to "fing." He was the apple of my mother's eye and her only grandchild. He excelled in school, and he played football and basketball well enough to make his old man proud.

I have tried to write, but for the first time I struggle with the words. I feel scared and sick at heart. I shouldn't have asked you. I had no right. Tears cloud my eyes to the point I can't see. I so anxiously await your answer that it has driven me a little crazy. I wish Amelia would come again. I am starting to look at everyone who enters my room in a most peculiar way, hoping it is her. Vince is starting to suspect something is going on. I want him to know you, but I worry that he won't believe me and will think I need a psych referral.

Dear heart, beloved of my soul. Did you open the small card first? One word was all I needed to answer you. I did not need to wait. I did not need to think about it. We have yet to make endless discoveries of each other, but what we know now is enough. I am not one who depends on hearts and flowers. What you have written from your heart means more to me than all the flowers you could buy—but you could pick for me a wild rose. Michael, I am yours.

My love, do you sense my joy? You have made me the happiest man alive, so ecstatically alive. I want you now! You have given my heart wings, with which I will fly to your waiting arms.

Darling, when we meet I will propose properly. You may not need hearts and flowers, but you *will* indulge me. We will write our own vows, say what is in our hearts in a small, intimate ceremony, with our children, families, and close friends in attendance.

I have just spent the most peaceful, contented time with you, sealing our betrothal. Our hearts, our souls, our minds were in perfect unison as you wrapped me in your arms in a mutual sharing of all that we have to offer each other. I *will* indulge you, Michael? Yes, I will.

You wrote that we will write our own vows, but I don't think we will need any words. We will simply look into each other's eyes and silently express all that passes between us now. The intensity and depth of our love will radiate out to include all who are gathered there with us.

Dear heart, I too want to shout it to the world. Vince will be the first to know when the time is right. I want to be free of the pain medication and some other drugs first and out of the hospice so I will sound more credible. They are here to start a new needle.

The scent you notice must be my aftershave. I often write soon after using it. I can't stop writing to you. I feel you so near that I am sure you must know what is in my heart before I put my pen to paper. Come to me—we will love as if tomorrow will never come.

I have arranged the last garden flowers of the season, baby white mums tinged with deep purple. I have lit some vanilla and spice candles and have poured myself a glass of a velvety red wine. The glow of the candlelight brings out the richness of my old oak table and the hardwood floors, a reflection of how your presence will enhance and enrich every moment of my life.

I have had a busy two days, no time to write of what I put myself through yesterday. I did resolve it, later in the day, so have debated whether to tell you, but it was so distressing that I don't want to keep it from you. I will tell you in the morning.

Michael, this past hour spent in your arms has brought back the awe and wonder of our first weeks together, your presence so strong I could close my eyes and believe you were here with me. Instead, I will take you back to my torment of two days ago: I walk with you on the island, suffused with joy, secure in our reality and in the promise of our future. I arrive home to find an alumni booklet in the mail. I notice it lists all graduates by decade and I tear it open, ripping the thin paper. I have to search for the name of my beloved in print, to see it and know that he is mine. Only one decade makes sense. I scan every year, go back to check each one again, name by name—yours is not among them. As I expand my search, I feel increasingly sick. The impact of seeing in black and white, or rather, of not seeing it, leaves me reeling.

Unable to think, to process the absence of your name, what it could mean, I sit unmoving, frozen. Fear sets in as my mind conjures a storm of dark possibilities. Could it be that there has never been a man named Michael? The implications are staggering. I am filled with dread, a leaden force that holds me in my chair. My heart is heavy, leaving my mind free to run rampant and weave its web of fear and deceit. It is an hour or two before I can weigh my fears against what I know to be true and realize there could be a logical explanation.

I do not seek connection with my spirit to confirm the truth I have known. I want to consult an outside source—the most powerful one of my experience. I feel some qualms, think it sheer audacity to try, but I reach out to Eli in the same way that I reach out to you. Is it even possible? You are here in the physical realm; he is not. I draw from the depths of my being and soften my heart until my mind is clear and can join in the effort. It takes longer, but I trust in the power that Eli himself proclaimed to us. After a time, I have a strong affirming sense of the presence we felt the night he visited us. I reach out to you and feel your love surround me.

As I write to you now, it is with that direct link that defies all doubt, but I cannot stay. I need to leave for the office, an early appointment with Sally, maybe a letter from you.

Michael—what have I done? Our letters will stop as of today. Did my brief doubts cause this? It is Zachary who told me, and he said Amelia was telling you at the same time. When I returned home, we cried in each other's arms, clung to each other, and then communicated our determination to fight.

Hope and heartbreak exist equally within me. I am going to take a short walk, an act of faith that we will someday walk those paths together. Then I will need to focus on clients again for a few hours, create some semblance of normalcy, even while I am crying inside. Amelia said she will return briefly at the end of my work day.

Good morning, my love. Did you sleep well? I feel you still. Yes, you are difficult to awaken. I still think you were faking it. Amelia is here.

I can't believe they are doing this to us. I thought they were here to help us. This is supposed to be some sort of a test, but I don't understand it. Why do they bring us together only to tear us apart?

Amelia is waiting for me to write this note, but she doesn't even know if it can be delivered.

How do I say goodbye? I can't. I won't. Have faith, my love. I will write every day as though there were no separation. I love you. No matter what happens, I will be with you, forever and always.

Michael, can you forgive my doubts? Amelia put them in perspective for me. "You were successful in your effort to reach out to Eli. He knows of your search for the truth and that you held on to your belief in Michael and to the reality of your experience with us. Other factors had much more to do with the decision of the Council. A review was inevitable considering the course of events since they first granted permission for you and Michael to correspond."

My love, as remission becomes a possibility for you, the Council realizes that, if we were to meet, it would touch many lives. We have thrown a stone into the pond of life—the ripples will be far reaching. They will determine if it is in our best interests, and in the best interests of others, for our contact to continue. They will even research the effects on several generations to come. Yes, this separation will serve as a test for us, but that is not its primary purpose.

Do you wonder how I could have said I would marry you and then doubt your very existence two days later? I was absolutely certain as I walked with you the other day, happy and secure in our love. It is not the first time I have been most vulnerable after I have given my entire life to you. Our experience has been so far outside of the norm that the solid black and white reality of a printed booklet left me catapulting between two poles—the magnetic force field was shifting and I was along for the ride.

Amelia is here now and waits as I write this. She asked me to tell you that there is no malice in the Council's action. "Child, there are reasons for this action beyond your understanding. Your brief doubts played a miniscule part in a decision that would have been made anyway." Michael, you are my forever, as I am yours.

I have vowed not to write in anger. I can't believe this. Our letters are my one tangible link to you. By what right can they keep us apart? It seemed the cruelest of jokes, but I could tell Amelia was almost as disheartened as I was. I will come to you no matter what, using my power to reach out to you.

I am feeling so down. I must try to reach you. I know you are surely feeling as I do. Can we try to comfort each other? I need to feel your arms around me—my tears come unbidden. Hold me close, my love.

My darling, do not chastise yourself for doubting. Do you think that I have not? I have wondered if someone here has written the letters to give me a thrill or to play some heartless prank on me. But I know what I have felt in your embrace—no one can make that up. Did I not comfort you as you did me? I tasted the saltiness of our combined tears.

Amelia had time to tell me a little of the spirit world. I feel that a great privilege has been bestowed upon me. She appears just briefly through an elderly woman who volunteers here. I hear this serene, peaceful voice coming from a body that looks like anything but that. Are you with me now? I feel your essence surrounding me.

16. The Council Decides

11/15—

"Way to go, Michael!" That was Zachary's response when I told him what happened. My attention was on a client, listening intently, when I felt your touch upon my cheek. It was so decisive a touch that I was startled and had to fake a cough to cover my reaction. Zachary said your success will strengthen our case before the Council. And, he said that Eli has declared his unequivocal support for us. The enormity of our situation begins to take hold in me, and I am filled with gratitude that our plea is even being heard. Of course, I would not be easily reconciled to a decision against us but—if I truly accept this entire experience—how could I be angry at them if we are denied?

Michael, it would be such agony to lose you. I expect we would both react like children, who recognize a parent's authority, know they are powerless to change a decision, but unleash a torrent of emotion at being denied what they want. I would throw some adult equivalent of a temper tantrum. I can imagine doing that, but the depth of my despair, once my anger was spent, is beyond my imagination.

My love, did you whisper to me of kisses sweeter than wine early this morning? How is it possible that our lips can meet so definitely? Knowing you will not read these words, unless the decision is in our favor, provides a pathway of hope—every word I write carries with it the expectation that you will read it.

I asked Amelia to help me with my power to reach out to you. She said, "You must trust in that power and in your ability to access it." Sometimes I try hard but am not sure if I have reached you, and then I make little effort and you are there. It is a complete and utter mystery to me.

Earlier, I lay down and softly called your name, a whisper on the wind. You came to me in a dream, my lovely Morning Star, with jet black hair and eyes to match, a dress of soft ivory leather with intricate beadwork around the neck, sleeves, and hem—a wedding dress.

Would you like to know more about the Council that holds our lives in their hands? I asked Amelia what she could tell me. "It includes two Sages, seven Masters, and three close to that status. It is led by Althea, who has been a Master for some time. She took a strong interest in your initial ability to reach out to Michael and in the strength of your subsequent connection, and she has already declared herself to be in your favor. Given her position, I find it quite extraordinary." It gives me great hope to know we have such a high level of support. We may need it. Amelia said some matters before councils require only a majority decision. In this case, the entire Council of twelve must be in agreement that our relationship be allowed to continue.

You may be thinking that we will find each other if the decision is against us. I would want to do everything in my power to go to you, but our attempts would be thwarted and our spirits would face severe penalties, a loss of status, if they supported our efforts. Our angels, now assisting us, would have to follow the dictates of the Council and act contrary to our wishes. (I find that hard to imagine.)

I haven't explained why my name wasn't listed in that alumni mailing. My ex was threatening to take Vince and go to her parents' in another state, so I transferred to a school there for my final year. Then my mother became sick and I insisted we come back to be close to her. I started graduate school and that is when we would have met. A year later my mother was better, so we left the state again and I got my second degree there too. Did events transpire to bring me back in order to meet you, to fulfill our destiny? I can hardly bear to think we missed that opportunity.

While I wait for the girls to get home, I will tell you a little about my family. My mother is still very active, spends half the year in Arizona. We weren't close as I was growing up, but we now enjoy shared interests and viewpoints, and we laugh a lot together. A devoted grandmother to the girls, she likes to tell how her heart fell when, age three, one of them flatly said, "We love our other grandma." Then her heart soared when after a long pause she heard, with more enthusiasm, "But we really, really, really love this grandma." I was in the next room and couldn't tell which of them said it, but she had perfect timing.

Amelia told me of a prior lifetime my mother and I shared (our only one) that sheds some light on our early relationship. I was my mother's servant, in a time and culture in which servants were often horribly mistreated. That pattern was not repeated, but Amelia believes the effect it had on our spirits affected our relationship, created distance on both sides. She said, "Most lifetimes include relationships in which past issues are to be resolved through the working out of the current dynamics." I think my mother and I have both learned that lesson.

Michael, the great privilege of having been given so much sometimes escapes me. When I stop to reflect, I appreciate that it is a gift,
and I am ashamed to admit my moments of doubt. I asked Amelia to
tell you they have vanished. I have felt you reaching out to me every
day—your touch so obvious it leaves no room for doubt. When I was
the one to initiate our contacts, I would sometimes wonder if I could
be imagining everything.

I gave Amelia a small gift to deliver to you, a token of the stone I
feel at my center. I relate to the intensity of it, the passion of the deeper
red in the middle, the sparks glancing off of the surface. I held it close
to my heart last night and this morning to imbue it with my energy.

I don't think I have ever described my body to you. I am six-two,
have a medium build, a somewhat long face with a rather square
jaw, and dark brown hair with a receding (just slightly) hairline.

Someday, *ma Cherie*, you will meet J.T., but not before you have
my ring on your finger. He considers himself quite the ladies' man
and he fits the image of one. I can hear you asking for details. He is
close to my height, extremely fit, charming, and handsome—all of
that, plus an excellent bedside manner. Back to the subject of rings,
what would you prefer?

This cessation of our letters is becoming more difficult with each
day that passes. I miss yours more than I thought possible. I am tiring more easily and Amelia says I have lost weight. I have a slight
fever, and the warden just dropped in to say they are going to start
me on IV antibiotics tonight, so I will be stuck here for a while.

Good morning, *ma Cherie*. I miss those beautiful words that I
know speak of love. At your request, Amelia asked me a curious
thing—if I had said anything to you about kisses. Are you referring
to kisses sweeter than wine? Yes, I murmured those words to you
shortly after this cruel separation was forced upon us.

Darling, these last few days I have been more certain of your
presence. When you have to leave me, the shift in energy is evident

and reassuring. Will you let me spend the night in your arms? We will pray that the Council is quick with their answer and that it is in our favor. I will not consider the alternative, my love. I will not.

Most years, some of my family have made it here for Thanksgiving, but today it was just the three of us, with enough food for a crowd—turkey and all the trimmings. I could feel you close and knew that our spirits were here with us. After dinner, we went through the girls' old school papers and artwork that I had saved over the years, laughing at some, filled with nostalgia over others. I read to them your description of Vince as a child—they want to know more. Then I showed them the picture Amelia said resembles him. Their first comments were, "He's hot." and "He's a stud." They wonder how he will react to your news and said it would have been difficult for them to accept it all at once. As we talked of you, Kenna said, "The two of you would have been such good parents together." I agree.

Yes, I will be with you and the girls in spirit. Vince and Tara brought me a turkey sandwich and some pumpkin pie, and they have just left. Now I want the staff to leave me alone so I can draw you near and spend the rest of the day with you. Are we having the traditional feast? Next year we will prepare it together.

My temp was down this morning, the IV is gone, and I am optimistic—but this waiting is driving me crazy. I don't know what I will do if we are denied. I will have to start making calls and try to find you. It shouldn't be that difficult. I will play the sleuth and follow the clues you revealed in our history, or I could hire a private investigator. We *will* be together, one way or another. You say our efforts would be thwarted, but I am not without some resources and a degree of cunning.

Thank you for the beautiful stone. It has kept me company today, and I slept with it under my pillow last night. I imagine it to be a part of you, the part that I strive to touch, to make mine, to take full possession of.

I think there is good news. I was awakened in the night by your strong presence, or perhaps it was your spirit who was close. There was so much joy and happiness between us that I think a decision has been made in our favor, and our letters will resume immediately.

Can you sense my excitement? Sally just called to confirm her appointment, and Amelia came to say that Eli wishes to speak to me this afternoon. I think that feeling I had in the night must have been accurate. I will know in a few hours.

Our wait is over—eleven days an eternity. Has Eli told you yet? He believes that, once you are in remission, the Council will grant our wish to reclaim our destinies. I am filled with hope for our future as I celebrate my love for you. The feelings linger, my lips tingle with the memory of yours. Are you asleep? I will nudge you, ever so gently, then ease myself into your arms.

Tessa, my love, I felt you close in the early hours of the morning. Your presence was more evident than usual and I heard you call my name. Is everything okay? I hate to leave you like this, but Vince is coming to take me out and about. I hope Amelia comes first so I can ask her what is going on. He is here.

It has been a long day and I am tired, a good kind of tired. I know I shouldn't overdo things, but I have felt as if I have been in prison—four walls and that pervasive odor that permeates all medical facilities. My supper is here and I am starved.

Thank God, and thank Eli. He was here! Eli was right here. I have to tell you, he scared the daylights out of me when he appeared through the warden. I was speechless, except to ask if it was a joke of some sort. It is no joke, my darling. We need only agree to the same conditions as before.

The warden just poked her head in to see if I needed anything. I will never look at that woman in the same light again. Eli appearing through her was a humbling experience. I will treat her with more respect—not that I was ever disrespectful, except under my breath, after she had left.

My beloved, I will never get enough of you. Did we not celebrate our joy? I have never felt such rapturous pleasure. There were tears in my eyes of sheer happiness. I adore you.

Michael, I have read your every word, twice. Could you sense my emotional overload a short time ago? It was a combination of relief, intense longing, hope for our future, and shame for my doubts—all firing a mass of conflicting neurons in my brain.

In this last hour with you, I have been reminded of the power of our connection: unbound souls unite...seeking, reaching past delights...crescendos undone, contentment overtaking...bliss, peace, spring will come.

17. Healing Powers

I said I would write of my leukemia, such a frightening word when I first heard it from J.T. I was devastated, thought it a death sentence, sank into what I call my "lie down and moan" stage. My type is acute lymphocytic leukemia, the one with the highest rate of remission. Darling, you should know that some of the treatments I am receiving might have long-lasting side effects—one of them is impotence.

Listen to me, my love. If that should happen before we meet, I will withdraw from your life. I could not come to you as half a man. I know you will say it doesn't matter, but my sweet, sweet love, it would perhaps come to matter. I can't stand the thought of ever disappointing you. It has grown late. Hold me, my love. I need you desperately.

I apologize for getting so maudlin, but I thought you should know the facts—enlarged lymph nodes, muscular/joint pain, and fever are all common symptoms. I noticed your letter was here last night, but I left it in my journal while I struggled with my right to open it. I question my ability to be everything you want and need. How can I ask you to take this uncertain journey with me?

I couldn't resist the pull of your letter. You spoke of hearing your spirit's voice. I am in complete awe of you. I have had no such connection with my spirit. Amelia wouldn't tell me his name, but she said it might come to me. "It was some time before Teresa was aware of Mahalia. It takes acceptance, patience, and a great deal of reflection."

Michael, I can only imagine what it was like for you to hear your diagnosis, come to terms with the illness, and at the same time try to fight it. Amelia and Zachary have assured me that it is possible for you to heal. You can direct forces within yourself to assist your medical therapies.

Have you ever practiced meditation—entered a state of being as opposed to doing or thinking? I start with yoga, or simply stretching, and then I take a few slow, deep breaths. As I feel the release of any remaining tension, I let my breath return to its natural flow. I place my awareness on each inhalation, not forcing it, and on each exhalation, the full process of each natural breath. It is that easy, but thoughts and emotions easily intrude. I acknowledge them without letting them take hold and then bring my attention gently back to my breath. It becomes easier with practice.

Once you have achieved a deep state of relaxation and awareness, you can add healing components. Visualize the Light surrounding you and breathe in its healing energy. You can direct healing effects to where you need them, even to individual cells or types of cells. Visualize one element at a time and create a detailed image to symbolize the healing process.

I use meditation to help me access my spirit and my powers of healing. I use a variety of visualizations to reach a deeper state, with greater effect. I then move on to prayer, the connection with my spirit helping me to access the Light. In recent weeks, I have then reached out to share that healing energy with you.

I talked to Amelia about my ability to beat this. She said, "You must listen to your body and become aware of even the slightest changes; only then can you effectively combat the effects of the disease and be rid of it."

Amelia said, "It is unfortunate that natural healing practices are now less valued. Early civilizations were given assistance to develop them; they were often of a spiritual nature, and believers saw better results. There are many healers among us in the spirit world. Some Masters take physical lives to share their knowledge; others work to bolster the powers of earthly healers."

I will take time each day to clear my mind and concentrate on healing my body. Amelia said I can channel my personal power into a healing force. She will guide me, but it is something I must do for myself. I must first have complete faith in that power and in He who gave it to me. I remember the Light. I know what it is capable of, and He knows what I am capable of.

J.T. has just left. When I told him of my plan, he said, "It's about time you started helping yourself." Maybe I've just been waiting for another miracle—it is up to me to make one happen.

My love, I want to tell you what your illness means to me. I ask myself who I would choose if I knew that another man was available—in perfect health, attractive, compatible, etc. Would I choose him over the man I love? I would not. Michael, I sense in you a virility that goes beyond the act of sex. You would still be a man to me, and I would still prefer you to any other. It is the sum total of your being that I want and love.

I have been doing some soul searching. I asked myself if I have the strength to stand by you, no matter what. The answer was yes. I then asked why I feel so strongly that I cannot desert you. The answer was clear—I want to *give to myself* the joy of knowing you.

I am working on getting more in touch with my physical self, to be fully acquainted with my muscles, organs, blood, arteries, veins, and lymph system. I did the breathing, as you described it, and managed twenty minutes. I believe it takes a lot of practice.

When Vince was here, I told him I need to talk to him when he can spare a couple of hours. I think it best to give him a little at a time, but where do I start? I guess at the beginning, with a woman who occupied not only my dreams but my every waking thought. That could be a little much. I will start with telling him about my near-death experience.

I took an outdoor walk this morning, the first in a long while. I turned in at a few stores, even stopped for a veggie burger. I found it exhilarating to be in touch with ordinary reality. It is not that I doubt our experience—my belief was strengthened as I realized that what we have together is just as real as the world I saw all about me.

A curious thing happened last night. I was deep in meditation, seeking your presence, when I heard you cry out. I thought something must be terribly wrong. I was confused, then worried when I didn't feel you close until early this morning. Amelia explained that you took a fall and hit your head, which interfered with our connection—the strength of it continues to amaze me.

You asked about a painting. Either I talk too much in my sleep or you are able to read my thoughts. I haven't told a soul about it, and I will say no more.

Michael, I do not want to write one more word to you. I want to talk to you. I want you to talk to me, talk back to me, talk circles around me, talk of love, our children, our past, our future, the weather. I want to do everything that will require no words at all. I will try later. Are you going to walk with me?

It could be spring here—melting snow, patches of green, air so fresh, trails of soggy leaves and then fine sand. I climb a ridge on the bank of the river and sit in the exposed roots of a tree with a double trunk, one long fallen and one upright and healthy. I sit with the sun full on my face, my legs crisscrossed, hands lightly clasped, the pads of my thumbs touching. I close my eyes and draw you near as I begin to meditate.

After a time, I draw on the energy of the earth, visualizing a golden cord extending from my core to deep within the earth. I draw energy up the cord to the base of my spine, to the crown of my head. Then I draw on the energy of the sun, let it flow into me and through me, and then I reach out to the Light. As these energies converge, I channel them into a healing force that I direct to the specific changes that need to take place in my body. I pray to the Creator to surround me and to infuse me with healing energy, and then I direct these powerful forces to join with your healing efforts.

Tessa, you fill me with your passion. I am totally under your spell. I long to hold you, touch you, feel you come alive to my administrations—in the earthly sense. I treasure the spiritual love we have, but it always leaves me wanting more.

I had a chance to talk to Vince yesterday about my near-death experience. He was interested and then very accepting of the truth of it and of the meaning it holds for me. The next time we talk, I am going to tell him that what I feel with you is of the same magnitude. Yes, it is far beyond our human understanding, but, nonetheless, it is real.

Amelia confirmed that my dream last night was a glimpse of our past life. I saw Morning Star in her wedding dress and then I saw a ceremony beseeching the Great Spirit to bless the union with many children, elk, deer, bear, and beaver. Our hands and wrists were bound, my right and your left, and then we were led to a special marriage lodge where food and gifts were laid out for us. A bed of animal skins dominated the center of the lodge near the fire. I knew we would remain there three nights and three days.

It is past midnight but I won't be able to sleep. The youngest of my brothers was passing through town and we met for coffee, too late in the day for caffeine. We had a good visit but it was short. It felt like a lie to say nothing of the amazing events of the past few months, but there wasn't enough time to even begin to explain.

Michael, are you sure you want to join this household? It is now two hours later. Callie's been talking with me about an obsessive ex-boyfriend who came to the door an hour ago wanting to come in, loudly insisting on it. He finally left, reluctantly. Then, a short while ago, I thought I heard his car and went to check. When I opened the door, Charkey jumped in the open window of the screen door with a live mouse in his jaws, which promptly escaped. He chased the poor, little, squeaky thing around and around the living room and finally caught it. I had to pick them both up and throw them out together, hoping the mouse didn't get away again and the boy wasn't lurking. It is quiet now. I may still find you in what is left of the night.

Darling, I haven't been feeling well. I tire more easily and need more pain medication. I try not to take them, for they interfere with my ability to reach you. Amelia has been encouraging me to use my powers of healing, and this is a good time to do that without any interruptions.

I spent almost two hours on it. I am now more relaxed, the pain is manageable, and I feel stronger. I started with the breathing, as you described it, and then paid close attention to each part of my body, becoming aware of any sensations of tightness or pain, if it was hot or cold or clammy, etc. I stayed with whatever sensation was present without trying to change it.

The funny thing is, they did change—the tension was replaced with peace and harmony. Then I visualized, in specific detail, my blood being purified by my power, gradually ridding it of diseased cells. I called upon the powers of my spirit, of our angels, and of the Creator. Together, we will be victorious.

Michael, you described in exquisite detail some moments I was certain had been mutual two nights ago, and I am reassured. Despite the intensity of our experience, my mind still insists on being the prime interpreter of it. Two sides of myself are engaged in a perpetual dance—my mind still insists on leading. When I am in touch with, and act from, spirit or intuition, logic refuses to follow, would rather sit on the sidelines, where it pouts and maintains a constant vigilance for any discrepancy.

Earlier, I was listening to the soul-stirring music of Sweet Honey in the Rock. Then I spent some time in a deep meditation, seeking Mahalia's presence. Thirty minutes into it, I heard a faint voice urging me to go deeper. I used a visualization, based on a favorite trail, that takes me down a steep mountain path, descending into a deep gorge, each slow step taking me to a deeper level of consciousness. After a time, I could hear her clearly: Tessa, what you have with Michael is real. It is important that you believe and that you have faith. For us to walk together, you must maintain contact and *walk with me*. It was a powerful message—she does not join my surface world of doubt, worry, and fear—I must meet her in the essence of being.

Who is Alexander? Were you dreaming of an old lover and saying his name? I heard it several times in my sleep and then again just after I woke up. I struggled for a while with the idea that I might have competition, then decided to let you answer my doubts. I called upon my power to reach out to you, with some urgency, and I felt you respond. If I listen with my heart, instead of my head, it tells me all I need to know. It's time for my tests.

I need you so, my love, just to hold me. I am waiting for J.T. to stop by with my test results. I don't have a good feeling about them, but I have been trying hard not to let the negative thoughts prevail. I don't want to draw too much on your strength for fear I may become a drain on your energies.

J.T. did not bring good news last night. I felt you reaching out to me, but I wouldn't allow myself to respond until early this morning. The tests showed an increase of cancer cells in the bone marrow. I am very disappointed. J.T. has ordered another change in the chemo, a more frequent and stronger dose.

Darling, have I been deceiving myself to think we might have a life together, to think I can rid myself of this disease? Have all of my healing efforts been in vain?

18. Take Heaven

12/18 - 12/31

The news this morning from J.T. and Amelia is much the same—not good. Amelia examined me and recommended a change in medication, which she will somehow bring to J.T.'s attention. He's the type of guy who thinks everything has to be his own idea, so I hope she can be subtle. I just wrote that as if Amelia's type of assistance is an ordinary, common occurrence. I have accepted so much—will others believe it when I tell them?

Have you trimmed your tree yet? I love the sprig of pine. Thank you for sending me a little piece of your Christmas. I put it in a glass of water to keep it fresh. The staff has decorated here and several groups of carolers will be coming. I used to sing in a church choir, sang solo for weddings, and was in a community men's choir. I miss all of that.

No, my love, I was not dreaming about an old boyfriend named Alexander, but I have always liked that name and wanted it for a son. I wonder why I have always been drawn to it.

Michael, I love you with all my heart, my soul, my being. Perhaps I should not presume to speak for my spirit. Zachary said they become somewhat amused at our efforts, and they don't always assist as much as they could, leave us to our own devices. That must be when we are most frustrated in our attempts. Apparently, we are like young children to them, new to this world and inexperienced. I would like to stay here, content in their presence, but I need to go to work.

It is a penetrating, bitter cold here that I can feel in every bone of my body. I am going to take a long, hot bath and dream of warmer weather. You mentioned skinny-dipping. I see the two of us on a secluded beach at twilight time, at one with the elements, not a thing between us and the air, us and the water. It is the month of June—balmy nights and delicately scented air—musical notes are carried whimsically by the breeze to unite lovers for the evening, or a lifetime. It is the hardest month for me to be alone. Will you promise me that we can be together by then? I know you can't. I can even think, at least by next Christmas, and be content—if only it were a certainty.

It seems that I have said your name as I slept. Vince heard it and asked me about you. I told him that you're the woman in my life and that I will tell him more when I am feeling better. So then he had to insist on details, like your full name, where and how we met, where you live. He was persistent, but I managed to do some quick talking and change the subject. You have piqued his interest, and it has given me the opening I need to tell him.

J. T. was just here with a positive report. My healing efforts may have had some effect after all. There is no increase in the white blood cell or toxicity levels this week, so he said I can go to Vince and Tara's for Christmas Day.

I think with sadness of all the holidays I missed while our girls were growing up. Would I have had a positive impact on their lives? I worry about meeting them, making a good impression. I would like to be cool but not too much so. What about the rest of your family—is your mother easily charmed?

The girls are similar to me in their insistence on reality over fantasy. Age five, a few days after Christmas, they called me into their room. Kenna, with a serious expression and the tone of an ultimatum, said, "Mom, we want you to tell us the truth—is Santa Claus real?" She spoke so in earnest that I could not lie to them. They were quiet a moment and then demanded, "What about the Easter Bunny?" A moment later it was, "What about the Tooth Fairy?" All their illusions were shattered in a few minutes.

Our Christmas Eve will be a quiet one, no travel this year. The girls and I will have a late meal and then open gifts. Christmas day, I will go to my cousins' and they will be with their father and stepmother. Church hasn't played a big part in our lives since they were confirmed two years ago. I know it has been an enduring presence in yours and will likely be a regular part of our life together.

I asked Zachary if the spirit world observes earthly holy days. "The Creator recognizes the differences in the primary belief systems and gives His blessing to all of them. Masters and Sages celebrate holy days that were familiar to them in multiple physical lifetimes. They also celebrate the diversity of beliefs that exist in your world and all that makes both mortals and spirits unique."

My darling, what beautiful gifts, the locket and the thought that it holds your love. I wore it through the night and am wearing it now. I felt you close throughout the night, our spirits rejoicing with us. Were we not consumed?

Did you feel me close today? Twice, Vince had to call me back to earth when I was trying to reach out to you. He wanted to know when he could meet you and, once again, asked me where you live. He didn't appreciate my vague answers. Then he took on the role of a stern parent. He sat up taller, squared his shoulders, and with an emphatic tone said, "Dad, we have got to talk." Soon he will know. Please come to me tonight. I need you so.

Thank you, my love. I knew at once that the painting was of Morning Star and Bear Hunter, and I felt a confirming response from my spirit, she who was the first to see it a few weeks ago and said that I must see it. To look at the deep love between them increases my longing to be in your arms, to lean my head upon your shoulder.

I am listening to "The Christmas Revels," the reading of a 1513 letter from Fra Giovanni to a friend of his. I will copy my favorite part for you.

> *"No heaven can come to us unless our*
> *hearts find rest in today. Take Heaven.*
> *No peace lies in the future which is not hidden*
> *in this present instance. Take Peace.*
> *The gloom of the world is but a shadow.*
> *Behind it, yet within our reach, is joy. Take Joy."*

You are such a joy to wake up to. They started the chemo last night after the warden lectured me about returning so late, like I had done it just to annoy her. She has most definitely lost the Christmas spirit. I am still wearing your locket—it rests just over my heart. Did you plan it that way?

Thank you for being at my side today. I felt your hand in mine while the bone marrow was being extracted. I am so fortunate that we have found each other. Had it not been for this divine intervention, I might have given up long ago. I had pretty much done just that in October, at the point you entered my life. I had accepted that I was dying. Teresa, you restored my will to live—my entire life has since been rejuvenated and redirected.

I've been thinking ahead to what this new year will bring—let's save Vermont for our honeymoon. I've tried to imagine sitting beside you in the confined, and public, space of an airplane and know that I couldn't manage it immediately after we meet. We will have to find a similar spot within a few hours' drive and leave as soon as we get the word.

I know the perfect mountain setting where we could meet. There is a small jewel of a lake, with a lodge and dining room, or individual cabins. Is your BMW the small, sporty type? It would be perfect for driving the sinuous mountain curves. Are you possessive of your car? I'm not used to being a passenger. I should warn you that I have a heavy foot, but it comes with a sixth sense that tells me when to ease up (most of the time).

Our meeting begins to seem imminent. I have an urge to go shopping, never my favorite activity, but I will enjoy choosing lingerie with you in mind. I am more likely, though, to wear your tee shirts. I imagine taking in the aroma of one at the end of a not-so-active day, just enough that your masculine scent has permeated the white cotton fibers.

Michael, I want to experience all of you, to feel your larger presence surround me. When we finally meet—*the mere thought of physical contact takes my breath away*—we will give such sweet pleasure to one another.

Great news! I can hardly believe it. I have had a complete turnaround from my last test results. When I told Amelia I might leave the hospice soon, she said she will remain close to me but her personal visits will be more difficult. I tried to joke with her, said I will cultivate a relationship with a widow-next-door type. She didn't laugh. Do they ever?

Vince is stopping by tomorrow to have that discussion with me, a major sacrifice considering how much he likes football. I don't know if it is more a matter of his curiosity about you or of his concern about my sanity. I hope you can be near so your presence will help me choose the right words, but how do I tell him about Amelia? How do I explain our relationship and leave her out?

Sweetheart, this year is drawing to an end. I read a few of your earlier letters as I held your locket in one hand and your beautiful stone in the other. This is the beginning of a new and wondrous life.

Michael, I have been reflecting on how our love has evolved, these last months and over many lifetimes. I see an image of a lightly textured fabric in rich, jewel-tone colors, interwoven with threads of pure gold. It is sometimes on display but often folded—only we are aware of its full beauty. Alone, we wrap ourselves in its warmth, when warmth is sought; sometimes it is gossamer light, caressing us. I am going to light some candles, draw you near, and dream of the year to come.

19. He Doesn't Believe Me

What a night to remember, and then, early this morning as I held you close, I heard our names and also Mahalia and Alexander. Yes, my love, I am certain now that he is my spirit. Had you tried to hint that he was? I'm waiting for Vince—a little nervous but excited to tell him all about you—he is here.

I am sorely disappointed. It did not go as well as I had hoped it would—quite the opposite. Vince made it painfully clear he doesn't believe in my experience. He wouldn't even consider that it might have some basis in reality. I have been replaying the conversation in my mind to see what I might have explained differently. I knew of no other course but to tell him the truth as I have known it.

I have gotten a message that "He has much to consider; you must give him time." Was that from you or from Amelia? I will write of the details tomorrow. Now I want only the comfort of your arms. Hold me, my love. I need you so.

Michael, I lie here in your arms filled with joy of body, mind, and spirit. A million connecting threads weave back and forth until we are bound to each other with every fiber of our beings. I will begin and end each day of this promising new year with you, my love.

I am ecstatic that you will soon leave the hospice—your next move will be here. Amelia is concerned that you may be too active and expose yourself to the risk of infection. In a similar situation, I would be apt to overdo things, try to resume my old life, tempt the fates. Will you please be careful?

I had a restless night thinking over my talk with Vince—an endless loop that got me nowhere. It might help to describe it to you. We were in my room, sitting in the two comfortable visitor chairs. He began with a look of sincere interest, leaning forward, eager to hear about you. First, I reminded him of the dreams I told him about in October. Next, I showed him your first letter, read parts of it to him, and told him of our brief encounter many years ago. Up to that point, he listened intently. Then, I told him we had missed our destinies and they are now uncertain. He raised one eyebrow. The clincher was when I said our being together isn't up to us.

Vince leaned back in his chair, away from me, his face frozen in an incredulous look of disbelief. I don't think his eyebrows could have gone any higher. "Dad, this can't be true. One of the staff, or maybe a volunteer, must be messing with your mind. They could easily put letters in your journal while you're sleeping." He also blamed the strong dose of painkillers I was taking then.

I tried to explain but couldn't get through to him. He left much earlier than he had intended after saying an awkward goodbye, not even looking me in the eye. My son is very much a realist; what I told him doesn't fit his perception of how the universe operates. I doubt he will even tell Tara—he thinks his old man is off his rocker.

Things have taken a turn for the worse. J.T. showed up, walking into my room with no hint of his usual upbeat attitude. I hadn't guessed that Vince would call him. We had a heated argument, ignited by his saying, "Michael, you've been through a great deal. I would like you to talk to a friend of mine. I think he can help you sort out what is real here and what is fiction. He's a psychiatrist."

I told him "I don't need to see a psychiatrist. For the first time since my diagnosis I have something to fight for. If you're my friend, you should be happy for me." He sputtered a few more words about me being taken in, then walked out, shaking his head in disbelief.

I wish I could pick up the phone and talk to you. I have never felt so all alone in the world. I have reached out to you in my need, but I get nothing in return. Where are you?

It is late now, and I still haven't felt you close. Have you deserted me too? Maybe my state of mind has something to do with it. I am feeling emotionally drained … desolate. Vince hasn't called. I have no idea what he is thinking, but it can't be good. I need someone to talk to, but there is no one who could possibly understand this. Goodnight, my love—wherever you are.

My love, I have not deserted you. Your pain is evident, but I feel helpless in the face of it. Both of us have struggled to see the truth of our own experience. Even now, I would find it difficult to believe a similar story told by someone else. I couldn't know their experience was real in the same way I know our truth. This would be easier if we had more frequent letter exchanges. My power to reach out to you has been diminished due to some minor surgery and a little infection. That is why I have been more distant. It would never be by choice.

The girls were full of empathy for Vince and grateful they had first learned of Zachary, and then Amelia. Your son might continue to doubt until the day we meet. When it comes to others, we can only share the strength of our own belief.

At least Amelia hasn't deserted me, but it seems she's the only one. She said, "You must be patient with Vince. As for Teresa, her power to reach out to you will return." There is little I can do but wait.

J.T. was here and left orders for me to be discharged as soon as I feel ready to go. He was distant, said only what was necessary, looked in my direction without quite looking at me. I could feel a distinct chill in the air, a first in our relationship. He is not used to encounters with something he doesn't understand—he will also need time.

Tomorrow I am going to look for a place to live, less excited than I had expected to be. I wish you were here. I wish even more that I was there.

A few weeks ago, I asked Zachary if it would be possible for him to speak to our spirits about our contacts. Today, he said Mahalia told him that she and Alexander will often be with both of us but sometimes with whoever is available, which explains our out-of-sync encounters. She admitted they have amused themselves at our expense but denied any malicious intent. And, she said they sometimes need to retreat, to rest, which explains our fruitless efforts.

When I think of how utterly surreal our story would sound to almost anyone else, and of how I once compared my initial experience to something out of science fiction, it is easy to understand that Vince is overwhelmed. Our love is strong enough to withstand the doubts of others—it has withstood our own.

Vince still hasn't called. It is four days since I told him, a long time for him not to visit, and you've had no way of knowing what is on my mind. I'm going out to look for an apartment.

Sweetness, I am back—in more ways than one. I gave a lot of thought to us, to our future, and to Vince. Being out in the world, knowing I will soon be living in it, changed my perspective. Our reality was as clear to me as all the sights and sounds of the city, the crisp winter air, the crunch of snow under my feet. Vince will come to terms with it in his own time. Amelia said, "This is an opportunity for Vince. It is an unexpected, but valuable, lesson for his spirit."

I found a furnished apartment four blocks from the hospital, across from a large park. Then I made some phone calls to arrange to have my things placed in storage and my house put on the market. It finally dawned on me that I won't be living there again. One change I made was immediate. I got my car out of storage. A short drive on the freeway reminded me of the exhilaration of those combined sensations of speed and power.

I have felt you close again, and I can sense your support and encouragement. Vince just called and said, "Dad, I don't like us being at odds with each other." Then he asked, "Exactly what do you know about this woman?" I told him that I love you and plan to marry you as soon as I am in remission and can provide for us. He was suspicious that you have an ulterior motive, but he was at least more receptive. We can be patient with him.

My love, I feel a stronger sense of you again and welcome your almost constant presence. I am composing a letter to Vince to help him understand our relationship, and I will enclose copies of a few pieces of paper that document my life, crossing out my last name and any clues to where I live. They may help convince him of my reality but will do little to reassure him as to my motives.

I just had a phone call from Sally. She is in enough of a crisis to need an emergency appointment, and I will see her soon. She has accepted that the alter personalities will be close, but now they urge her to express herself and act to meet her own needs. She is uncertain, not fully trusting either them or herself. It is all part of the process of her growth and integration. If Amelia comes, I will give this letter to her, and Vince's.

Good morning, sweetheart. It is a warm, sunshiny day here. Will

you be walking on your usual trails? I plan to drive to a similar spot I have found here, just a bit closer to where I think you are. I am better able to reach you there, away from the city and more attuned to you and our spirits. This is quite a large city, close to half a million in population. (I hope it is okay to tell you that.)

Vince and I had another talk. It went better this time, largely due to your letter. He is still skeptical, doesn't want to hear any talk of guardians and angels, but he is at least thinking about us. J.T. just called and invited me out to dinner, so I will have an update on him later this evening.

We had quite a conversation. At first, J.T. took a patronizing tone. He couldn't accept our delivery system, kept repeating some version of "Michael, just think about it—listen to reason." He said, "There are a lot of scam artists out there, not to mention unbalanced minds. Someone is taking advantage of you or maybe has an unrequited love for you." Then he started spinning dark variations on the theme of *Fatal Attraction*.

I decided there was only one way to stop him. I had to play my trump card. I told him how Amelia has appeared to me using his body. That left him speechless, a first in my experience. I could see the wheels of his mind turning, wondering if he needed to make an immediate referral to the psych ward. I think it was a close call, but he opted to hear me out. I described Amelia's visit, in detail, and must have been persuasive. In the end, he said, "When can I meet this woman of your dreams?"

Michael, I picture you driving your car and I smile with happiness—for you, and in anticipation of our future. You are out and about, buying groceries, going to the library, coming back to life, coming to me. I want to give you directions and then expect you to be here by morning.

I am glad Vince called and was more receptive. What about J.T.? Does he still want you to see a psychiatrist? I looked through my official diagnosis manual to see what one might try to label you. You would no longer qualify for Brief Psychotic Disorder as it has exceeded one month; Delusional Disorder would be a possibility, including a special relationship to a deity; and Shared Psychotic Disorder (*folie à deux*) exists when you join in another's delusion. I hope J.T. will listen to you more as a friend than as your doctor.

Teresa, I am a little concerned that you are trying to label me with a psychotic disorder. If I hadn't talked to J.T., just last night, I would think the two of you were conspiring against me. I already have a medical label that will be hard to shake. I am at a loss as to why you would even suggest it.

Thank you for the little book of healing quotations you sent. Your thoughtfulness and generosity overwhelm me, as did your beautiful note. Do I have to be careful not to compliment you so much? Will you think I have some obsessive disorder?

I won't be able to write words you want to hear until I can understand. I have struggled with it all day, so give me some credit for trying to dismiss it. What conclusion am I to draw from your attempts to label me? Have I said something that indicates a problem? Until I hear some explanation, I can't write what is in my heart—it is overshadowed by the doubts in my mind.

Darling, forget what I wrote. It is two o'clock in the morning. I have given it a lot of thought and I know I am wrong. Please forgive me. I've been under a lot of stress. Come to me in my dreams.

Michael, as much as I enjoy your words of love, the wider range of thoughts and emotions in your last letter reveals more of the man I have grown to love and makes him even dearer to my heart.

Zachary cautioned me last week that the final outcome for us is unknown. He is concerned that I could be setting myself up for possible heartbreak—it strikes me that his words of caution have come a little late in the game. I did give it some serious thought and told him today that I want to know you to the fullest extent possible. If I have to someday mourn you, I want to know who and what I have lost, every facet of your being.

Sweetness, it has been a long day, arranging my move. If Amelia knew, she would chastise me for doing too much. Do not fear. I took time to rest between tasks, then took a drive along a scenic route north of the city, along the major river that flows through here. I stopped twice for a short walk. Did my eyes behold sights similar to those you enjoy? I felt you near.

I am just back from a long drive along the river. I immersed myself in the crystallized winter landscape, diamond points of brilliance in all the colors of the rainbow. It reminded me you wrote that the Light is made up of all colors—magnified, diffused, one with their source. It was in stark contrast to the nearly black trees, illuminating the simplicity of their winter silhouettes. Such scenes touch me deeply; it is how I know myself.

I looked for more of Khalil Gibran's work at the library today. He was an artist as well as a prolific writer and philosopher, was influenced by Christianity, Judaism, Sufism, and Islam, and was friends with Rodin, Yeats, and Jung. How I would have loved to have been in a café in Paris or New York listening to the four of them at the next table, or to any two or three of them.

One Gibran quote mirrors our experience. He writes that the soul, in its glory, will follow a truth that the mind rejects. By contrast, the mind, in its worst moments, will fight against the path of the spirit. It is exactly what we have written, though he puts it more eloquently. We first blindly followed the dictates of our spirits, caught up in their joy at having found each other. Then we sometimes fell into that lower state as our minds sought to prevail and rise up against the truth we knew in our hearts, informed by Alexander and Mahalia.

Your letter is here, delivered shortly after you wrote it. Were we driving along a river at the same time, enjoying the beauty? Could it be the same river? Were we traveling toward each other? If we knew that for certain, how could we stop from meeting halfway?

I wasn't able to write today, but I pray that the words in my heart reached yours, on angel's wings or with the wind. I felt you close throughout the day. My move went well, except when I put the wrong soap in the dishwasher and had suds all over the kitchen. This will be short. I am exhausted and wish only to seek the comfort of your arms.

Welcome, my love, to the first day of the rest of your life. I am filled with hope for our future knowing you have left the hospice, its purpose so contrary to what lies ahead for us. You were quite insistent with your wake-up call. I did not intend to be cruel, but I waited for you to reach out to me twice more before I responded. I wanted to feel the full force of your desire before it merged with mine, and I did—and it did.

Michael, I have felt a deepening of my love for you. I think of a long-lived tree, a giant oak, the many years it continues to grow and change, unobserved, within its depths. Our love is like that, already formed at a spiritual level, then blossoming anew in each lifetime together—aspects of our love concealed from us, then suddenly unfolding.

I love the way you make analogies of our love to nature. Do you think we will be aware of Mahalia's and Alexander's influence when we are together? Will our love flow and extend to those around us? Will it diminish our faults and enhance those qualities the Creator hopes to see manifested in all of His children?

Guess what just happened? The building managers are an older couple, Maeve and Henry, two doors down. A few minutes ago, Maeve—a plump, white-haired grandmotherly type—came to the door with a casserole for me. You have probably guessed by now that Amelia appeared through her. She is more similar to my vision of Amelia—wise, kind, and gentle. I guess an apt description would be to say that she is more angelic; the volunteer at the hospice could be a bit crusty. Amelia said she will be available if I need her.

I wrote my last note in haste, no time to explain why I played around with a diagnosis. Michael, consider this—if you are psychotic, what would that make me? I am so sorry to have caused you anguish. I was mocking the medical profession, questioning if they could see beyond the accepted view of reality as we have had to. There is a long history of mystical and surreal experiences being interpreted as symptoms of mental illness. In some cases, that is exactly what they are; many doctors would not look beyond that.

Whatever are we going to do with ourselves, with our ups and downs, our missed connections, our misunderstandings that can take days to sort out through our letters? Do you feel, as I do, the lack of any reference points, of any prior experience to guide us as we blindly go through uncharted territory?

I like thinking that it may be the same river, that we are connected by such a force of nature. I think I am upriver from you but too far away for us to meet by chance, even on a long drive. If I were to put a note in a bottle and throw it into my river, would you look for it every day in yours?

20. A Winter Melancholy

01/19 – 01/31

Teresa, your locket is still right here, where it shall remain until you can see it, feel it between us, and then be the one to wear it. Have I told you that I raise it to my lips whenever I take my leave of you?

I have been thinking of how my life has changed since you came into it. I am a different man. I reflect on life's mysteries more often and experience the world as more welcoming. I am more tolerant, patient and, I hope, loving. I want you here with me. Do you feel my need, my desire? I could cry with the frustrations of this separation, and yes, I would look every day for your message in a bottle.

Some wrenching moments earlier—the pain is still with me. As our relationship deepens, Michael, I grieve with a greater knowledge for our lost years, lost love, lost family. I miss you to a depth I hadn't known was possible. I want to curl up somewhere, retreat from the world, exist only with you in the presence of our spirits, but others keep calling me away, needing me.

Today is better. I feel a quiet peace. If you were here, there would not be a lot of chatter, just the contentment of being in the same room with you. It touches my heart that you bring my locket to your lips when you say good night. I questioned at the time if it was the right gift—it is so *not* masculine. Now I know it was perfect.

I took a nap, meditated for an hour, and then was able to concentrate on my work. I became so engrossed in it that I didn't realize the time until it started to get dark. I'm within a few days of finishing my software program. If I can sell it, neither of us will need to work again. To that end, I am putting together a proposal to send to six major companies.

You do not have to hide your pain from me—it is familiar. We both sometimes feel the despair of our situation, but more often we revel in the joy of shared moments, of loving and being loved. Do you get a sense of what the spiritual world is all about? During my near-death experience, it was the overwhelming sense of love that enticed me to stay.

Sweetheart, to keep anything from you would make a travesty of our love. Not long after you came into my life, I lost my hair from the chemo. I begged Amelia to describe me as she had first seen me. Then, every day I would look closely for any new growth. This morning, I noticed a fine bit of fuzz, no more than what you would find on a peach. Can you love me with no hair?

I feel a winter melancholy, a letdown from the intensity and seemingly endless discoveries of our first months together. We should be moving on to the next stage of our relationship. You are out on your own, living a normal life—your home should be my home.

It is twilight. I stand at the window wrapped in a natural-fiber shawl that reaches to the floor. I stare out at deep drifts of snow as five deer slowly pass in single file across the ridge of the hill, stop to sniff the air. I wait. A great horned owl descends from the sky to take his perch on the highest branch of the tallest tree. I wait. The wind comes up and swirls the snow around, obscuring the break in the trees. I wait. I am Morning Star, drawing my blanket around me, looking for Bear Hunter, returning home.

What I sense is a discordant note. During our first months together, we were caught up in a joyous symphony that should by now be reaching its climax and resolution. Instead, I am struck by the incongruity of our separate lives.

I am anxiously awaiting your letter, the first since I told you of my hair loss. It is difficult to talk about my leukemia and its side effects. I want you to think of me as the man of your dreams. I want to be strong for you. I do look better—my clothes no longer hang on me and you can't count my ribs unless you really try.

I need to tell you of the dream I had last night, another glimpse of our past lives as Bear Hunter and Morning Star. You were pregnant for the first time and close to giving birth. An old medicine woman of our tribe spoke to me of her concern for you—the child was large and you had a small frame. She urged me to seek a vision. It is not clear how long I remained in the Medicine Lodge, praying, before a white buffalo appeared to me and said, "Your wife will live and you shall prosper. Your son will one day take your place—he shall be named Talon Qua." Our son was born the next day. I wept at the sight of him.

Michael, this is not easy. You are here with me and then, suddenly, you turn and walk away. You grow smaller and smaller, then disappear into that final dot of perspective where our path meets the horizon. I try to call you back, to no avail—you keep retreating from my sight, deserting me.

I take my misery to the river, drive out forty some miles on a rolling, curving road. The skies are low to the ground, weighted with thick clouds in shades of gray and bluish black that reflect my dark mood. I have to make an effort to shake it off and come into presence with my surroundings. I can see now that the somber hues of the clouds make up a color palette—there is light contained within their darkness.

The ground is snow covered; native grasses add accents in ochre, taupe, burnt umber, and sienna. I am entranced by their many varieties and colors, the grace and beauty of their forms. It reminds me that Emerson referred to beauty as "the instant dependence of form upon soul." It is a truth I recognized when first I read his words.

I turn off the highway and stop to look out over the river, shallow here, a frozen, wind-swept expanse of blackish green. I look up to the river bluffs, their contours defined by drifts of snow caught in the shadows of cliffs and ravines. Close by, a red fox darts across a stretch of open prairie. I roll down my window to the sight and sound of honking flocks of low-flying geese, instinct guiding their ever-changing V-formations. I gaze at them and think of how they mate for life.

Winter is hardly my favorite season, yet it touches me deeply, has its moments. In spring, it is the nascent quality of life itself that calls to me. I reach out to embrace the world, feel myself come to life with the whole of all creation. Summer brings the contrast of early mornings and late evenings with the oppressive heat of the day, the silver linings that remind me to find them where I can. Then, as autumn mixes its rich, pungent blend, I feel a oneness with the earth. It is in the dead of winter—with its cold, stark beauty—that I know a piercing intimacy with the pain of the world, and with the elemental forces that stir my soul.

Michael mine, as I write it is once again as if I am talking with you. It was only this morning and somewhat yesterday and that day last week, an hour here and there, sometimes two or three, that I had lost that feeling. One minute is enough to know the utter desolation of being separated from you.

Have you just been here with me? Is your question about your hair answered? Did you feel me caress your head, kiss it, and brush my cheek against its new growth? It will not matter in the least.

I felt your presence today during the chemo. The biopsies, and the bone marrow and spinal taps, are scheduled for next week. Darling, do you realize that when I am in remission I will still need frequent tests? My sweet love, you need to know how emotionally trying that can be, waiting for the results. I'm suddenly not sure we should be planning our future together. I am going to take a drive up along the river and consider all that I am asking of you.

Sweetheart, I have come up with only heart-wrenching alternatives. I know this: I love you with all of my heart, it seems beyond all reason. Do we need to let reason prevail? Help me, my love. I can't bear the thought of letting you go. Please think carefully before you answer this letter. My mood has gone from bad to worse—to write of the details would serve no purpose.

My love, if you were close just now you know my answer. I hesitate to write so soon, lest you think I haven't given it enough consideration. I will let last night's dream inform you. I was to be married to one of two men, but it was not to be my choice. One man was you; the other one was a bit younger, attractive, perfectly healthy, etc. I was in bed with him, not intimate, but close. I was repulsed, afraid they were going to choose him. I woke up before their decision was made, still apprehensive, wanting you.

Michael, I ask myself: how much time would I need with you to believe it worth this agony? The answer is: any time at all. I then ask myself: what if it were only for one day? The answer is the same—if it were for one hour—if I were to reach your side in the final moment of your life.

Sweetness, you were with me last night in a dream. I was not consciously reaching out but was inexplicably being drawn to you. I did not protest but allowed myself to be transported until I felt us merge as one. I can no longer question these encounters.

My hair is definitely growing back, but it still looks a little funny, like the haircuts we used to get as kids in the fifties. Did I ever tell you about my weekend in San Francisco before going to Vietnam? It was an experience I'll never forget. I saw Judy Collins in concert at The Forum. Downtown, everyone was protesting the war. After one of us was beaten up for being in the military, we left and spent the next two days in Carmel. I didn't have much hair then either, so it wasn't easy to blend with the crowd in San Francisco.

Your letter brought strong affirmations of all we are to each other. How can I continue to think as I have been? I believe you when you say you have given careful thought to your decision. I need to stop wasting precious time and get myself in remission.

21. Love: it is an imperative

February

Michael, you once wrote that the spiritual world is all about love. According to Amelia, there is one lesson common to every lifetime—each of us is to learn a lesson of love. While the experience is often a romantic one, it might be love of a different kind. She said, "The Creator's purpose was to give mankind the capacity to love, not only in relationship to themselves, but selflessly."

Love is one of the four essential attitudes. You will recognize the others: Faith, Hope, and Charity. She said, "The greatest of lessons are those of maintaining these four attitudes—under a variety of circumstances that are increasingly difficult. It was the Creator's intention that these attitudes would positively affect brain processes and lead to higher levels of physical and mental health." I wish I could say they are my constant focus. Over my lifetime, I have held them generally, but I do not intentionally cultivate them as often as I might, and I do not consistently draw on them to guide me. It is easy enough to do so in the abstract, removed from the world, but it is in the nitty gritty of life that we are called to apply them.

Amelia also spoke of the future of our planet. "It is of the utmost importance that this message be conveyed—you must practice and embody these four attitudes—for the sake of each other and for the sake of the world you have been given to survive in." Her tone conveyed her deep conviction in the necessity of us doing so: *it was an imperative.*

Vince stopped by last night, and he was the one to bring up your name. He finally accepts that we have a long-distance relationship through our letters—he didn't mention our delivery system. Am I wrong to let him accept what he will without trying to explain the significance of our angels? He is anxious to meet all of you, even said, "Imagine that, Dad, I'll finally have some sisters to pick on."

J.T. called to say he is stopping by soon with my test results. I am worried, my love. I have to remind myself that my symptoms are diminished, and I rarely take any pain medication. Except for the tests, and some horrendous headaches I've had lately, I almost feel like my normal self.

I have felt you close since J.T. left. Can you sense my excitement, my strength? The results were very good. There is no evidence of cancer cells in the spinal fluid or in the testes, and there are fewer in the bone marrow. I am not yet in remission, but I am confident of our future together.

Last week, Amelia told me of some scenes from our secondary lives, what might have been if you had taken my class twelve years ago. You made an excuse to come up and ask me a question but couldn't understand why you were drawn to me (so much for any sex appeal I thought I had then). She said that you were nervous and felt awkward and that I was aware of your discomfort and a little amused by it. You maneuvered to sit next to me at dinner and then asked if I would like to go to the lounge for a drink. It wasn't long before you asked me to come to your room. I am only a little surprised at what she said my reply was, that I had been waiting for you to suggest it.

(Out-of-town propositions were not infrequent, but yours was the first I accepted.)

As Amelia described what she saw, Mahalia and Alexander drew so close that I could have been recalling an event from my past. I can picture us both then, in our early thirties, vibrant with energy and good health. How do we accept that there was wisdom in the intervention that caused the class to be canceled? There must have been other possibilities—a one hour delay in leaving, a different route taken home … something.

Michael, you write of a loss of yourself as we part. I too feel that. As I write, your scent reaches me from your last letter, your physical absence a gaping hole in my center. I want this wait to be over. I don't want to leave you, but I need to go to work.

Can you feel my joy? As positive as I have been, I did not react with a calmly stated, "I knew it." After Amelia told me, I needed to speak with Sally again, so I had to set my feelings aside. When I got to my car, I turned on the radio. Guess what song was playing? I was smiling and cheering most of the way home, and then I was crying—tears of relief, tears of joy. It is late, the end of a long day of celebrating our love and our future.

J. T. is coming soon. We are going out to lunch, and then I hope to persuade him to come in for a while. Amelia is concerned about my headaches and suggested it will give her an opportunity to appear and do an exam.

It worked according to plan. Amelia did not tell me much, except that there are some tests she will somehow convince J.T. to order. I didn't dare test his credulity by telling him of her visit, that she used his body again. I don't know how much he can accept. Will you spend the night with me? Tomorrow is a chemo day.

It is late. The chemo still makes me sick but not as much as before. Thank you for the card with the white buffalo and the explanation that it is held to be sacred and a sign of hope. How is it you know exactly what will raise my spirits? I kept the image in mind for most of the day. I am very tired—will you be content to just hold me tonight?

I have been making two small gifts for you and should finish them in time to leave for my afternoon appointments. I will likely see Amelia and will ask her to include them with this card for tomorrow's celebration of love.

My beloved husband, my life's companion—there is no doubt that we will find each other in the world beyond this one. It is in this world that we did not recognize each other until, with the help of angels, we were given another chance. We celebrate a love that has transcended time and space, that has lost and grieved and grown stronger, that is teaching us a meaning of itself that deepens with each passing day. Let us celebrate our love—as one.

My darling Tessa, I am hopelessly in love with you. I want you in my loving embrace, now and forever—to love, protect, and cherish above all else. Come live with me and be my love.

I have admired your gifts and have read your card. To know that I am so loved is a gift in itself. I have finished the entire book of quotes about love, and I put the mix tape in the first thing. Did you feel my tears? It is a little early in the night to let you know that I want you, need you. I will wait.

I love that you took the time to find the lingerie. I had guessed from your hints what you were looking for, including the rose and the ribbons. Did you have my stationery in mind? Will you keep your eyes on the pearls and the satiny ivory fabric as they reflect the soft glow of candlelight? How will the beads feel as they slowly traverse the midline of your body? Will you promise to let me keep it on long enough to find out?

How did you know what I had in mind as a gift? Am I that transparent? I had to go out of town yesterday to wrap up the sale of my house. On the way back, I stopped at my favorite men's store and bought a suit for our wedding. It is a light gray with tiny black flecks through it, with pleated slacks. I plan to wear a white shirt with a tie that you choose for me. Have you given any thought yet to what you will wear?

This letter is not going to be as light-hearted as I would like it to be. Maeve brought me a plate of cookies and then Amelia came. She said, "I have consulted with those in the spirit world who specialize in assisting with medical issues. They believe it is necessary to convince J.T. that you should have a CAT scan or MRI as soon as possible. I want you to tell him more about the headaches when you see him tomorrow. I will take it from there." I am going to tell J.T. that the pain is now excruciating—it will not be a lie.

Amelia brought up the topic of love again today. "One kind of love is that found in human relationships—you must contend with the individuality, flaws, and weaknesses of others. Can you nourish the capacity to see both the person and their spirit? Can you recognize their struggles, withhold your judgment, and believe that their choices have not diminished their innate worthiness? I am once again humbled as I recognize my failure to consistently practice this form of love.

I am just back from a long walk, more than my right leg could take. It was such a gorgeous day that I ignored the first warning twinges and kept going through the mud, slush, and ice. I had to trudge back, limping, trying to focus on the beauty all around me. I don't want to accept that I have to set limits on myself. Will you keep me in line or let me go my foolish way and then suffer the consequences?

Amelia said we are not allowed to send photos, but it would be okay to send you a small copy of a painting showing two girls about the age Callie and Kenna were in 1983. Everyone assumes it is them. They were as sweet as the girls in the picture and they still are at heart, even let it show at times.

Sweetness, do you have my letter by now? Do you like my tee shirt? The picture you sent of the two girls was my undoing. If you tried to reach out to me last night, I was beyond consoling. I would be proud to be their father, and I am angry that I wasn't given the opportunity many years ago. I would have been there for them as they grew up. Damn the unfairness of this! I can't write now.

You may know before you read this that I am having surgery tomorrow. I wanted to keep it from you but Amelia, in her infinite wisdom, said, "Michael, do you not think the two of you have come too far to do that?" Yes, my love, you have every right to know. She said she will inform you as soon as the results are known.

The girls came home as I sat down to write. Whenever they notice I have a new letter, they ask, "How is Michael doing today?" We were eating lunch, spending some time together, and now I'm sitting here in my corner chair, listening to them in the kitchen ... they just had a skirmish over clothes but were teasing and laughing as they went out the door.

I too cry out at the unfairness of it all, and then I remind myself there are many others whose destinies have not been fully realized. We may be unique—in that we were told what we have missed—but I would not exchange our experience for the bliss of ignorance.

You get one guess what I am wearing, caressing. I buried my face in your tee shirt as soon as I opened the large envelope, drinking in the scent of you. I love the idea of wearing what you have worn next to your skin, within limits. I will wear it to bed tonight, hug it to me as though it were you. How I wish that you were in it, that our wait was over, that we had spent the last twenty years together, that we had been allowed to meet in November.

My dearest love, you have likely been told by now that I am okay. The problem turned out to be a large cyst at the base of my brain. It was easily excised with the new laser techniques, but it could have caused serious problems if it hadn't been detected early. I have Amelia to thank for averting a delay in my recovery, or worse.

Your letter is here, but I am not past the first page. I have read it three times and still delight in every word. I can't stop picturing you in my tee shirt, drinking in the scent of me.

I've hesitated, but now I feel compelled to tell you that I have figured out where you live. I have spent a lot of time there over the years. Don't worry, I have no intention of telling Amelia. It is my contingency plan. I know where you walk and have taken those paths myself. We will soon walk there together.

You have your suit and I have some lingerie—is that all we will need for our wedding day? I picture you on the road, stopping at the menswear store, looking at suits—touching them, stroking them, imagining my hand caressing you through the fabric. To know that you are anticipating and preparing for that day brings me great ... I am looking for a word between satisfaction and joy ... it is a quiet, deep pleasure that I feel to the core of my being.

Michael—your name is still as music to my ears, the sweetest, clearest tones. There is a quote I like from ancient Hindu scripture that fits: "When we love our husband/wife/child more than we love ourselves, we are loving the Lord in them." I once used the word reverent when writing of you, my husband—this is what I meant.

22. Success and Forgiveness

Can you sense my excitement? Do you remember that I wrote to some software companies about my program? One of the largest of them is interested in producing it and will send a rep here next week to meet with me. Sweetness, if I can sell them on this, we will be set for life.

It has been a long, tiring day. I met with my attorney, had lunch with J.T., did some shopping, and now I am exhausted. The news hasn't all been good. Maybe Amelia has already told you of the test results—the bone marrow test was a disappointment.

I have just sought my inner sources of strength and power, and it has left me in a reflective mood, more aware of the changes taking place in my body. I have gained twelve pounds, my skin has a healthy color, and my hair is growing back. I have better muscle tone and the dark circles under my eyes are gone. The changes have been so gradual that I hadn't noticed them.

Michael, you were the star of my dreams last night, a series of three. In the first, I am running along the edge of a lake, splashing in the water, energetic and happy. You are the reason for my joy, my *raison d'etre*. In the next, I am sitting on top of a piano, ecstatic, looking at sheet music. I hold one up and read the title: "The Greatness of the Male Body." Whose body but yours can it have been written for? In the last, I am lying on my bed, crazy with anticipation. You are running down the hall, coming closer, calling my name. I woke up expecting to hear your footsteps. As I faced reality, I reminded myself that it won't be long before my dreams come true.

My love, I haven't written much about my father. He is an alcoholic who was physically and mentally abusive to all of us. His sister in California just called to tell me the alcohol has finally taken its toll. He is now in a nursing home and is incoherent much of the time. Her call has brought back a hoard of unpleasant memories that I had sealed off in some dark recess of my mind.

I wish you were here, darling. I want to lose myself in you and not think about this. I hadn't spoken to my aunt since my father was in legal trouble, five years ago, and I refused to pay for his defense. Now she thinks I should pay his expenses, what isn't covered. I don't want to have anything to do with him. I feel nothing for him, not even hatred anymore. There was a time it wouldn't have been wise for us to be in the same room; he is the only one I have ever thought I could be violent with. I wish you were here. I wish my mother and Danny were alive. I wish … I wish ….

My sweet love, I could feel your pain as I read your letter. Imagine that you are here with me—you can hear the love in my voice and see the caring in my eyes. I know you are feeling anger, and I expect beneath it is a feeling of loss, for besides the physical and emotional pain your father inflicted on you, he robbed you of your childhood.

I think it is natural for you to feel no obligation to help him, to feel you owe no duty to one who was not the father or husband he should have been. I wonder if it is possible for you to see him, not as a father, but as a fellow human being with all of his flaws. Can you see within him some remnant of the young man with whom your mother fell in love?

Zachary once told me that forgiveness is a lesson of almost every lifetime, but it is not easy when the other hasn't taken responsibility for their actions, which may not be possible now. To the extent that you hold on to the pain and anger, give them a place in your deepest self, does that not prevent love from flowing and exerting its healing power? Not that forgiveness can be given lightly, as simply a mental construct—it is soul work.

I have made some presumptions. I make no claim to know exactly what is in your heart. Michael, can you feel my love? It recognizes your pain but wants you to be free of it. I want to be there to give you the support that words cannot give.

Amelia somehow knows about my father and that I have my presentation today. With her usual calm, she said, "Michael, it would be wise for you to take all matters one step at a time." So first, I need to get through this meeting. I am wearing a gray tweed jacket, black slacks, and a black and gray striped tie. I have never given a presentation like this or one with so much at stake.

It is over—now we wait. I think I did fairly well. I went through the program and then fielded their questions for nearly two hours, and now I am mentally exhausted. They made no offer and they took no material with them. It would be almost impossible for them to pirate the project, but it has happened to others so I have taken some precautions. I have invested over three years of my life in putting this all together, and I want to protect that investment—our future.

I had been doing a lot of soul-searching, even before I got your letter. You are right in everything you said. I could feel the love emanating from the pages as I read your words. As I try to sort out what feelings, if any, I have for my father, I imagine you are here with me. I knew, before I read your compassionate words, what tone you would take. What had the most significance for me was when you asked if I could see in him the young man with whom my mother fell in love. I have decided to cover his expenses, but I still don't know about forgiveness. Darling, that may take a while. I have not yet worked through my past with him, have preferred to ignore it. I will reflect on our relationship, and the emotions it triggers, and try not to run from them. I have been doing that for a good part of my life, not wanting to face my feelings. Now it is time.

"How do I love thee, let me count the ways. I love thee to the depth and breadth and height my soul can reach." My soul has reached new dimensions in my love for you.

Michael, "I love thee to the level of every day's most quiet need, by sun and candlelight." I had run across those words last week, surprised that neither of us had yet quoted from that love sonnet by Elizabeth Barrett Browning. My favorite lines are these and the ones you sent.

The girls got up early for a Saturday. We were talking and carrying on, silly stuff, having fun, when Callie said, "Look at us, three girls who all look alike, sitting around not doing a thing." Earlier, Kenna had noticed your tee shirt and asked me about it. She kept pressing me for details so I finally told her, said she might think it was kind of lame. She laughed and said, "That's not lame, that's just dumb." She had to tell Callie as soon as she came upstairs and then they both had a good laugh over us two old lovers, or maybe they think *too old* to be lovers.

Thank you for telling me that your father and I would have been close and that the three of us have shared several past lifetimes. I wish I had known him. I wanted Amelia to tell me more about our secondary lives, but she said, "I question the wisdom of that. Is it not enough to know that you would have been happy together?"

I asked her, if we would have been so happy, then why were our destinies altered? She said, "Happiness and contentment do not always promote learning. Discord and unrest keep that pursuit alive." I don't understand it, or maybe I just don't want to accept it. I would gladly sacrifice some lessons to have had our life together, but I wonder if Alexander would say the same.

I fully endorse, and am looking forward to, every item on your list, but I can't believe my handyman skills don't rank in the top ten reasons why you want me there. Besides household tasks, I will be more than happy to help the girls with their car. We were out working on Vince's one day this week. It felt like old times—a six pack of beer, two guys, and a car. I did limit myself to one beer.

I am just back from a twilight walk along the river. I spent a few agonizing moments longing for you, then decided to stay in the moment and be present to the beauty of the night. The full moon rose against a backdrop of indigo blue—above a narrow band of gold that might have been mined from the depths of the earth. It epitomized the words and feelings of an old song, "Where the Blue of the Night Meets the Gold of the Day ... someone waits for you." When I play it, certain chords bring tears to my eyes, so poignantly do they evoke the lyrics, set a mood that matches ours. I sense you waiting for me now, the sweet pleasure I take from your presence tinged with the bitter reality that you are not here.

Do you remember I once wrote of going to the mountains, disappointed that I couldn't hike as I had wanted to? I started my moonlight walks the evening I returned, that September. I walked out on the island at dusk, still missing the challenge of climbing. I kept going, listening to the hooting of the owls and a chorus of chirping crickets, walking through the perfect mixture of warm and cool air currents. So determined was I to fulfill the longing of my soul to experience the elements, that I ignored the obvious. My walk back was in full darkness with just occasional patches of moonlight peeking through the clouds. I had to stop often and stare up at what little light there was and then could see the path for a short way ahead. I've kept up the walks since then. If I feel a frisson of fear, it is easily defeated when I let myself be present to the magic of the night.

I have heard from a second software company, in California, that wants to fly me out to discuss things, and there's word about my last blood test. It's about the best I have had, an increase in white blood cells but with few antibodies—my immune system is trying to make a comeback. It is great news, on both fronts.

Yes, my love, I can hear your concern as if you were here with me. I have considered the down side of the trip, but I can think of no other way to present my project to them. J.T. said, "You're nuts to even consider it," but he didn't absolutely forbid me to go.

I have been on the phone all morning. The most important call was from J.T., with the news that my other test results were also excellent. They were so good that he dropped his professional role and let a hint of excitement into his voice. The biopsies and spinal fluid were negative for any cancer cells; there are still some in the bone marrow, but significantly fewer. I am almost there!

I love you, sweetness. Of all the events in my life, including my illness, nothing has humbled me as much as your love—the truest, purest love I have ever known.

Welcome to spring, my love. If the first day of summer does not find us together, we will wait—sometimes patiently, sometimes not. Earlier, I was reading a novel and had to stop, overcome by tears when an everyday scene described a woman straightening her husband's rumpled collar. I long for those simple gestures as much as the more romantic ones. Are you coming to bed with me? I have a long day tomorrow.

No time to write and I am not in the mood for it now, so I will summarize my thoughts of you today: your tests tomorrow, how I will be close; your clothes, as I glanced at a men's catalog, picked out what you might like; your body, both in and out of the clothes; your girls, could I send them to you for a week; tulips, are there any outside of your building; and your trip, can you fly first class so you have less exposure?

Yesterday, I wrote "your girls" because I didn't feel much like claiming them. I walked in the door to the sounds of a shrieking, physical fight that had started over each wanting to go along when the other has plans with a mutual friend. As close as they are, their fights have an equal, but opposite, intensity. I don't think I've mentioned that they both have earned black belts, but they fight without regard to any rules. Today, all is well, the usual pattern.

It is pure joy to me to picture you and Vince out working on his car, doing such an ordinary father and son activity, working and laughing together. You are physically stronger, engaged with life, feeling like your old self. I want to get in my car and go to you, share some stolen moments. I could never leave you.

Darling, can you sense my excitement? Did you feel me reaching out to you with the news? I wish with all my heart that you were here to share my joy.

So now they are my girls? You can't imagine how much I would welcome their visit. I wish I could be there to help you at such times, but I've gathered from you that my mere presence will change the dynamics between them.

My trip is all arranged for me, flying first class. I am feeling much better, so I don't want you to worry. I will have two or three meetings, and I will have to find time to go see my father. I am not looking forward to it, but I hear an inner voice telling me that I need to come to terms with my past. I have an early flight, so I will say goodnight now and write after I arrive.

Michael, can you tell how thrilled I am with your latest test results? I have been bubbling over with excitement all day, having to suppress it when with clients. Our future could be just a few weeks away.

I will be thinking of you and will be close these next few days. I wish you well with your meetings and with your visit to your father. I wish even more that I could be there to look after you. *Vaya con Dios.*

Sweetness, it has been a long, exhausting day. My presentation went well—they made no attempt to hide their interest. One of their board members asked what I thought my program was worth. I said that it was more a question of what value it would bring to their company.

When I returned to my room, there was a message for me to call my attorney—the other company has made an offer and a rep will be in town next week to discuss the details. I'm going to meet with a consulting firm before then to have them evaluate my program and help me assess its worth.

I felt you near when we went to dinner. Perhaps it was because of Felicia, the dark-haired beauty who works for the company, though I think she had dual roles tonight. Was your spirit here and jealous on your behalf? Felicia was pleasant enough, but she kept touching my arm or placing a lingering hand on my thigh to emphasize her words. Her intent was obvious.

You must be curious how it went with my father. I was shocked—he is but a shell of the man I once knew; he can no longer hurt me. As I sat and watched him, and listened to his gibberish, I thought, what if he is trying to apologize or explain things to me and I don't have a clue? Tears came to my eyes, angry tears of frustration and then sad tears for him, for my mother and Danny, and for myself. It was emotionally draining, but I am glad I made the visit.

About your girls—now you can have them for a month. I had denied them permission to go to a Nine Inch Nails concert, four hours away, mid-week, friends driving, and they went anyway. Their one redeeming act was to call me, halfway there, and let me know where they were. They had a good time, but they will be limited to work release for a while.

I walked along the river today, thinking we will soon walk there together. I saw two bald eagles near where I saw one last winter swoop down and grab a fish from a small hole in the ice, then fly away with it in his talons, all in a few seconds. I kept a lookout for a fallen feather to save for Vince, our Talon Qua, our Brave Eagle.

A few tense moments as we waited for a thunderstorm to pass before landing, but I am back home now, closer to you again. I have to tell you more about Felicia, how I wasn't comfortable fending off her advances. It would have been easy to take her to bed and pretend that she was you, but I couldn't do that to you, and I couldn't sell myself out so easily. I finally had to take both of her hands in mine to keep her from touching me. I told her she's a lovely woman, but I am deeply involved with someone. She said you were the lucky one, but I begged to differ.

Amelia was here earlier today. She is concerned that I am pushing myself too hard and said I must rest and return to my regular meditation. It won't be this busy for long, and then I will take as much time as I can to rest. J.T. called, wanting to know all about my trip. He, too, said I should take a few days off.

Michael, I can feel you close. As I took a shower this morning, I thought of your test results and imagined hearing soon that there are no new cancer cells. I almost collapsed as I stood there under the streaming water, sobbing, gasping for breath, overwhelmed with emotion as excitement mixed with relief. I am not counting on those results this time, but it is possible. We could be together just days from now.

My dearest love, I was reading from my little book—a beautiful passage of a love sustained while the lovers were parted—when I felt a breath upon my cheek. The calm serenity of your presence descended upon me like a soft, warm blanket, enveloping me, quieting my mind. I couldn't tell where you left off and I began.

23. Running on Faith

April

My dearest Teresa, it is too early to awaken you, just before dawn. I have had such disturbing dreams that sleep has become a source of anxiety. I find solace in thoughts of my love for you. I would rather endure the pain of my illness again than this agony of being apart. I fear I will never know your touch, your kiss, your sweet embrace.

As the day goes on, I am feeling even worse. J.T. wasn't available so I tried his pager, but he hasn't called back. I try to write but the words do not come. Will you allow me the luxury of falling asleep in your arms? I will try to obliterate the demons. *Je t'aime, ma Chérie*

Michael, I have one wish—that you will come back to me. I was told that Vince found you, unconscious, with no idea for how long. Amelia knew but Maeve wasn't home, so all she could do was influence Vince to stop by. Now she and Zachary will do all that is in their power, and they have asked Eli for his assistance. I am staying positive and hopeful. My fervent wish is to be there by your side, to hold your hand, to speak to you of my love. I know that you would hear me, you would feel my touch.

I have several clients this afternoon, so I will need to turn my thoughts to others for a few hours. I have no choice but to put each disparate element of my life in its own compartment, to briefly shut you out. I trust that Mahalia will be there with you.

I now know details—a virus has invaded the membrane that surrounds your brain, likely caught on your flight home from California. Amelia is assisting your doctors, influencing them to act according to her greater knowledge. She said she will write a message for you when you are able to speak. I will treasure even one word from you. I know you are trying to come back. Did you feel my kiss upon your lips, your brow?

I need to go out of town tomorrow to testify in court, to where I am quite certain now that you used to live, a four-hour drive. How do I not drive four hours more and try to find you? It is only because our future would be at stake that I dare not take that risk.

It was still light when I got home. I stopped outside to pick some April flowers, sturdy grape hyacinths that speak to my hope and faith and love. Is your music there now? I asked Amelia if she would arrange it. I have been listening to "Running on Faith" from Eric Clapton's *Unplugged* album, the chorus a wish and a prayer as I reach out to you.

My love, I know you have been worried. Vince and Amelia have both offered to write for me, but I know how much it will mean to you to have this from my hand. Thank you for your unwavering support. Yes, I did feel your touch, your hand in mine ... this is all I can manage.

Sweetheart, I want a future with you and our daughters so very much that it is all I think about, but now I must face an unbearable reality. Amelia said the experimental drug I am on was made available through Eli's powers. I hope their efforts have not been in vain. I don't seem to have the strength to fight any more than I am now. It has taken me awhile to write this much. I can't keep focused ....

Time has stood still. I have no conscious memory of this past week. You will have to excuse my writing, which looks almost impossible to read, but I am very weak. I have been aware of your presence, kissing me softly. I love you, sweetness.

My dearest Michael, I wish for you all the miracles in the world. I chose this card because I know our angels are doing all that is within their power. Amelia said, "We have not worked on your behalf all this time only to give up now." Zachary said, "Eli would not be so eager to help Michael if he did not know the Council's final decision will be in your favor." I am filled with hope and gratitude.

Dear Teresa, Dad fell asleep while writing this letter. I found it here beside him. The beautiful card you sent is in his hand. He loves you a lot and I guess you must love him too. I can't pretend to know how all of this is possible. I'm not even sure I believe everything, but as long as the two of you know what is going on, I guess it is okay with me. The one thing I don't understand is why you are not here. He really needs you now. He said you can't be together until he is in remission. What if that doesn't happen? He's starting to wake up again. Vince

I see my son has taken some liberties with my letter. Don't worry about him, darling; he doesn't understand. I sent him to get me a soda so I can put this where Amelia will find it. I have felt you near. *Je t'aime, ma Chérie.*

My sweet love, you deserve so much better than this. What do I have to offer you? The thoughts I have are breaking my heart. I can't stop them, so I will rest now and be with you in my dreams, where all is right with our world. I have felt you reaching out to me … so near … yet so far away.

Dearest heart, first I will answer your question of what you have to offer me—you need offer nothing more than yourself. It is you that I want, Michael, not a perfect specimen of good health or a guarantee.

I am enclosing a letter to Vince, to explain a little of our history and to ease his mind as to why I am not there with you. I realized as I wrote to him that I already think of him as my son. As much as you envision life with me and our girls, Vince too will be a part of our family, even if he will not be living with us.

I am pleased that you have liked the cards and my new fragrance. I agree that it is more sensual, even erotic—why do you think I chose it?

This virus has taken a larger toll than first thought. Certain tissues are more susceptible—the membranes surrounding the brain and the heart. So far, the drug has only had access to my brain, but they have now obtained it in IV form. I can't help but wonder what will be next. Why is this happening to me now?

Maeve was here with Vince and Tara. Knowing Amelia would come, I sent the kids to the cafeteria, and she talked to me about resuming my meditation. I have tried to, but I can't concentrate. She said you suggested that I start to meditate before I rest and then let the process continue in my sleep. I will try it.

Sweetness, have I told you how much I like your new scent? It clings to the heavier paper of the cards, imparting a richness that your writing paper does not. It isn't a floral scent, or a spicy one, but some subtle combination, plus some citrus notes, that I was instantly infatuated with.

Dear Teresa, I am at a complete loss as to what to say. I don't know anything about the supernatural, but I do know you are the best thing that has happened to my dad in a very long time. I'm inclined to think I don't care if you're the Virgin Mary herself as long as whatever you're doing keeps helping him. Dad said I will meet Amelia, but someone has always been in the room when Maeve has visited. She probably thinks I'm a geek for looking at her so weirdly. This is all a little bizarre, if you don't mind me saying so.

I am grateful to you for the support and love you have given my dad. I believe you have made all the difference. Something very positive happened to turn things around for him at the hospice last fall. I don't think it was his chemotherapy. Do you mind if I write again? As ever, Vince.

I have had a wonderful dream. Before I went to sleep, I thought of ways to fight the enemy within. I asked myself: what in my life have been the most powerful influences? First and foremost was my encounter with the Light; it was a life-altering, all-encompassing experience. Second is you and our love; you give me strength, happiness, and intense fulfillment. Third is Vince; his love and support are unfailing. He has my blood in his veins and is my legacy—our son. I called upon the power of the Light, the strength of our love, and the tenacity and vitality of youth to overpower my enemy. The battle was fierce, but when the smoke cleared we stood among the ashes—ready to resume the fight.

I felt your touch last night, and then again this morning, as surely as I felt your locket in my hand. I remove it only during the scans. Every day I touch it to my lips. It holds within it your essence. I like to think that Mahalia inhabits it when she is close.

This card speaks of the earth's treasures, of peace, and of the harmony of nature. Michael mine, you are my treasure of this earth. We have a natural harmony that is reflected in the places we love, in which we *will* love. I will find true peace and stillness when you are here with me. Until then, I will seek you among the beauty of nature, and I will reach out to you for the peace I find only in your presence.

J.T. just left. There is still fluid building up around my heart, but he thinks it is manageable with the medication. I am allowed to go the few steps to the bathroom but that is it. He has scheduled an MRI for tomorrow.

Amelia suggested that I add a more realistic approach to my meditation by visualizing my body—muscles, bones, organs, down to their cellular structures—growing stronger. She said, "Total relaxation, conscious breathing, and a positive attitude are all important. If you enter the dream state with those factors, plus the belief that your body is stronger than the virus, your subconscious will have the right ingredients for effective healing while you sleep." Exactly what I had been focusing on at home.

I do feel better, stronger than I have in a while, and the pressure in my chest is less. I dreamt of making my body stronger, muscle by muscle, cell by cell. I saw my tissues repelling the virus, becoming immune to its attacks, and I dreamt of peace and serenity calming the inflammation. I feel less afraid.

Sweetness, there are so many ways that you replenish me. The words "Michael mine" make my heart swell with pride and so much love for you. I am yours for eternity.

I was so pleased to get a letter from Vince and will write to him again. I was amused by his reference to the Virgin Mary. He doesn't know that I am often as confused by all of this as he is. I understand his not wanting to read the "mushy" parts of our letters, so I will keep it to a minimum. I've read parts of his letters to the girls. They are looking forward to having him in their lives, and they often ask about you and send their love.

Dear Teresa, it is difficult for me to write to you under these circumstances, but I know Dad would want me to. You probably already know that he had a severe heart attack during his MRI. We aren't certain how much damage was done, but his mitral valve doesn't close as it should. He isn't strong enough to tolerate any more tests. He says your name a lot while he is sleeping. The two of you must have something real special going on. As I told you before, I think you're the best thing that has happened to him in a long time. Vince

Sweet Michael mine, you have brought new meaning to my life, have touched unknown chords deep within my heart, my soul—at the very center of my being. Let my love surround you, enfold you, give you strength and comfort; feel my kiss upon your lips, the touch of my hand in yours. Let me lie by your side, and hold you close.

I know we have been together in your dreams and that you reach out to me. I have felt the essence of your love, sweet and tender, strong and enduring; your body is weakened but not your love, or mine. I will wait as long as it takes for you to come to me.

You may not be able to write for a while, so please remember this—I know that you love me, that you will do all that you can to come back to me, that you say my name and call me sweetness.

Teresa, we were on the same wave length. I saw the letter with both our names on it by his bed, and I read it to him as you asked me to. I must have really murdered the French, because he smiled as I stumbled over that part. It is a beautiful letter and, might I add, that is some pretty dynamite perfume. Dad asked to sniff the paper and that really made him smile. He held it to his face for several minutes before he kissed it where you had. He asked me to tell you that he "loves you more today than yesterday," and then he mumbled something that sounded like "weakness," but I'm not sure that was it.

I can tell from your letter that you really do love him and that you would be here if it were possible. Just keep doing what you are doing. I don't understand it, but he feels that somehow you are with him when he sleeps. I'll just fold this and leave it here in the same place yours was and hope whoever does the delivery will take it to you. Vince

Michael, I have been lost in reverie of precious moments we have shared, savoring the experience of having been so well loved by you. We share so many memories—the incredible, the romantic, the intensely physical, and the deeply spiritual. I know you are fighting to come back, that you want to add to our memories. I am fighting with you, reaching out to you with love and support, faith and hope. Were you with me as I sat in the sun in a clearing in the woods? Did you sense the energy and healing I sent your way? Do you know how great a part you are of every aspect of my life, how empty it would be without you? I pray that I will never have to know your absence from my physical life. You will never be absent from my heart.

Dear Teresa, Dad is doing better, getting a little stronger every day. He read your letter tonight by himself. I'm glad I didn't have to read the French out loud again. You are right that I love him very much. We've been through a lot together. I've thought so many times that he wasn't going to make it. I would try to prepare myself for the possibility, but I don't think anyone can be ready for that. I think you are right about a few other things too. I've given it a lot of thought, and I think we would all make one hell of a nice family, kid sisters and all.

Dad is sleeping again now, so I had better get back to the floor. Would you please tell Kenna and Callie hello from me? I would say something big brotherly to pass on to them, but they will probably gang up on me when we meet, so I better not. I am an only child, so it is kind of fun to imagine life with two kid sisters. Have I told you that Dad really likes your perfume? Me too! Love, Vince

Michael mine, I am relieved to hear that you have been steadily conscious and off the respirator, but best of all was to hear your message, passed from Amelia to Zachary to me, that you love me. It was like music to my ears to hear it from your lips, more or less, within minutes after you spoke the words.

I sense a greater strength now when I reach out to you—there is more energy at the end of whatever wavelength we are on. You will gain strength every day and we will have our life together. To know that we almost lost you has given me a new perspective, more patience. I am thankful for what we have now—the rest will come in time.

Hello, sweetness. I am not very steady with my hand yet, but I hope you can read this. I am getting stronger. I try to spend a little time when I'm awake reading my cards and inhaling your beautiful scent. They've had me sitting on the side of the bed and standing for a few minutes, so I'm a little shaky and tired right now. Before I go, I must tell you that I have felt you near—in all the ways we've been close these past months. My dreams have been of our past, our present, and the future that awaits us.

What a beautiful gift, your letter. I know it took a lot of effort for you to write. I am grateful for another gift you have brought into my life—a son.

You are right that I have never been far away, but I expect it is sometimes not my presence but that of Mahalia you sense. I know she communicates my thoughts and feelings when I cannot, and she brings her own immeasurable love to you and, of course, to her Alexander.

My dear, sweet love, I have felt you so near throughout the afternoon, have heard you say my name, and have thrilled to the sound of "Michael mine." Do you have my letter yet, sweetness? How can

I bear to let you go? You deserve so much more than this.

I have read your letter, twice. Darling, thank you for what you said about Vince. I think often of our other son, have dreamt of him, and wonder if he is waiting for me. I think you're right that Mahalia is often close, for I hear Alexander's name in my dreams. I love you so very much.

24. Hope Returns

May

Michael, I am thrilled with Amelia's report of your progress. She also told me of your thoughts of releasing me. My sweet love, it is in your power to release me—it is not in your power to make me go. You will not be rid of me so easily. As I write, I look out at a profusion of rosy pink blossoms on the crabapple tree I planted ten years ago; the clump of river birch I planted last year, its unfurling leaves lit by the sun; and a plump, red-breasted robin pulling a worm from the rain-soaked earth. I see you here with me—before the leaves have fallen from the trees.

Sweetness, it is either late at night or early in the morning. They have tried to get me to go back to sleep, but I begged them to let me write for a while. I am sorry to have written so stupidly about you letting me go. The depth of your love is evident. I will fight with all the power I have to come to you.

Have I told you that Maeve shaves me every morning and spoils me with baked goods? I am sending her some flowers for Mother's Day. One of the nurses said that I am lucky to have my mother come every day—I didn't correct her.

I am finally out of the ICU and in a regular room on the 6th floor, with a view of the parking lot. I watch the people far below and wish that I was one of them. Had you missed the scent of my aftershave? You were right that I need my daily fix of your scent.

My mother is here for a week, back from Arizona. We've been catching up, spending time with the girls, and going to every nursery in town for garden plants. Early this morning, we walked on the island, where the air was filled with the sweetly sharp scent of chokecherry bark. I plan to tell her about you, that a former colleague played matchmaker. I want to share my joy with others and hear them ask me about you.

Last week, I told Sally a condensed version of our history. She remembers when I reached out to her, that she was aware of a positive force, not realizing until now what it had been. It was so distinctive a memory for her that she knew immediately the time to which I was referring. A few weeks ago, I informed her that Zachary is her guardian, which fits better with her experience of him than that he had his origins within the depths of her unconscious mind.

Sweetness, I have pictured myself holding our babies in the same way as the man on this card. I think of you as the mother of all of our children—Callie, Kenna, and Vince. You are the woman I would have loved to make our babies with, the woman who has given me many lovely children, past and present. I loved you then and I love you now. Happy Mother's Day

Vince took me down to the gift shop in a wheelchair to look for something special. I saw this card and couldn't resist it. Now I have to go for another walk around the corridor. Every step I take brings me closer to you.

My mother has been helping me with some painting around the

house. As we relaxed this evening, I told her about you, starting with the more ordinary, but inaccurate, version of our story. Then, out of the blue, she started talking about guardian angels and past lives, which I took as a cue to tell her more. She asked if "all of this is a New Age thing." I told her that I don't consider it to be, but that that term is an umbrella for a wide variety of beliefs and practices. Amelia said she has reservations about some of them. "It is always good to explore possibilities, to seek truth, but the best intentions can go awry when leaders demand unquestioning followers. It has never been the Creator's intent that unthinking obedience be a part of belief. Inquiry brings about dialogue. The Creator wants mortals to question and thereby to learn."

Amelia also shared that the Council, when they met in November, considered allowing us to meet immediately, but their eventual consensus was that the needs of others outweighed ours. If we had met then, you likely would not have contracted the virus. To dwell on that is to be torn apart by the anguish in my soul.

My love, I am recovering from the chemo, but my attitude has deteriorated. The cardiologist was in earlier … I will never again take to the ski slopes. I can't write now.

I must apologize for my poor mood this morning. When he told me of my limitations, I focused only on them. I had to know if I will be able to make love to you. The answer is yes! When he asked what activities I had enjoyed—shook his head to skiing, racquetball, and tennis—I got a mental image of myself as a vegetable. He said I will be able to go for walks, ride a bike, swim, and play golf, all within reason. He didn't say that I had to make love within reason, and I wasn't about to ask him.

Michael, I do wish for your sake that you will be able to resume your favorite activities, but I have had some qualms about my ability to keep up with you. I will take you in any physical condition. I prefer that you be able to walk and talk and make love to me.

Could you possibly be any more dear to me? Kenna shared the letter you sent her, and I have read it twice. It is just right. The card—the big bear holding the hand of the little one—prompted tears of loss, then joy. She has needed someone to hold her hand, to be there. To read the words "your mother and I" brought more tears and the knowledge that I am no longer alone as a parent. Callie is looking forward to her letter.

Your beautiful letter is finally here, and you have told me exactly what I wanted to hear—we were in sync Wednesday night. Sweetness, when it comes to making passionate love to you, moderation is not in my vocabulary. If my doctor insists that I take my time, I promise you will not be disappointed.

Amelia was here but she had to leave abruptly. I want to ask her a question, but there is never enough time. Would you ask her this for me—what lessons are to be learned from all of this pain and suffering?

25. Eli Visits

6/1—6/24

Sweetness, I spoke to Amelia about my recovery. She said, in that more serious tone we both have heard, "Michael, you are the master of your destiny." I promise to do whatever I can to secure our future—it is almost close enough to touch.

J.T. was just here with good news/bad news. The good is that I can be discharged soon! The bad is that they are getting some flak from the insurance company. He asked how I would feel about returning to the hospice or going to a convalescent facility. I can't go back to the hospice, sweetness. I don't want to be surrounded by death again.

Mon cher Michel, I felt you close as I was lying in bed this morning after a restless night. The girls were at the lake with friends, got stuck in the mud, and couldn't get back until after daylight. I fell asleep waiting for them but woke up in the middle of the night. Wanting to feel you close, I took down the box that holds your letters and started at the beginning.

My sweet love, our life together defies description. Yes, we did think it surreal, beyond our imaginations, but those first weeks brought their own truth. This is what I wonder—if we had met years ago, under more ordinary circumstances, would we have experienced the full power of our love? Would we have recognized the presence of our spirits? I will reflect on that as I drive to work.

What wonderful news, but it should be me caring for you when you leave. Amelia said you are more in touch again with your healing powers. I will be optimistic and think you will be able to fend for yourself until you can come to me.

I've been on the phone to both computer software companies this morning. My attorney has been handling things, but they want my assurance that I'm improving and that we can still negotiate.

More great news! My attorney just called to say both companies want me to sign a letter of intent. They have their offers ready and want to send reps here to the hospital to negotiate. J.T. said an emphatic no, and my attorney agrees. If they are this anxious, they will wait until I can talk to them on my own terms. I will be out of here in no time—the future will be ours.

Sweetness, it thrills me to read you felt me near the other day and to learn you were in the sun as I had known you were, but I hadn't pictured you on the beach in your swimsuit. I used to have a man-type bikini but always felt self-conscious in it. What do you prefer? If you want me in something skimpy, it will be on a secluded beach for your eyes only. Our meeting is once again imminent—we can plan and picture events just weeks from now.

I am sitting in my corner chair where I usually write, but it feels as though I'm lingering in bed with you, wrapped in your arms and in your love. I have been listening to "Running on Faith," remembering how I would listen to it every night when your condition was first so precarious. I could not write, then, of my anguish, my helplessness, how it felt to not be able to go to you. I was told you weren't likely to survive, might manage to hold on for another day, maybe two. I still can't write of it , except to say that I continued to reach out to you, seeking the Creator's blessing and a miracle.

I will change the subject, to Amelia's answer about the lessons you might learn from these last two months of illness. She said that the virus, and all that followed, was not destined but due to your chance encounter with it. As to what might be learned, she was not as direct as you might have expected. "It is not for me to answer. There are many lessons possible in these circumstances. When Michael someday returns to the spirit world and processes this experience, it will be in relationship to the lessons he had chosen for this lifetime."

I mentioned what seem like two obvious lessons, those of maintaining one's faith and hope. "Those are certainly possibilities but Michael, during his previous lifetimes, may have already learned them sufficiently." When I told her I had hoped for something more specific, she said, "I will tell you this: Michael changed a great deal after the onset of his illness. That is perhaps one lesson he has learned, the importance of finding time for the type of self-reflection he has lately engaged in."

Amelia went on to tell me more about her conversations with you. "Michael wants closure with every topic he brings up, and he questions me to that end. He is reluctant to have me go, but it is important that I leave him with questions, that he reflect and work things out for himself."

I asked Amelia to explain the difference between destiny and fate. "Fate is the intended end point of a life, absent the effects of reckless behavior or unforeseen circumstances. It is an approximate time within a span of several years. Alexander knows the time allotted to Michael. He will be alert for any circumstances that might lend themselves to the lessons yet to be learned." I take hope in the phrasing of Amelia's answer—there are still lessons for you to learn here, with me.

Just a few words before I go to sleep—it has been a long and trying day. They came early to get me for the bone marrow test. I felt your kiss upon my brow, or was it the touch of your beautiful spirit, Mahalia?

I am feeling much better this morning. The catheter is out, the monitor is gone, and I am going home soon. J.T. made a convincing case for keeping me here until then. I am fortunate to have him as a friend and look forward to the day that I can introduce the two of you. I hope we have a chance to get together soon after we meet, before our wedding day.

You weren't kidding when you said I had a surprise coming. I couldn't imagine what Maeve was bringing me and then noticed the box looked familiar. It was Amelia, saying you had asked her to bring your letters to me. Sweetness, I have to go take my walk, and then I will meditate for a while before reading some old love letters.

Like you, I picture us together within weeks. I even called the lodge to see if they have cabins available about six weeks from now. Only a few, so we may have to change our plans. Also in anticipation, I am cleaning out my closets to make room for your things and working on getting in the best possible shape.

My love, your words of longing and desire touch similar chords within my heart, my soul. Do not be concerned whether you will elicit a response from your woman. That you will satisfy my every need and desire is not something I question. Were you here with me in the last half hour? I felt your presence and knew the sweet, rich promise of your love.

A positive sign! Tara is going to my apartment today to clean and air it out, ready for my discharge. She is a very thoughtful person and a take-charge one. You will like her. I already think of my home being with you—my apartment will be just a stopping place for a few weeks.

More good news! I can go for a drive with Vince and Tara tomorrow. J.T. said the nurses won't be happy about it, but they will cap off the IV with a heparin lock. I am sick of looking at these four walls s, and my daily walks around the corridor leave a lot to be desired.

The drive yesterday was perfect; today has been another one of good news/bad news. The good is that the virus has been defeated. The bad is that my heart valve has not healed as much as they had hoped. I have tried to write several times today but have not found the words. To try to explain how I feel is too depressing to contemplate—suffice it to say that I've had better days.

Have you been trying to reach out to me? I know you can't begin to imagine what it is like for me here. I have to sometimes weigh carefully what I write so you don't realize how depressed I get. I want you here. I need you. Sweetness, I love you with all that I am.

How do I love thee … let me count the ways. Michael, one of the many things I love about you is that you have been such a wonderful father and that you will be still to the girls. I look forward to knowing Vince, in part, because so much of who he is has come from you. I want you to know Kenna and Callie and they want you in their lives. Together, we will be the family that all of us have wanted. Happy Father's Day

I'm glad you had the same experience of us being together the other night. It reaffirms my faith in us, in our ability to connect. It is a great comfort to let our love, our spirits, surround me—almost like a shield, secure and protective.

We went for a drive again today, followed the river and stopped where I have felt so near to you. It was a spectacular, sunny day and I was able to walk around a bit. I am filled with hope that soon we will walk together.

I showed Vince your card. He got tears in his eyes too, a chip off the old block. They gave me a new putter I've been wanting. With these positive vibes around me, how can I lose? Sweetheart, keep your faith in our future and I will too. I love you beyond reason.

Michael, I know so well what I am missing, no less than if we had spent our lives together. Can you believe I will have patience, will wait as long as it takes, if I tell you I need you so much it hurts, until I sometimes think I can't stand it? I think it will be like the pain of childbirth, forgotten when it is over, endured in the knowledge of the joy it will bring. The pain is less now, but my longing for you remains and will only increase until I am in your arms.

I must tell you about my visitor. A priest came into my room, an older man, a kindly expression on his face. I thought it was a routine visit, but then he said my name, and yours.

He knew everything about us. He spoke of how we are being tested and said that our love will endure these troubled times. He asked if I believe all that I have been told by Amelia. When I answered yes, he said, "Then know that you and Teresa hold the key to your destinies." As he turned to walk away, I asked, "Father, are you Eli?" He turned around and, with a beneficent smile, said, "Yes, Michael." I still feel sort of tingly all over and two feet off the ground.

Can you believe it, sweetheart? I feel as if I have been touched by the hand of God. I can only compare it to my near-death experience. I feel much the same as I did then, when I first woke up from it.

I have been reading random letters, reminded of the man I first came to know, his substance and his essence. We met so gloriously in autumn's fair breeze and then came through a winter melancholy. Spring was almost our undoing, but now warm summer winds promise to bring us together before the seasons have come full circle.

When I think of how soon it could be, the length of our time apart fades to insignificance.

Sweet Michael mine, when we meet we will already know each other, even as we begin a lifetime of discovery. A short while ago, I reached out to you, and I am now filled with love and contentment. It is all that we have experienced, and there is something more—a larger presence surrounding us—our invisible choir.

Good morning, sweetness. As you can see, I didn't get back to this last night. My attorney found me on the deck and we finalized some paperwork. As I was about to write, Vince came and spent his break with me. I felt you intensely close again when I went to bed, just like old times, and I woke up with you in my arms this morning. I adore you.

I asked Amelia about Eli's appearance. She said, "I had no prior knowledge that he would be here. Eli is not one to announce his plans." I feel truly honored by his visit. Eli has given us his blessing and his assurance that I can recover. I will, sweetness.

Were you out walking today? It is cool here for late June. I intended to write more but was interrupted by a phone call from my attorney, and now dinner is here. I will eat, then take my walk around the corridors, and write more later...

PART III

A Search for Truth

26. A Predator Stalks

MICHAEL ... I AM NOT ready to say goodbye. Never again will I read your words of love ... never will I hear you call me sweetness. I struggle to express what is in my heart. I can't. I won't even try. You know—and now you know what might have been. Can you see us with our babies?

I can hear a procession of honking horns a few blocks from here, in celebration of a wedding. Just yesterday, the prospect of our meeting imminent, our girls and I were talking of the day that we would be married. One of them said, "You're going to look so pretty standing there with your beautiful daughters." Now I will never see you in the suit you bought, so full of hope for our future, so certain you would be wearing it that day, Vince and J.T. by your side.

6/26

I am back, my love. Last night, a moment of relative calm could not last as I pictured us, just weeks from now, in the place we had made plans to meet. I finally slept a little and woke this morning thinking my tears had run dry. I was soon proved wrong and now they have come again. I will try later.

It is almost midnight. I am not so much calm now as spent, but I am unable to sleep. It was a few hours earlier, two nights ago, that Zachary came to the door, a first for either him or Sally. I thought she must be in a terrible crisis. Puzzled, I merely nodded when he asked if he could come in. He stepped through the doorway, paused, and asked, "Are your daughters home?"

I knew then, but I did not let myself know. I answered that the girls were at a friend's for the night and invited him to be seated, going through the motions of civility. He took an old oak captain's chair, its solid simplicity suiting his nature. I sat on the loveseat opposite and waited for him to speak.

I was still trying to ignore an insistent, internal alarm when Zachary bluntly stated, "Michael is dead." There would have been no point in his trying to soften the blow. My immediate reaction was a futile attempt to deny your reality. I almost asked Zachary, "Are you tired of playing your little game? Have you had enough of maintaining this fiction?" I did admit to him that I wanted to deny your very existence, that it would be easier than facing the truth. I flashed back to the day in April when I was told you were dying—this time there would be no reprieve. I will tell you about it.

Zachary is here for less than ten minutes. I know what is coming for me. Not wanting to face it, I return to the book I had been reading and finish the last ten pages, aware of keeping at bay what I do not want to feel. There will be no going back.

I am crouched far back in a cave, knowing that pain is lying in wait—there is no escape. It will stalk me relentlessly, like the predator it is. That pain exists before and beyond any words, a primeval cry rising up from the earth itself, cried out to the unknown forces that control our fates. I see an image of earth-red streaks, a naked figure, a ravaged face howling into the wind.

I sit, unseeing and unfeeling, as the reality of your death slowly settles in, and the life force that courses through my body morphs to a slow-moving sludge. Time passes. I force myself to get up. I call the girls, woodenly ask them to come home; they want to know why. I can only repeat, with more intensity, "Just come home."

They arrive ten minutes later. They know but, like me, they do not want to know, to confirm what is written on my face. I tell them what Zachary told me—you collapsed while taking your walk, a few minutes after your last written word to me. Your death was quick. There was no hope of saving you. Their faces look bleak; they are two lost girls. Kenna cries out, "What will we do now?" I attempt some motherly platitudes, but what brings them a modicum of comfort is my saying, "We will still have Vince in our lives." They respond with sighs of relief. Callie says, "That's right. We will still have Vince. He can tell us all about Michael."

6/27

Hello, my love. I am not yet ready to give up this tie to you. Do you remember how we often wrote in close synchrony, the content transmitted and received in real time? Our letters did not bring news, only confirmed what we already knew. You walked with me; we laughed together, cried together.

I am thinking of driving out to the island. Can I bear to go there now, without you? How can I not? I drive slowly, drawn to the place, but I don't know what waits for me. I want to find some comfort, but I know that agony will first have its way with me.

My steps are slow, each one a reminder that we will never walk here together. I give voice to my grief, cry out loud, a mournful keening from my depths. I cry out your name. I don't have the strength to vent my grief, or my anger, in any forceful way that rises to the level of the feelings inside of me. I pick up a small branch and break it against a tree. I pick up another and then another, but my arm is weak. I am acutely aware how paltry are my efforts.

I want to break weighty branches, hurl large rocks into the river, run myself to exhaustion, pound my feet into the ground. I want the trees to absorb the pain in my body, the pain in my soul. I want the water to flow over me and through me and gently find its way to my ravaged heart. I want the wind to bring you back to me. I want comfort—and I want to rip myself to pieces.

Spent and emptied, I walk on, making my way slowly to the shelter. Since I was last here, my world has slipped from its axis. I pause, steady myself with one hand on the warm wood of a large, solid support log. I take a deep breath. With hesitation, I sit in my usual spot. I look out at the water, take a deep breath. I lift my eyes to the river bluffs, take a deep breath. My center holds. I can let myself remember—how I would reach out to you from here, our spirits so close it took no effort.

After a time, I am able to settle somewhat into meditation, enough that I can feel the presence of our invisible choir—they have been here all along.

It is evening now. Amelia called earlier and asked to meet at the office for a few minutes. She gave me the letter you had left for me and told me more of your death. She said she was listening as J.T. told Vince it was "a fluke." It was not indicated by your latest test results. You sneezed, and the weakened valve in your heart briefly, for a nanosecond, failed. A sneeze! A fluke! After all you have been through, your fight for life, your fight for us to be together.

Amelia knows that, if the valve had not failed in that instant, it would have functioned perfectly for six more years. That is why Eli spoke so positively to you about our future just a few days ago—this was not to be. Left reeling from the pain, and my incomprehension, I could not read your letter until just now.

My dearest friend, lover, wife. It is the first of May. I am getting better, but if you are reading this it means I have failed you. I am truly sorry. I know it must be difficult for you. I want you to know that I always felt, always knew, that you were my greatest support, my greatest comfort. I loved you for that, one of many reasons. The fact of the matter is, Sweetness, that my body was not able to withstand the onslaught of this disease.

Dearest one, take comfort in knowing that I will be happy and that I will watch over you until we are together again. I will be there to greet you when you come home. I have loved you in lives past and in our secondary life. In this life, I have loved you even more and have received the gift of your love. Forever and always your friend, your lover, your husband. Michael

My love, do not think that you have failed me. I know how much you wanted to be with me and how hard you tried. As I turn the page, I am reminded that I will never send these to you. I remember all the pages that passed between us. I thought we would exchange our letters for something more, that you would be here with me. I still await your arrival. Will you come and read over my shoulder?

6/28

Michael, it is an hour since I woke up, and I am now calm enough to sit and write. Your service will be held this afternoon. I asked Amelia what clothes were chosen for you to wear. She said I might not want to know, but I already did. I don't think of you as being there in a grave; that is not where you are. Still, I want to be a part of it, should be a part of it, sharing with Vince and our girls the grief of losing you.

It occurs to me several times a day that no one is bringing food to the house—no casseroles, no cakes, no cookies, no matter that it is too much. There are no cards or letters of sympathy, no late night phone calls for me to make, no funeral arrangements, no gathering of families and friends. The rituals of your death are being denied me by the same forces that denied your physical presence in my life.

Vince, Tara, J.T., Maeve, Henry, and all the others who knew and loved you, are gathering now for your service. I know two things: your body will be interred in a cemetery in the city; Amazing Grace will be played. And I know this—we are not there, your girls and I. It is not right. Michael, I miss you so.

6/29

Good morning, my love. I will need to put some distance between us today. I had cancelled all appointments for two days but have scheduled Sally and one other client for this afternoon. Despite my feeling that it's not possible, it appears that my life does go on without you. I am going to leave now to do some errands around town. I need to create a buffer zone between my grief and the rest of the world.

Michael, do you know what has been done? Can you understand it? I had thought my pain could be no greater, until Amelia told me that Vince's memories—of me, of our relationship, of the letters he and I have exchanged—will be erased.

My mind went blank. I sat numbly, silently, unable to comprehend. I now have a visceral understanding of why someone would cut themselves in an effort to feel something, anything. My emotions receded to some deep place where they could not rise up and destroy me. I don't know how much time passed before Amelia gently nudged me back to life with her words. "Tessa, I understand. I know how much Vince has meant to you, in this lifetime and in others. It may help you to know that he will be with you in your next one."

Amelia's words do help, on one level, but it is not on the level of my present existence, in which I can neither accept nor can I understand. If you were here you would see the holes in this notepad, made from the sharp point of my pencil as I bring it down again and again in a feeble attempt to vent my anger and frustration. If it were to miss its mark and enter my body, the resulting pain would not approach what I am feeling. I am going to take a walk, try to meditate, and thereby gain some acceptance. I have no choice.

I did find a degree of calm—that of a mother who knows she has to remain in control for the sake of her child. I have just finished my letter to Vince, the tracks of my tears leaving faint traces on the paper. Amelia said that he is writing to me, for one last time. I asked her why this has been done to us. Why this senseless cruelty?

"Vince was not directly involved in the approach made to you. His knowledge of your contacts, and of the assistance given to you and Michael, was second hand. He would not have been approached on his own. If you and his father had met, he then would have known everything, as your daughters do, but it would have been incidental to that primary relationship. It would not have been the result of Vince's own search for truth or what had been destined for him in this lifetime."

The logic of Amelia's explanation does not escape me, but it is not an argument that reaches the mother in me. I wrote that I will someday find him and will tell him that I had once been close to his father. I said we will share memories of you and maybe he will know, in his heart, who I am.

The girls were here when I got home. They understand it even less, feel as devastated by Vince's loss as by yours. He would have been both a brother to them and a link to you. We all feel a deep betrayal and cannot see beyond the unfairness of what has been done.

My love, this has taken me a while, long pauses as I dissolve into tears or sit here and try to come to grips with our loss. I know you are not yet close, but Mahalia is, and I feel the strong presence of several other spirits. It is all that makes it possible to have any acceptance of losing you, and now Vince. I can distinguish at least two spirits, their energy filling the space around me. I am aware of an increase in the density of the air and the most subtle of vibrations. I feel a slight warming around me and the qualities of love and support. I know that you are not among them, but their presence, and the process of writing to you, talking to you in this way, has brought me some small measure of peace.

6/30
Good morning, my love. I am beginning to accept that I will never turn to you and say those words, will never awaken to your touch. It is a fragile acceptance, for even as I write this it all comes back. I

could force my attention elsewhere, but I want to relish my memories, our hopes and dreams—it is too soon to give them up. To some extent, the utter finality of death makes it easier to accept your loss than Vince's ... I cannot go there.

I had to schedule two clients for this afternoon, so I will need to keep some distance from you again. It will not be easy to see and talk to colleagues I have known for years and not share my loss. I am close to two of them, yet even they know nothing of the great love of my life.

I must go now, sweet heart. I need to take Callie to work, and then I will walk awhile with my memories. It is a cool, cloudy, windy day—somehow that will make it easier, to be out in the elements.

Michael, I am back, feeling like the proverbial camel that has had one too many straws placed upon its back. As I walked, I realized that your last name had escaped me. It was on my mind just yesterday as I was thinking of searching for Vince. I assumed my forgetfulness to be a temporary effect of my grief.

Amelia was in the waiting room when I finished with my last client. She stepped into my office but said she did not have time to sit down. She had managed to retrieve your locket from your personal effects at the hospital and she gave it to me, in pieces, and explained that the chain broke when you fell, in the last moment of your life. You reached for it, clung to it, as you realized you might be dying.

She gave me Vince's letter. There was no time to read it then or to question her further about why his memories had been erased. It would have been futile—no answer would have satisfied me. She said she had to leave but I quickly, insistently, asked about your last name, could she remind me of it. She said, "Child, I must tell you, your memory of Michael's last name has been taken from you. I would have told you when next we met. And now, I cannot stay a moment longer."

It was just as well. I would have found no comfort in her explanations as I felt the weight of this final straw pressing down upon me. I made it home, the drive a vague memory. Then, through my tears, I read Vince's heart-wrenching letter. I feel the enormity of what he has lost and of what the girls and I have lost, but there is no force behind my lamentations. I am too weak now. The pain eases a little as I write to you, talk to you.

I keep your locket close to my heart and will get a new chain tomorrow. I touch it to my lips, as you did to yours, and then I touch it to my cheek to capture your essence. I sit here, longing to be where it has been these last six months—nestled against your chest, pressed to your lips.

Dear Teresa, this is the hardest letter I've ever had to write. How do I say goodbye to someone I've never met? I did not say to someone I don't know. I feel as though I do know you. The few letters we have exchanged, and what Dad read to me from some of his, have told me a lot about the kind of woman you are. Amelia told me why you can't be here with us. I'm trying to understand and accept everything, but it is hard. I don't think it is fair that you can't be here. I don't think it is fair that I can't visit you or even know more about you and Callie and Kenna. I had almost come to think I had a family somewhere.

I used to kid Dad about his phantom girlfriend. Now I'm sorry I ever did that. I don't think you're a phantom. I think you loved my father as much as he loved you. Teresa, he did love you. Whenever I asked about you, this look came over his face like a look I had never seen before. I wish you could have seen it.

I don't want to stop writing. I don't want to say goodbye. I wish we had known each other better. I don't want

my memories taken away. I asked Amelia, if I ever met
you someday, would I know you? She said probably not.
I think I will. I hope I will. I will miss you and Callie
and Kenna. Good bye, Teresa. Love always, Vince

7/1

Michael mine, is your first journey almost complete? I told you I
have sensed a very definite presence, sometimes more than one, yet
there is nothing of you in them. Zachary tells me there have been
several, most often my father's spirit and that of his mother, who I
don't remember. They have come to comfort me.

This is the longest I have been awake, a little over an hour, without being overcome by tears and sobs of grief, saying your name,
asking why. I still can't put it into words that are adequate to convey the depth of my loss and longing. The emotions of my deepest
grief exist at some primal level—technically, in the limbic area of
the brain—that has lost communication with the cerebral cortex, the
origin of more sophisticated expression. By the time I write of a moment, an hour, a day of grief, I have already lived it. I have distilled
the raw pain down to something I can carry with me without having
it destroy me. It is easier now, the sharp, jagged edges of my grief
have softened a little—sorrow remains.

A full week has passed since I heard the words "Michael is dead."
To write them now brings back the tears. I hold on to your locket …
my link to you.

7/2

I wake up to a perfect summer morning—a hint of moisture in the
air, the mere suggestion of a breeze, the sun warm not hot—the
earth giving up its essence. I am tending my flower garden, returning to life, when I am brutally assaulted. The stillness is broken by
the soft, plaintive cooing of a mourning dove, so aptly named they
might have been created to give voice to the grief of all humanity. It
is the second call, in response to the first, that does me in.

I need to get away, to walk, to move fast. The island air adds the scents of the river and of thick vegetation, ripe with summer, but there is no escape—the trails remind me that I will never walk here with you. The pain intensifies. It pierces me at my center, where you would reach the stone that has now lost its resonance. It radiates from there to my heart as I cry out in grief and sorrow. I turn off on an old forgotten trail, blinded by my tears. I cannot bear this pain—and I cannot outrun it.

I am walking as fast as I can, trying to distance myself from the pain, when I crash into a barrier—there is a solid wall in front of me. I fall halfway to the ground from the impact, struggle to regain my balance, then pause in the stillness. I see now that there is no physical barrier; the path before me is clear. The energy that stopped me in my tracks now envelops me. I feel it infused in me, in every cell of my body. I know it is Eli. As I stand in place and allow a fuller awareness to develop, I am lifted up and supported, surrounded by love and healing—a moment written indelibly on my soul.

It is late in the evening. I am still filled with the wonder and strength of Eli's manifestation. It was as if he had materialized in front of me, as solid as a physical presence. I recall the visit he made to you a week ago that filled you with awe, brought back memories of your journey to the Light. We have been blessed.

7/3

My love, to write as if you are still in this world has been a necessary transition—to continue will serve less purpose. As the pages add up, I am reminded that they will never be sent. You will never hold them in your hands, will never reply.

Michael, you are always on my mind. Sometimes I think I have achieved a calm acceptance, and then I am once again in tears, mourning your loss, the future we had planned, and the past twenty years that might have been ours. The pain of those lost years would have eased if we had met—now it is mine alone. I know that the pain of losing you will surface again. I will tempt it as I leave the present moment and visit the past or future. I now sometimes invite the pain, need to feel it to signify the magnitude of our loss.

You are surrounded by the Light, and you understand much that was not clear to us. I wait for you to return to me, to make your presence known. I will not say goodbye. It is too soon for that. I cannot yet imagine that time will ever come, but I know that it must. You will need to move on in what is now your world. I will need to move on in what I can only define as a world without you.

My sweet Michael mine, *ne manqué pas de revenir me voir. Au revoir, mon cher. Je t'aime.*

27. Alexander is No More

TEN DAYS SINCE ZACHARY BROUGHT the news of Michael's death, and I have moved the mementos of our time together to my bedroom, visible but not constant reminders. Two items were missing from what Amelia returned to me—the red stone and his favorite card.

I keep two cards near. One I had bought an hour before Michael's death and planned for him to have before his next tests. The front shows a little girl on a beach, sand running through her fingers, and the familiar words of William Blake:

> *To see a world in a grain of sand*
> *And heaven in a wild flower*
> *Hold infinity in the palm of your hand*
> *And eternity in an hour.*

I thought each day would be infinity to us—we would have looked together at nature's beauty and known we shared a piece of heaven on Earth. The inside message is a wish for miracles. I read it and almost lose my belief in them. I cry out loud my question of why there could have been no miracle for Michael. I have not forgotten that we were blessed with miracles throughout our time together, but why could there not have been one more?

The other card is the one Michael sent me for Mother's Day. It pictures a man similar to his younger self, shirtless, a newborn cradled to his chest. As much as I mourn my loss, I mourn for our children. I ask Amelia to tell me what she knows of the son who is lost to me. Kenna and Callie are a comfort, more so by returning to their everyday lives than by mourning with me. They ask thoughtful questions and put up with my tears. The first week they spoke often of their own loss but less so now—my knowledge of Michael was not theirs.

7/8

As I sit in my office waiting for Sally, I wonder if I should tell her today about Michael's death. No, it is too soon. I could not keep my composure and maintain my role as her therapist—she is here.

Amelia comes to tell me there is just enough time for her to place Michael's death in the context of his near-death experience almost a year ago.

"Then, Michael was granted a return to life because there were several lessons he had not yet learned. One was to have loved unconditionally, another was forgiveness. After you entered his life, he was able to learn both to the extent he had been meant to in this lifetime."

I ask Amelia how long Michael would have lived if I hadn't reached out to him in October.

"He would have never recovered from the weak state he was in— he would have died last December."

I hadn't known that for certain. Amelia tells me more.

"Michael's initial recovery brought him into the lives of Maeve and Henry and helped them achieve closure with regard to their son's death in Vietnam. There were other lessons Michael learned in that time and other lives he touched, among them the young man at the hospice, Ethan, and his parents."

I am grateful to know that my reaching out to Michael gave him more time and aided the growth of his spirit. There is just time to ask Amelia if she can confirm my encounter with Eli.

"Child, you are quite adept at knowing the truth of your experience."

It helps me to see clients, to inhabit my professional role, but I am drained after a few hours and schedule accordingly. I have become expert at reducing the red, puffy eyes my tears leave in their wake— cold packs, tea bags, and cucumber slices. Whenever it seems my tears have run dry, I am soon reminded they come from an inexhaustible reservoir.

I leave the office, turn my car radio to NPR, and hear the harmonic voices of a men's chorus. I can pick out Michael's among them. It is so real to me that I think Mahalia must have heard him sing in our secondary lives, and she recognizes similar tones. I should pull over. I am gasping, tears cloud my vision, but if I stopped my life every time some incident ignited my grief, I would do nothing and go nowhere.

I have returned to some of my less than healthy eating habits, using food to distract me and fill, to some little extent, the deep void I feel. My weakness is a sweet tooth, and then I balance the sugar binge with anything salty and crispy. My favorite is what I am eating now—chocolate ice cream, a pint at a time. The icy cold hits me first, then the sharp bite of chocolate, and finally the velvety texture that makes of it a comfort food. It is not the worst vice, and I do not chastise myself.

7/11

I see Sally today and tell her about Michael's death. I acknowledge my grief, but I do not share it. Over the years, I have mentioned bits of my personal life to her. She once complained that it is always superficial, that I do not share important or difficult events. Like other long-term clients, it is hard for her to accept that she opens her entire life to me, and it isn't balanced by my own disclosures. Now, she conveys her sympathy and says to take what time I need with Amelia.

I cannot help but compare my experience of grief to that of others. I do not presume that my loss is a greater one, but the circumstances are different than most. Except for my daughters, and now Sally, there is no one who knows. I sometimes feel that I am being shunned, purposely ignored in this most important aspect of my life—my grief a hovering ghost.

How can I share my loss with others when their sympathy might be tinged with doubt? If I had told close friends, months ago, I could turn to them, but only if they had accepted the truth of my story. To present them now with the surreal account of my life with Michael, expect them to take it all in and then to share in my grief, is more than I dare to ask. So I reply to the standard question the expected answer that "I am fine" and hide my sorrow.

My mother I do plan to tell, but I can't bring myself to call her. Even though she had seemed to accept Michael's reality, I can't predict her response. It is usual for me to call her every week, but I am restrained now by uncertainty. In ordinary circumstances, I would have made notification calls immediately with the expectation of a knowing sympathy.

7/13

Pain, that predator, still stalks me, but it doesn't cut as deeply, even as I come to a better understanding of that analogy of grief to physical pain—to being sliced open, flayed to the bone, raw flesh exposed to the air and the salt of my tears. It is easier to write those words now than when I felt them every day, every hour, when a deep chasm opened between the part of me that feels and the part that puts feelings into words.

In the early morning and late evening, I walk on the island, seeking connection with nature and with Mahalia. These times are the most peaceful, the light less harsh, the sounds muted. I feel in the air an energy not unlike that of the spirits who have kept me company. The calls of the mourning doves are now soothing murmurs that suggest a response to some unseen presence, but they are only being who they are.

This evening, I walk far out on the island, beyond the trails and old forgotten paths. I sit on a narrow stretch of beach in the last rays of the sun and meditate to the sounds of gently lapping waves and distant sea gulls, hearing in their muted cries echoes of my pain. I pray to the Creator—for strength, to be replenished, to know serenity, to accept. As I make my way back, in a walking meditation, I hear the name Jacob and sense it is the name of the spirit who would have been born to Michael and me. I will ask Amelia if she can confirm it.

7/14

Michael is back. There is no mistaking his presence with that of the other spirits I have experienced. It is stronger, more definite, the essence of Michael. His presence is familiar but his physical aspect, so apparent while he was living, is absent now. It is obvious to me that a spiritual/physical relationship is no longer possible, that it required two spirits and two physical bodies, acting in concert.

I first feel Michael's presence as gentle warmth, as an energy that surrounds me. Then I feel his touch, soft as a feather but unmistakable, on my arm or cheek. I can sense his presence when I return home, like the hum of a small bee reduced to the lowest possible level, to where I can't say if I hear it or feel it. I think that he has been waiting here for me, letting his essence accumulate so as to be more noticeable. Such is the force of his presence that I sometimes enter a doorway and collide with him. It is noticeable, but it does not stop me in my tracks as did Eli's energy.

I know that spirits of higher status have a greater ability to make their presence known. They can control the degree of their power, and they can stay at a distance or come close. I think that Michael is appearing with all the force of which he is capable and that he comes as close to me as possible.

7/15

In the minute before Amelia appears, I am aware of Michael's energy next to my chair. I say only "hello" to Amelia. She greets me, then turns her head slightly and looks to where I can sense him.

"Hello, Michael."

She appears to listen to him, then turns back to me.

"Michael has completed the first two stages of transition, of which there are seven."

She glances again to the space he occupies beside me.

"Michael is eager to say something to you, but I want to first tell you that not all spirits are able to return in this manner or so soon after their physical death. Michael's high status, and his conduct of this recent lifetime, has allowed him to have this access to you. Your spirit, due to her high status, has the ability to make you aware of his presence."

Amelia turns away from me to listen to Michael again.

"Yes, I know that you are impatient and frustrated."

She listens to him for a longer time, then looks at me and conveys his message.

"Michael is intent on finding another receptor. He does not want to appear to you through Sally. He is looking for someone more suitable—a male who is quite similar to him in age and physical characteristics."

I immediately picture someone who so closely resembles Michael that I could almost believe it is him. We spend an hour or two together, and I get a sense of having met him, talked to him, touched him. There is a minute left to ask Amelia about the name Jacob. She confirms it is the name of the spirit who would have been our son, then listens to Michael.

"He says that he has spent time with Jacob, who had not yet given up his hope that you would be together and might yet have a child. He was among the young spirits who brought Alexander's message of the light."

Our time is up. I say my usual goodbye to Amelia and a tentative one to Michael, knowing he will remain close.

7/16

Michael's presence has been less than constant. I know he leaves to search for a receptor. I wonder, when I meet a man on the street or out walking, if he has found one. How will I react if someone speaks to me, says my name, and I realize it is Michael? Though I am expecting it, I will have to pause and catch my breath.

Sally calls to see if I have time for a short session this afternoon to address a minor issue. Near the end of it, I can sense Michael's presence, and then his energy moves closer to her chair than to mine. I expect Amelia to come, but it is not she who inhabits the body before me. I know it is Michael. He looks at me with eyes of an intensity I have never seen—a concentration of all of the energy a body might contain, and more. All of the energy of his lifetime is there, of many lifetimes.

I wait for him to speak, but he says nothing; he doesn't need to. He is present for a minute, maybe two, and then Amelia takes his place. As if chastising him, she faces me and explains.

"I declined to assist Michael in this, so he approached Sally's spirit, Thalia. It was she who allowed it. The Council has not given him permission to speak to you, but he could wait no longer to have some physical connection."

While Amelia is speaking, I can feel Michael's energy next to my chair again. After she withdraws, he takes her place for another minute, still without speaking but with an even greater intensity. I know it is Michael—he touches me to the core of my being.

This is the first I have heard the name of Sally's spirit. I am grateful to Thalia for having allowed Michael to appear. She would not have agreed had it been explicitly prohibited, but I have learned that spirits are capable of pushing the limits of what is allowed, pursuing personal agendas, and following a favorite maxim of mine: act first and ask permission later. If a spirit goes too far, they will be reprimanded; a loss of status could result from an egregious flouting of the rules.

7/17

I am working in my perennial garden, pulling weeds, when the phone rings. I brush most of the dirt from my hands and reach the house before it stops ringing. I answer and hear a voice similar to Zachary's. I know it is Michael, and I am not entirely pleased. My first thought is of my client, if he has disrupted Sally's evening. He reassures me.

"I made a promise to Amelia that I would make no more contact without her permission, but I could not wait. I have yet to find a suitable receptor, but Thalia has again cooperated. She was close to both of us in several of the past lives we have shared, and she wants to assist us."

He confirms that he is still near, close to me and the girls.

"I have wept as I observed them and knew what I was missing."

I ask him about the stone and the card that Amelia couldn't find. He says he retained them as he made his journey to the spirit world, but he plans to return them to me. I ask him if their return will be a message, a sign it is time for us to move on.

"You are correct that it will be a sign. And now, sweetness, I must go. I promised I would take only a few minutes. There is too much at stake for me to push the limits. I will continue my search for a more appropriate receptor, a male."

I sit here, somewhat stunned and unsettled by Michael's phone call, by having heard him call me "sweetness" in a voice so close to Sally's. It is only when I think back to his convincing presence in my office that I am able to accept the voice as his.

7/18

I am excited at the prospect that Michael will soon find a suitable receptor. A man close to his age and body type might be too much to expect, but any male receptor would give me a better sense of him than if he were to appear to me again through Sally.

I walk this morning, serene, knowing Michael's love. I sit at the shelter and cherish the memories of reaching out to him from here. I let them wash over me—there is no pain.

I continue my walk, take a faint trail, then leave it when I notice a mossy area off in the woods. I walk over, drawn to it, and am aware of a strong energy field, similar to that of spirits but with a distinctly different quality—of the elements, rising up from the ground. A large log, from a tree long fallen, is well on its way in its gradual return to the earth that once nurtured its growth. Its velvety sides are textured with lichen and moss in blended shades of copper, brown, and green. Its top surface, half its volume, has been leveled by time, its core turned to a rich mahogany mulch. I stand on it and feel as if I am walking on air. I am reminded of when Eli's presence surrounded me and lifted from me the weight of the world. I will come back.

This afternoon, Amelia tells me there has been a change of plans.

"Permission has been granted for Michael to appear to you, this one time only, through Sally. He has become frustrated over his futile attempts to find a more suitable receptor."

My wish for Michael to find a different receptor is not as strong as is my desire to speak to him, to experience again the intensity of our last encounter. But when he takes Amelia's place, I am disappointed—the eyes that look at me are not the same. The degree of difference is that of a light bulb that has been switched from its brightest to its dimmest setting. I feel an ominous sense of trepidation. Who is this? I put my unease aside and ask him to what extent he is speaking as Michael, the man, and to what extent he is now Alexander.

"Alexander is no more. I have taken the name of Michael."

That does not exactly answer my question. We talk for a few minutes but, without that earlier intensity, I am aware that I am holding back. There is too much to say, and too little time, as we try to establish a connection. We have not yet succeeded when Michael ends it.

"I have agreed to keep our meeting short. Our chance of further contact will be at risk if I do not comply. I will continue my search for a different receptor—*this* is *not* how I choose to appear to you When Amelia returns to say goodbye, I am once again aware of Michael's familiar presence next to my office chair.

7/20

Two days since I have been aware of Michael, and I assume he continues to look for a receptor. I consider our options: Michael could continue his search for a different receptor, a man; he could speak to me directly through Sally again; or he could let Amelia convey his words to me. There is a fourth option: Michael could abandon his efforts and continue with his full transition to the spirit world. I could mourn as others do—with no expectation of speaking to their loved one. Would that be the wiser choice? I will never know. I cannot turn away from this opportunity.

7/22

Shortly before I expect Amelia, I am once again aware of Michael's presence. A moment later she has news for me.

"Michael has now been granted official permission to communicate with you through me. He will make his thoughts known to me, and I will then convey them to you."

She looks attentively to where I can sense Michael, then speaks his words.

"I went before the Council to plead my case to appear to you through a different receptor."

Amelia interrupts to tell Michael she wants to say something, then turns back to me.

"The Council is concerned that Michael has not yet made a complete transition to the spirit world, that he has retained too many of his human qualities and desires. He was in danger of being declared an errant spirit."

She turns to Michael, listens, then repeats his words to me.

"I told the Council that I am aware of my need to complete my transition, that I am not an errant spirit. They were eventually satisfied that I understand both my limits in this world and my responsibilities to theirs. They gave me permission to continue my search for a receptor, but they refused to assist me."

When I ask if one of them can explain errant spirits, it is Amelia who responds.

"An errant spirit is one who chooses to live outside of the rules, is incorrigible. They tend to be either young spirits or those who pursue a course of action tied to their recent physical lifetime. They are capable of influencing human subjects, urging them to act contrary to their original intent."

Amelia turns to Michael, listens, then repeats his words.

"Errant spirits are more likely to try to influence a person who is engaged in destructive or negative behaviors. I wish no harm. I know that my status could be affected by my actions and that has helped me stay within the rules."

Our time is almost up. This is my last appointment and I expect Callie and Kenna to stop by. Just as I faintly hear their voices from the waiting room, Amelia turns abruptly to Michael—he is no longer there. A minute later, I hear her sharply admonish him.

"Michael, you are not to leave my presence while we are engaged in conversation."

Amelia repeats his reply for my benefit. I hear no note of repentance in his tone or in his choice of words.

"I will not miss a single opportunity to be close to my daughters."

Michael and I communicate through Amelia for a few more minutes. His presence is obvious to me, distinct and apart from her. I feel a sense of relief—I do not need his appearance through a different receptor as proof; however, I would not pass on that opportunity.

I visit with the girls for awhile, then sit in my office and consider our dilemma. I do want Michael to find a receptor similar to his physical self, but would that make it more difficult for us to accept the limits of our relationship? I expect it would, but I can't help but anticipate the possibility of him appearing to me through a man.

7/25

Michael is next to my chair again today and communicates with me through Amelia.

"I am disappointed and angry. There are few receptors in this entire area. I have found only two in this city. One of them is a man, a homeless alcoholic; the other is a frail, elderly woman in her nineties. I do not wish to use either of them. If you agree, I will request permission to appear through Sally again."

I tell him I am disappointed, but I would choose for him to speak to me through Sally if the only alternative would be no further contact between us. I remember Zachary once said it isn't meant to be easy for spirits to speak through mortals, and I can imagine the havoc if it were a common occurrence, but my mind is not eased. Amelia turns to me and provides some insight into the Council's reasoning.

"I expect it was meant to be a lesson for Michael. He was not misled but merely allowed to go his own way, to discover for himself the futility of trying to connect with you as if he were still in human form. And now, I must leave you."

It is just as well that we are out of time. I would want to press her for more of an explanation of why we were led down this path. I feel betrayed. We were led to believe that it was only a matter of time before Michael would find a receptor. Our hopes were allowed to grow with each passing day. The possibility has been dangled in front of us, then jerked away whenever it was within our grasp. We have anticipated a reunion, of sorts, between a physical man and a physical woman.

It is hours still until dark. I need a change of scene, but the island, with its trees in full leaf, will press in on me, suffocate me. I need to breathe. I drive home, change into my swimsuit and some old denim shorts, then drive twenty minutes up to the lake—miles of shoreline and a seemingly endless expanse of water. Trees are a scarcity, killed off in the years of high water. The marine air is fresh, not stultifying. A light breeze carries the mysteries of the water's depths and the mingled calls of kingfishers and red-wing blackbirds. Against the backdrop of a clear blue sky, vultures glide in the air currents far above, alert for carnage.

I walk along the shoreline, bend to pick up small, polished stones, put the best ones in my pockets. I imagine their origins: chipped from boulders, churned and tumbled in a tumultuous journey, their rough edges worn smooth. I feel like one of them—tossed about at the mercy of unknown forces. When will I be polished?

Michael is not close. Into the vacuum of his absence returns the feeling of betrayal. It infiltrates my mind, attaches to my grief, and demands proof. Why has the Council done this to us? I dwell on my unmet expectations and the idea that we have been misled. I can't shake it off.

It seems I am in the middle of some crazy card game in which every other player can see their cards—mine are laid face down in front of me. The others know the rules of the game—only I do not. I can't even see the other players. In a mixing of metaphors, I see myself as a pawn in a game of chess: moved about at the whims of others, expendable, the first to be sacrificed. My thoughts propel me on a downward spiral.

I feel again the pain of hearing that Michael is dead—the least compensation would be confirmation of his existence. The pain intensifies. I want to pluck it from my heart and cast it away. I want to watch the vultures descend and devour it. But to excise the pain, I would have to take the whole of my heart, cut it from my chest, and fling it, still pulsing and bleeding, onto the rocks. There is no compensation.

I catch myself before I spiral completely out of control. I came here for a fresh perspective, not to be embroiled in this tempest conjured by my mind—which still can't accept there is a realm beyond its understanding. I need a diversion. I kick off my sandals, slip out of my shorts, and feel the bite of the cold water as I swim out as far as a steep drop off. The shock clears my head, and I remember—my mind is not the arbiter of my belief.

I walk awhile to dry off, then find a smooth spot in the sand, warmed by the sun, and sit in a lotus position. I enter into a deep meditation and draw on an inner guidance that knows what reason does not. I am aware of my spirit and, after a time, of her message: *you must rest in what you know.*

I recall my intuitive belief in my spirit when she first spoke to me last October and wish I could immediately interpret my overreaction to every discrepancy as arising from the limited capacity of my mind to understand. I once wrote that the influence of my spirit is ultimately stronger than that of my mind, but I do not make it easy for her. I ask Mahalia's forgiveness.

My surroundings suggest an analogy—my belief to a deep lake, still and serene within its depths, the place of spirit. The surface is vulnerable to the onslaught of heavy weather. When doubts, or dashed expectations, intrude most strongly upon my belief, my mind seeks to prevail, and I find myself sitting in a small boat upon the water. I do not seek refuge in the deepness of my belief, in what I know to be true, but allow myself to be tossed and turned about, at the mercy of the storm.

28. Not One; Not the Other

I AM TAKEN BY SURPRISE TODAY when Amelia tells me there has been a change of plans.

"Michael has finally accepted that he is not going to find a different receptor, and the Council has granted him permission to speak to you directly through Sally. You and he are to have three one-hour meetings, the first one today."

I have to make a quick mental adjustment, not an entirely successful one—this is not how either of us wants to meet.

Michael greets me by name, with quiet emotion. The fullness of my greeting is once or twice removed from that of my desire to speak to him. How do we accept our circumstances? I cannot connect his loving gaze to the man I had known. How different the look on my face must be from the one of pure joy he would have seen if we had met.

I struggle to get beyond the obvious—the body before me is nothing like the one I had longed to touch, to feel surrounding me in pleasure and in comfort. There is a mere suggestion of masculinity, just the other side of gender neutrality. There is nothing of the male heat, pheromones, or virility of Michael so apparent when we were together with our spirits. He is not one; he is not the other.

It becomes somewhat easier. As we move past the barriers that separate us, I gain a greater sense of who he was in life. I can hear him in his voice—it carries a tone, cadence, and inflections similar to those that came through in his letters. I see him in facial expressions and gestures that fit the Michael I knew. I consider closing my eyes to make it easier, but I would miss too much of the man that was. Then my sense that this is Michael speaking to me is threatened by something he says.

"I had wondered, when I anticipated our life together, if you were a good cook. I enjoy watching you now as you prepare a meal, and I can tell that you have a fair amount of skill."

In a split second, I am again aware only of the body before me, only of Sally. Michael's words were so generic as to have no meaning. Why did he not mention a particular meal, the pasta dish I made last night? My mind jumps to con artists and charlatans, to how they speak in generalities. I shake off the doubts, take a deep breath.

When Michael suggests that I will someday move on with my life, that my grief will have an end, I share with him what Amelia told me last week—our relationship has not changed the new destiny that had been set for me twelve years ago. I am not expecting his anger, the grimace that rearranges his facial features, the tightness in his raised voice.

"I do not know the human identity of this man. I do know his spirit. He was my adversary for your affection in two previous lifetimes. I can't stand the thought of him taking my place by your side. I won't have it."

I observe his spontaneous reaction—it is that of a jealous man. I recall Amelia saying that spirits in transition retain their human emotions, and then I hear a softer tone.

"Sweetness, it would be difficult for me to see any other man in your life but most especially my arch rival."

Michael's emotional outburst enhances his reality—anger is easier for me to accept this way than words of love. Then, just as he begins to seem more real to me, it is time to say goodbye.

Our spirits fueled the intensity of our initial experience. It is not something that can be replicated now, hardly hinted at, but it has been a subtle presence, providing the context in which I am able to recognize Michael. The one hour we have been allowed, for all its frustrations, is over too soon.

8/1

I do not expect to meet with Michael today but, as I am wrapping up my session with Sally, I am aware of the scent he used. It is obviously a masculine scent, but I can't help asking if she is using perfume, though I've never known her to. She tells me that she has used no scent, but that she, too, has just noticed one in the room.

I am perplexed and unable to disguise it, disturbed by this over-lapping of Michael and Sally. She leans forward in her chair, and I can tell that the scent is nearer to me than to her, on the side of my chair where I have sensed Michael's presence. I realize now that he is here too, has brought his scent. A moment later, Amelia explains it to me.

"Michael wants me to tell you that he was able to replicate his scent, which is not uncommon when spirits return to this world. He has done it to please you."

I am disconcerted, anything but pleased. Why does he make his scent known in Sally's presence? How could he not anticipate the effect it would have on me? There is no time to express my thoughts. Amelia is telling me she cannot stay, that she came only to convey a message from Michael. She looks in his direction again, then back to me.

"Michael says he is anticipating his next meeting with you, and he will remain close for the rest of the evening."

I look forward to Michael's scent accompanying him. I go to my car, do not notice it there, but I fully expect to be surrounded by it when I walk in my front door. I open it to the usual scents of home, nothing more, but his presence is so strong that I do not dwell on the absence of his scent. He is still close when I go to bed and as I fall asleep.

8/2

I wake to find Michael gone, a distinct emptiness where last night there was its opposite. I am busy with long-neglected yard work all morning, so it is not until a midday rest that I flash back to the scene in my office yesterday. I can focus on only two things—the scent and Sally's physical presence. They are inextricably linked in my mind, which is no surprise. The sense of smell is first registered in the primitive limbic area of the brain, and our reactions are based on emotional associations. To me this scent equals Michael, his letters to me, my love for him. Inserting Sally into that equation distorts it and threatens to destroy my truth.

I begin to torture myself. I see a detailed image of Sally—at a particular store, standing before the display of men's cologne. I see her select the one I know. Then I see her in my office, applying it through some sleight of hand. I flash back to Michael appearing to me through her body and then further back to seeing each of his letters withdrawn from her bag. The implications are devastating. I flash on every possibility, every permutation of the facts as I have known them. Have I been wrong all along?

I remind myself that the scent was simply there in the room, did not emanate from Sally's body, wasn't noticeable until the end of our session, and it was next to my chair where I could sense his presence. These facts make no impression upon me. I rail at unknown forces for allowing the doubts to be triggered. I cry out to them: "Isn't it enough that I have to endure the pain of Michael's death? Why must I be faced with conditions that fuel my doubts?"

I allow this episode to overtake me. I think of how I have talked out loud to Michael when I have known he was close, yet in our conversations he has made no reference to what I have said. I know there are restrictions—he is not allowed to confirm my experience—but I speak from my heart of my deepest feelings and he ignores them.

It is Friday afternoon, no clients to divert my attention. The girls are at the lake with friends. There is no one I can talk this out with, no one who shares my frame of reference. I make no attempt to connect with a spiritual resource. Once again, I place myself in that small boat upon the water—without a paddle—and the winds are fierce. I let myself be tossed and turned about, caught up in a maelstrom of doubt. I do not seek the lifeline that is always here, within my reach. I do not seek to rest in the deepness of my belief.

8/3

My misery of yesterday is not resolved, but I do not let it take hold today. I make a conscious effort to immerse myself in a large project I have contracted with a local agency. It is a change from client work, uses knowledge and skills from when I worked with organizations, with people as they function in groups, a step or two removed from any personal issues they might have. As I research new material in the field, I feel relief to have this external focus. I am lifted out of my angst—or that of anyone else.

I take a break, drive up to the lake and turn off on a dirt road in the opposite direction. I maneuver my small car over deep ruts until I come to rolling hills. This is pure prairie, tall grasses turning from green to burnished gold. I open the car door and am hit by the ubiquitous, aromatic scent of deep lavender monarda, recognizing that it is similar to my scent with its notes of bergamot, jasmine, lavender, and sandalwood. I bite into a minty leaf, then pick some spikes of purple gayfeather to use in dried arrangements and collect tiny seeds from the smiling yellow faces of black-eyed Susans. Then, facing the sun, I do some standing yoga routines, the last one a meditation. I am replenished.

I decide to attempt a challenge that has defeated me these last three years—climb the hills. I try one, not too steep or too tall, but formidable. I make it to the top, go down the other side and up the next hill, then back. My success is heralded by the crystal clear notes of a meadowlark's song as he tilts his head to the heavens from his perch atop an old, weathered fencepost. I stop and listen as he takes an encore, transfixed by its purity.

Exhilarated, I return to my car and drive on to a cluster of choke-cherry trees, their sun-drenched fruit hanging in bunches. I eat from the ripest and juiciest, my fingers staining a blackish purple. I strip handfuls of the pea-sized fruit and listen to their distinctive clatter as they drop into the empty bucket. I anticipate their full-bodied, fruity aroma as they slowly simmer to a thick syrup that will flavor my Greek yogurt for weeks to come.

I am interrupted by the unmistakable warning sound of a rattle-snake, in close proximity. I freeze in my tracks, then look down at it—coiled inches from my feet, rattles still aquiver. One more step and I would have forced him to defend himself. I take a slow step back, then another, and then stoop to pull up my short, lightweight socks. I laugh at the absurdity of it; they offer no protection. I take the dubious precaution of moving on to the next tree, hoping that the rattlesnake was a lone traveler. This is my summer experience of an atavistic return to a time long gone. I will not be denied this pleasure.

8/5

As I wait for Amelia, I can sense the remnants of my emotional tailspin of a few days ago, but it is not she who appears. Hearing Zachary's voice, tinged as it is with emotion and concern, my tur-moil returns full blown.

"Tessa, I know of your recent torment. Some members of the Council are adamant in their belief that it is in your best interests, and Mahalia's, to be given no sign of Michael's presence, only that which you know in your heart and can sense when he is near. They have interfered with his efforts to make you aware of his scent. It is not that they wish to cause you any further pain—their intent is to assist in your growth."

I reply with my now too familiar refrain: understanding is easier than acceptance.

"Amelia is here with me. We entreat you to believe—not in us but in the Creator, and in the greater purpose for which you and others have been approached."

I tell him that I realize the greater importance, and I do, but at a deeper level than where I have allowed this episode to impale me, caught on the sharp tenterhooks of my mind. Zachary shows his understanding of my dilemma.

"You have had to accept, and believe, much more than we had initially intended. Your relationship with Michael, and then his improvement to where a life together was possible, became a barrier to your belief when his death left you with no physical proof. You were tested in many ways before being approached, but it was never our intention that you be tested in this very personal manner."

His answer does little to satisfy me. My logical self persists in wanting to know why—if Michael had achieved remission, allowing us to meet and providing the ultimate proof—I cannot be given some proof now. Why did both, Michael and proof, have to be taken from me?

"Had Michael achieved remission, and the two of you had been allowed to meet, it would have been a gift, one blessed by the Creator."

To recognize it would have been a gift does not bring me the peace I crave. The tension of trying to accept the Council's reasoning combines with the stress of the last six weeks, and I give vent to my accumulated anguish. "All I want is to have Michael take me in his arms and tell me that everything is going to be all right." Knowing that we are the only ones left in the office, I allow myself to give voice to the depth of my pain, a guttural and then higher pitched wail. It is a needed catharsis, this crisis the catalyst. In that one moment is all that I have not been able to express to another person. Amelia comes, looks at me with compassion, and adds her support.

"How may we help you, Child?"

I can only reply: "You cannot give me the one thing I want."

As we continue our conversation, I am more in touch with my spirit and again centered in the depth of my belief. I am comforted by the deep concern shown by Zachary and Amelia, but even more so by how they reference the Creator and a greater purpose—in their authenticity is revealed their truth.

8/12

My second meeting with Michael, and I can't help but speak of my reaction to his scent. He shows his irritation—not so much with me as with the Council, that they would interfere with his efforts. I ask him how he would react if our roles were reversed. What if he had to accept me appearing to him through a male—say, a large bearded man with a deep gravelly voice. What if my scent, the one he was so enamored of, was obvious only in that man's presence?

"I have not considered that possibility, but I know it would be just as difficult for me, if not more so."

It is easier then to move on. I am beginning to hear and see the Michael I knew in the body before me. He tells me of the lessons he learned in the months that his life was extended after I reached out to him.

"My love for you was more complete than any I had known, in this lifetime or in any previous lifetime. It was unconditional. Also, I found forgiveness for my father and for a superior officer in the army whose actions had led to the death of two of my friends. He had reminded me of my father."

Michael speaks to me of his experience of death, of again going to the Light, how it was a familiar journey.

"In my near-death experience, I wasn't told that the reason I needed to return was for the lessons yet to be learned. This time it was made clear to me—because I had now learned those lessons, return was not possible."

My face must betray a wish that it wasn't so.

"Sweetness, please know that, as a man, I would have chosen to achieve remission and come to you, but, when death came and I returned to the spirit world, my desire to be with you was not a factor. The decision to stay or return does not depend on relationships or other desires of this world."

I am aware of wrestling with myself as we talk, caught between conflicting desires. I wish it was Michael, the man, here with me—and I want to accept him this way—to quiet my mind and simply hear him. The first is impossible; the second is nearly so. It becomes easier as we talk of our children, our mutual love for them a bond that bridges the distance between us.

"I have been close to all three of them. Vince's grief is less now. He is focused on medical school and on his life with Tara. Please tell Kenna and Callie that every day, without fail, I give each of them a hug."

Michael says he has been aware of my grief. I don't like to think of him observing me in tears, incessantly blowing my nose, and I express my regret that I can't always bask in the sheer pleasure of his presence. He makes an intriguing comment that I think is his way of giving me a message, some small physical proof. As he speaks of being close to me at home, he deftly slips in a comment about chocolate ice cream and then moves quickly on—he has said more than he should have. He has noticed my indulgence, my coping mechanism, but he is careful to not be too flagrant in his breaking of the rules.

I have just noticed that our time is almost up when Michael refers to the one he calls his adversary.

"I was too quick to react the last time we met. He is a good spirit, and a strong one. In previous lifetimes we have been both friends and brothers. I know you will be happy in the life that lies ahead for you."

In effect, he gives his blessing. I cannot yet imagine a new relationship, but I will call back his words when the time comes. We have swiveled our chairs a little closer and occasionally reach out to touch the other's hand. As we say our goodbyes, we are more accepting of the limitations of our physical contact in this world.

8/15

I return from a morning walk and go to my bedroom, see something on my pillow. I go closer. It is the red stone and the card that Michael took with him. I gasp in dismay. He told me their return would be a sign it was time for each of us to go on with our lives, spiritual or temporal. I quickly calm down and plan to ask Amelia about it later today.

I have only a minute with Amelia. She tells me that Michael's intent was to please me.

"You may think that spirits have a perfect memory but, especially for one in transition, caught between two worlds, it is easy to lose track."

I ask her how he could have taken the objects with him; it seems an impossibility to me.

"It is not unusual for spirits to take items with them when they leave this world, but it requires the strength of a higher status—the process defies explanation. There exists, on the plane of transition, what you might compare to a set of safe-deposit boxes, in which items can be kept until they must be returned."

I have read of loved ones not being able to find a treasured object and then thinking it a miracle when they find it, weeks or months later, in an unexpected, improbable, place. This would explain it.

8/21

I walk every day seeking the serenity of nature, Mahalia's presence, and Michael's. Lately, I more often go to the lake but this evening, when the heat of the day has passed, I drive to the island. It is easier to be here now, to be at one with my surroundings, to know peace.

I reflect on the process of my grief, able now to take a step back and observe its course. It has been a journey within a journey. I have traveled to the depths of longing, the depths of despair, have discovered hidden dimensions to my soul.

I see an image of a physical path—a rocky ascent, beset by obstacles. My path eases, until I stumble into a deep crevasse; it eases again, until I get stuck in the quagmire of my mind; and then back to the beginning to repeat the sequence. I think I have now reached an extended plateau, no more peaks and valleys, the way is easier; my grief has entered a phase of fond reminiscence. And then—just as I am thinking that—I am decimated anew.

Coming toward me on the path is a couple about the same age as us, similar in looks, holding hands. They say polite hellos and must wonder why I ignore them, why the stricken look on my face. I move past them, grasp for some memory to hold on to, but the ones within my reach are anything but comforting. I reach out for an image of Michael's body—it is not his that I see. I reach for the sound of his voice—it is the voice of another that I hear. I reach for the memory of his touch—it is clouded by the body that has been imposed between us. Then the assault escalates—every discrepancy that has ignited the slightest doubt comes tumbling down from whatever high shelf on which I have stored them. I am trampled under their weight as they stampede over my certainty that I know truth.

I am close to the shelter and stop, overwhelmed by this onslaught. I am knocked out, feel it as a blow to my solar plexus. Too upset to sit or meditate, I catch my breath and then make my way to where a faint path of flattened grass leads to the far end of the island. After five minutes of a slow walk, I am calm enough to bring my focus to my body, to feel the strength that is returning to my legs, even to run for half a minute. By the time I reach my destination, I once again feel connected to myself.

I think now that I can meditate, but as I enter into the initial calming stages the feelings return—anger, loss, betrayal. Minutes pass as I hold them in awareness without fighting them or encouraging them. They want to be recognized, and that is enough. I reach a deeper level of meditation and the feelings are gone. More time passes. I reach out to the Light, to the Creator, and pray: *open my heart to thy presence; strengthen me to thy service; sustain me; guide me on the path that is thy desire for me. Renew in me serenity ... truth ... purpose.*

I repeat my prayer, make it my mantra, and then continue in silent meditation, aware now of the spiritual energies that surround me, Michael among them. A short time later, I am aware of an intense white light that lasts for more than a few seconds. I feel an opening of and lifting up within my heart and a distinctive presence—warm and comforting, of the most gentle intensity. I sense a message, so clear that I can easily put it into words: *I am to believe in my own experience and in all that has been revealed to me.*

I do not doubt that I have reached out to the Source, the Creator, the Great Spirit, to God—and I have been answered. I express my gratitude for all that has been given to me: opportunity, knowledge, trust, and faith.

8/22

Today is our final meeting, and I am aware of keeping at bay the incongruity of our circumstances. It is impossible for me, still, to immediately recognize Michael in the body before me. Apart from these meetings, I have such a strong sense of his presence that it now creates a jarring sensation. I proceed on faith.

We talk of the life, the joy, that might have been ours. I have brought with me a dozen photographs of Kenna and Callie through the years. Michael looks at them with love and longing, holds them tenderly. He has seen images of our life as they exist in the spirit world, but the tangible paper snapshots of this world return him to very human emotions.

Michael gives me glimpses of what would have been our future.

"If not for the fluke that caused my death, I would have left the hospital two weeks later and continued my path to remission. We would have met early in September in the place that we had planned, and we would have been married there a few weeks later. We would have built a house in the country, overlooking the lake, and we would have traveled a great deal, always staying in places surrounded by nature."

Hearing his words, I am caught up in an emotional pinball machine. I experience again the angst of learning it was a split second that determined Michael's death, mixed with a deep, penetrating loss for the life we might have had. My emotions collide, ricochet, ping, glance off the edges of my soul, drop down to be hit again. My feelings are short-lived, just a remnant of what I experienced at the time. Michael looks on, with concern but helpless, constrained by the limits of what he can do to comfort me. I take a deep breath and wait for him to speak.

He tells me more about the life we would have led, both of us quite active, our love the key to our strength. I want to give him one pure experience of being the woman he has seen in that future, untouched by grief. I want to ignore the stark reality of our circumstances.

A short time later, I tell Michael that I want to keep his memory alive, even if there is to be another man in my life. When he questions if that would be realistic, I reply, "It is not unusual, especially when there are children involved." I speak spontaneously, as if we had shared a full life and had raised our children together. It is almost the moment that I had wished for, that I could respond to Michael as himself and be the woman he loved.

As we relax into a greater sense of knowing each other, it is obvious that there are insurmountable limits to the expression of our feelings. I tell Michael that the sense I get of him when he is near has made it even more clear to me how completely I would have loved him, would have given myself to him.

Our time is almost up. It has become painfully apparent that further meetings would frustrate us more than satisfy our desires. In our last moments together, we join both hands, gradually let go.

I sit at home now, wishing we could have had even one moment together before Michael's death. I want a memory of his face, his voice, his touch, a physical image I can call to mind in the years ahead. I cannot go to my bed, cannot face being there alone. I lie down on the couch, make an effort to stay in the moment, and soon can feel his presence, warm and comforting, surround me. I think now that I can sleep, as close to being in his arms as I will ever know.

8/23
Michael is not here, must have left while I was sleeping. He said he would now have to devote his time to completing his transition. I will need to be careful to not let myself fall into the dark hole of his absence.

I am distracted by plans to spend a week with my mother and seeing other family. This annual August trip will put some distance between me and all of the memory-provoking places in which I have been close to Michael. It feels as though I will be leaving him, but it may be helpful. I am looking forward to having more concentrated time with Callie and Kenna as we retrace the road trips of their childhood, likely one of the last times in which we will travel together from here to there. It will be difficult, though, to arrive where I had thought Michael would accompany me, to catch my first sight of those I had looked forward to introducing to my love.

8/29
We had a good trip, the three of us, and enjoyed reconnecting with family, but my mother greeted me with no indication that I had suffered a recent loss. When I had some time alone with her, I brought up Michael; she did not acknowledge either his reality or my grief. With no prospect of his imminent arrival, she is now skeptical. She was not blatant about it, but I could read between the lines. I was

disappointed, and hurt, but I can understand her reservations.

I have wondered if it would be helpful to have one last meeting with Michael after he has completed his transition. Will it be more evident, then, that we inhabit different worlds? I will ask if it is possible. He has not been close. His presence had been so obvious and constant that it now seems he has moved out of my home, has packed his bags and left me.

8/30

I am back to work and meet with Sally today. She can now easily go an extended time without contact and is ready to make the shift to weekly appointments. I take this moment of transition to tell her of my meetings with Michael and to thank her for the time taken from her life this last year. When I add it up, it comes to just over twenty hours. She tells me that is nothing compared to the hours I have been available to her for crisis calls and emergency appointments, and says to take whatever time I need.

Amelia comes long enough to say that Michael was given permission to write me a letter using another receptor, the elderly woman. He has made brief visits here, to the physical realm, and the woman's spirit allows him access. Amelia says she will deliver his letter to me later this evening. I ask her why she can't give it to me now, but she refuses to explain.

I sit here in my corner chair where I have been all evening, looking out to the street. I write a bit, but mostly I wait. I look out the large picture window as a hundred cedar waxwings descend as one and briefly inhabit the hedge. I see young children at play on a swing set and can hear older ones, up the street, call out to each other. A man jogs by, two neighbor women visit across a wooden fence, and Charkey patrols his fiefdom.

Two hours, and there has been no knock on the door, no sound of the unmistakable screech of the mailbox since I opened it when

I arrived home. No one has walked up the driveway, clearly visible through the window. It finally occurs to me to check the mailbox. Michael's letter is there.

Dearest Teresa, I have asked Amelia to deliver this to you in the same manner she would deliver your letters to me, by some unseen force. I remember how mystified I was, at first, to discover one in my journal.

Were you aware of my presence after our last meeting? Being so near to you, my longing became unbearable. As I watched you sleep, I was grateful for the time we were given to laugh and talk and cry together. I didn't want to go, but Eli summoned me upon the rising of the sun, and I had to leave you.

As I reflect back upon my human needs, it is even more apparent that I must complete my full transition and leave behind my earthly wants and desires. I am continually expanding my knowledge. When I have completed the current phase, and my spiritual body is stronger, I will again be close to you and my daughters. There is so much I wish I could say to them. Please tell them I have been near only to watch over them, never to judge them. They must grow and learn from their experience, including their mistakes.

My beautiful love, it is several days since I have written. I must finish this and leave it for Amelia—she has been my strongest ally. Sweetness, I pray that you will keep me in your heart as I keep you in mine. Forever and always, Michael

The handwriting is obviously Michael's, but it now has the wavering quality of an elderly, trembling hand, and I am reminded of my grandmother's writing. Having read it once, I absorb its essence, bringing back memories of favorite passages from his letters, of the strong sense they carried of the man who wrote them. I mourn the ordinary memories we might have had. I treasure the extraordinary ones that were ours.

29. Man Becomes Spirit

I WANT TO EXIST OUTSIDE OF time—where I do not have to face this month when we would have met. I imagine the preceding weeks. Michael's tests show he is closer and closer to remission; anticipation is coursing through our veins, impossible to convey in our letters. We meet in the mountains as we had planned. I see the drive there, our first sight of each other, and invite my grief to return full force. It is not our lost past that I mourn—we would have shared these very moments.

I immerse myself in images of our life together, knowing that time will wash over the eight months we shared while Michael was yet in this world. It will mellow and fade the highs and the lows, leave in their place a chiaroscuro print of light and shade. I am not yet ready for that. I need to let myself feel the full force and depth of our experience.

It is easier now for me to be present to my grief, to not be caught unaware in the jaws of the predator, ravaged by its torments, defenseless. I can visit the past for a moment or an hour, be intentionally present as I remember past delights or feel again that all is lost to me—a willing embrace of tears and laughter.

It was a year ago today that Zachary revealed his role and purpose to me. I could not have predicted, then, the amazing journey that lay ahead of me—one in which I would learn of the world of spirit not only from him but from personal experience. I journeyed far into unknown territory, without a map, but I did have a guide.

I once referred to Mahalia's search for Michael as an odyssey—it ended when Amelia told me of our destiny and I reached out to him. I had no idea, then, of the new adventure that would unfold. What started as a quest for knowledge, to being open to Zachary's teaching, segued to a pursuit of love, to reclaim a lost destiny. My final journey has been a search for truth—a truth my spirit has always known.

9/3

Sally's session. In the moment before I expect Amelia, I am surprised to feel the energy that is Michael beside my chair—a welcome reminder to me of the distinct and palpable difference between his presence and his non-presence. Amelia says hello to both of us, then turns and listens before repeating his words.

"I am nearly finished with this part of my transition. A final meeting with you has been approved for after I complete it. I have recently met with Amir, the spirit of Kahlil Gibran. I am greatly impressed with him and have been granted a second meeting. I am honored, for he is within the inner circle, the ten spirits who are closest to the Creator. He expressed interest in our experience and in the significance of his writing to us, and he has given me a message to convey to you when we meet. And now, I must say goodbye."

Michael has changed: his energy is more contained, not attempting to merge with mine; his words are simple statements of fact; and he departs with none of his former reluctance. He has but a single focus, came only to deliver his message. The stark contrast prompts an image—man becomes spirit.

9/8

Michael is back. His arrival is so definite that I don't question it. I am sitting in my chair, engrossed in a novel, when I am engulfed by a dense energy, impossible to ignore. I feel his essence surround me, a stronger energy than before—he has completed the plane of manifestation.

9/11

Michael has been close all afternoon as the girls and I share our recent experience of him. They, too, have had some awareness of his presence. We work side by side to prepare one of their favorite dinners, chicken curry on jasmine rice. The doors and windows are wide open to air that is equal parts sun and earth and the sight of autumn perennials in rich, saturated colors. I savor the earthiness of vegetables from a local garden, breathe deeply the essence of cut peppers and onions, admire the form of a perfect pear and apple. I marvel at the alchemy as their flavors blend with pungent spices.

Michael's presence, the outdoors coming in, the timeless quality of making a family meal, the delightful companionship of my daughters—all combine in a synergy of elemental forces, infused with love. So strong is Michael's presence that, when I reach for plates to set the table, I find myself counting out four of them. He could hardly be more present if he were physically here with us.

9/12

The battle is over. The most rational, logical part of my mind now accepts the truth of Michael and demands his appearance, expects him to show up on my doorstep, to share my bed—last night he did. I was lying there, still awake, when I felt Michael's strong essence. Then, for a long minute, I felt his physical being lying next to me. It was as obvious as any body that has ever lain beside me.

I reflect on my past doubts, the times I would zero in on whatever did not meet my expectations. I would focus with a zoom lens on some isolated part of the whole and be stuck there, could not zoom out and see the larger context. Those doubts most often lasted minutes, not hours, with some notable and painful exceptions. They did not, ultimately, compromise my belief, but they did cloud it. I had to return again and again to my center, to rest in what I know.

9/13

Amelia comes long enough to say that my meeting with Michael will be today. I had already sensed his presence next to my chair. When he takes her place, his eyes immediately tell me that he has achieved a greater peace. We greet each other with more certainty—accepting our limits, we are more secure. I am about to say something when Michael speaks first.

"I have completed three more of the seven stages of transition, including that of manifestation."

As he speaks briefly of each stage, I remember how Zachary and Amelia have described them to me.

The Seven Stages of Transition

Initial Transition: A spirit is welcomed by a pathway of light that helps them break free of all earthly impurities. The spirit becomes lighter and freer as human attitudes and mindsets are left behind—as if the spirit is wearing heavy layers of old coats and one by one they drop off and away. A spirit becomes more aware of their purpose and able to go forward and process what has been learned, including what the next lifetime should offer. The spirit meets, and is embraced by, loved ones from this and previous lifetimes, and then remains in a state of rejuvenating limbo until beckoned onward to the next plane.

However, if the lessons of this lifetime have been largely incomplete, there is a difference in progression. The wandering plane is the destination for those who have taken the life of another, or their own, and also for those who have wasted the lifetime, are in a period of indecision, or simply desire a break. There are various levels and degrees of experience available, depending on the circumstances. A sojourn there is not an easy one, but it is not meant to be a punishment. It is a place to realize where one's actions or attitudes have led and to make a course correction. Its name comes from the process—spirits wander from one resource to another, seeking assistance, and are given whatever is needed to get back on track to a spiritual progression. There is even joy to be found there, in finding one's way.

Renewal: The spiritual energy expended during the lifetime is renewed. It is a longer and more intense experience for those who have suffered greatly during their life, a time for healing and replenishment. Upon completion of the first two planes, a spirit may choose to pursue other tasks in the spirit world before progressing further with their transition.

Learning: A spirit reviews, with assistance from Masters, their completed lifetime: the intended lessons are compared with what was learned; every thought and action is replayed, sorted, and put in order of importance; and a more thorough assessment is made of what the next lifetime should include. Master spirits help the returning spirit to be objective and honest as they decide what is relevant. Not all memories of the lifetime are retained, only those relevant to their spiritual growth and related to their future needs—negative as well as positive memories. The experiences of the recent lifetime are used to further forge and develop a spirit's identity.

Decision: A spirit decides what previously learned material would be valuable to take to the next lifetime and what lessons must be learned in the spirit world before then. Some spirits take a long time between physical lifetimes, either because they need to focus on the lessons of the spirit world or because they prefer to wait (some for the equivalent of several hundred years). This plane must be completed before the next lifetime is taken.

Awareness/Manifestation: Spirits are able to make their presence known in the physical world. This is possible to some extent after completing the first two stages, but now their presence will be stronger and can be maintained for a longer period of time—their ability to do so is related to their status. Some spirits will not complete this plane until they have taken more physical lifetimes.

Reflection/Recollection: Similar to the plane of learning, but this stage includes all previous lifetimes. Relevant material is reviewed, with less emotion but with greater awareness of the effect it had on others. The spirits of the individuals involved may be present to give their perspective, but it is not required. A spirit will gain greater insight during this phase and realize what they might have done differently.

Restoration: After fully processing the material from the most recent lifetime, a spirit transitions to the higher status level they have earned. Spirits are questioned by a number of Masters and Sages; those of higher status may be summoned before the Creator. There is the spirit world equivalent of the granting of awards and honors and a listing of credits, after which a spirit is restored to their full spiritual essence. Upon completion of this stage, a spirit may request a stint as a guardian or as an assistant to Master spirits; younger spirits may request a transfer to the angel realm to be messengers.

Michael explains to me how completing his transition has changed him.

"I have accepted my role in the spirit world and have given up most of my human characteristics. I now speak to you more as the one who was Alexander, with the addition of the pertinent memories of this last lifetime. As important as this lifetime has been, and will always be, as Alexander I had lived many lifetimes and retain experiences from each."

Michael, speaking now from the perspective of Alexander, tells me how he and Mahalia rejoiced at having found each other last October. He is at his most intense with what he says next.

"We have spoken of the doubts that sometimes assail you. Teresa, I want you to know this—it is of the utmost importance that you believe. To not believe in us would be a repudiation of all you have been taught and of the many opportunities opened to us. They were a gift. For you to fail now in your belief would interfere with our being together in future lifetimes. You would lose status and our path ahead would be altered."

I am flooded with relief—I have already battled with my doubts and have reaffirmed my belief. Just as, in my twenties, I could not accept Pascal's wager, I cannot now base my belief in Michael, and in all that I have been told, on the consequences of disbelief.

I have been anticipating Amir's message for me, which Michael has committed to memory.

"I once wrote that we are all toys in the hands of fate when speaking of the cruel blow dealt to my beloved and me. You must think that fate has treated you the same. Do not dwell on that which has been lost to you in this life, but rejoice in what you have shared with your beloved Michael. Take heart that you found each other, if only for a brief interlude. Eternity approaches. You shall not be denied the joy of love or the glory of youth.

Through my living word, I will live in death. Let my
words be a comfort to you and live within your heart."

I do take comfort in Amir's words, and I am deeply honored
to have received a personal message from one within the inner
circle, closest to the Creator. I am especially touched by his reference to "your beloved Michael." There are so few who can speak to
me of him.

As always, our time together is up too soon. This farewell meeting
has had both a greater finality and an easier acceptance. As we say
our goodbyes, the air between us holds the knowledge that we are
bound and encompassed by our eternal love.

9/18

When Amelia comes today, we discuss her changing role. She will
remain in close contact with Sally but has begun to pursue other
assignments in the spirit world, as is typical of most guardians. She
gives me an example of a recent natural disaster in which over a
thousand lives were lost; she was among those spirits who assisted
others with their journey to the spirit world.

"There was a primary window of opportunity that we knew would
close at this time. And now, I have a question for you: what do you
imagine Michael's physical appearance will be when you first see
him in the spirit world?"

I mention what Zachary once told me, that spirits have a vaguely
physical form.

"The appearance of spirits is not at all ghostlike, and we are not
wisps, but neither are we solid. We have the appearance of a physical body, but we lack substance. When you first see Michael, his
appearance will be what was described to you, with brown hair and
eyes and of the same height. Later, you will see his true spiritual
self—his blond hair and blue eyes have been common to most of
his lifetimes, and he is almost as tall as he was in this last lifetime.
Certain aspects of appearance are similar over all lifetimes."

I tell Amelia that descriptions from near-death experiences vary greatly, e.g., those who report seeing Jesus describe widely dissimilar physical features. Some use this as evidence that such experiences exist only within the mind of each individual. She gives me a logical explanation.

"Those returning to the spirit world are meant to see what they expect to see. A spirit will have been greatly influenced by the physical life. It is important that they receive validation of their human experience so that the memories of that lifetime can be processed during their transition."

I ask what more she can tell me about the appearance of spirits.

"Each spirit is surrounded by an aura; with gains in status they become larger and more intense. It is how we recognize each other. No two are so alike that they cannot be told apart. Masters and Sages are immediately recognized to be such by the size and quality of their auras."

Amelia hesitates, then asks if I have questions related to my visit with Michael last week. I ask if she can give me any examples from the life material he processed in his transition.

"As you know, Michael is of fairly high status, but you cannot assume his transition would be an easy one because of it. Still, he found it easier than a young spirit would have, and it took less time. Michael completed his transition in a matter of weeks; younger spirits can require up to several years for the full process."

She pauses a moment, eyes closed, then looks at me.

"I can give you one example. Michael may have spoken to you about Vince's mother, of her inability, or perhaps it was her unwillingness, to embrace the maternal role. He judged her for that, and he took advantage somewhat to demonstrate his greater skill and suitability as a parent. In the stage of reflection, he spent considerable time reviewing how he might have handled that situation differently. First, he had to recognize how his actions and attitudes might have contributed to hers; then, he had to identify what he might have done to assist her. It was he who was in a position to teach and guide her, but he failed to do that."

I ask her if there are other benefits of higher status. Is it rewarding in itself? Amelia looks at me intently as her demeanor takes on both a softer and a more serious aspect.

"It is the goal of all spirits who assume physical lifetimes to strive to become more like the Creator."

I remember now that Zachary said something similar, what seems a very long time ago. Amelia pauses, and then I hear a tone in her voice that I have not heard before. It is a subtle distinction that conveys a strong sense of purpose and anticipation. I see in her eyes a reflection of the truth she knows.

"Promotion in the spirit world is a joyful process that brings one closer to the Creator. Spirits of the highest status are in the inner circle, followed by Sages and Masters, and then others. What you know as the Light is visible to all in the spirit world. As spirits grow in status, they draw ever closer to the Creator, and the Light is of a greater intensity and power. Spirits are aware, during the most arduous moments of their physical lives, that the lessons they are learning will bring them closer to the Creator."

Our time is up and we say our goodbyes, with more finality than usual. The timing of Amelia's next visit is uncertain.

As I walk tonight, I reflect on what Amelia said about a spirit striving to be closer to the Creator and on how Zachary once told me that spirits can become weary and depleted by what happens in a mortal life, by man's inhumanity to man—a spirit will suffer as the human life suffers.

I think of stories of great hardships overcome, how the spirits of those individuals often shine through. Is it their awareness of that closer presence that illuminates their features? I remember how the Light appeared to Sally, Michael's experience of the Light, and my own. I have some sense of that striving, of that desire to come into greater presence.

My thoughts go to what has been conveyed to me of the spirit world and to the role of each individual life. What I was initially told by Zachary left me feeling that all of the blanks had been filled in. Not that I had had a list—and not that I was told all there is to know—but I had been aware of a vague sense of incompleteness that vanished then.

I am flooded now with images of the spirit world that came to me on first meeting Eli. I wrote of it as being a resonance, within which exists purpose, and that the Light illuminates everything and infuses it with love. Adding all I have since learned, I am overwhelmed by the immensity and symmetry of its design—its intricacy and its simplicity.

9/20

I have told two colleagues my story, and I wrote a lengthy account to a friend who is also in this field. All three were open to the truth of my experience and two of them shared their own encounters with the world of spirit. I will be alert now for opportunities to share it with others.

I consider reading our earliest letters—will they bring pain or comfort? I know it will be both, but I retrieve the box that holds them from a shelf in my bedroom. Since Amelia returned them to me, I haven't looked at those I wrote to Michael, the ones he held in his hands. As I read one, then another, the undeniable reality of our experience washes over me. My timing is right—comfort outweighs pain.

My reflections take me to the Greek myth of Eros, the god of love, and Psyche, the personification of the human soul. When they first meet, Psyche is not allowed to see Eros by daylight. She must accept that he is love in its purest form—based solely on her nightly experience of him. Her sisters are suspicious and convince her that Eros must be a monster. Determined to see his face, Psyche takes a candle to his bed. Eros wakes up, sees the distrust in her eyes, and flees. Psyche wanders, forlorn and bereft, until a series of difficult tasks is assigned to her. She is assisted by the gods and is finally reunited with Eros.

I see a similar lesson in my love for Michael, a reason to be denied any absolute proof. In our first weeks together, like Eros and Psyche, we experienced love in its purest form. It is important that I retain the certainty of what I knew then. My belief will be rewarded with the fulfillment of our next destinies together. We have been assisted by angels, not gods from Mt. Olympus, and not to the end we desired, but we were granted as much assistance as was in their power to give.

I write of proof as if I have had none at all, and yet I have. Early on, Zachary knew of the book I was led to at the library, and he later knew what song Michael had been listening to. Amelia mentioned the tall trees before I did, described details from my life twenty years ago, and spoke to Michael in my office before I told her I could sense his presence. Michael knew I had been eating ice cream every night and which flavor. Objects appeared on my bed and a letter in my mailbox. Not one of these—or a number of others—was absolute proof. As a whole, they were convincing, but my mind was always quick to point out the most remote possibility of a lucky guess on their part, a faulty memory on mine, or the involvement of a third party. The appearance of the light sent by Alexander, that star come to earth, was of a higher magnitude—it is my touchstone. My personal experience of the Light, and of other sources of spiritual presence, has also been affirming.

None of these proofs provided what I have wanted—tangible evidence that our lives have intersected. I have yearned for something as solid as Michael's physical body, made known to me by my five senses, not my sixth. To persist in my desire for that absolute proof is the equivalent of Psyche taking her candle to gaze upon Eros.

9/21

Michael has been close some days, absent others. Amelia had mentioned that he would be given a short assignment in this realm. He and other spirits are attempting to influence the leaders of a well-known religious organization, to guide them away from a path that would distance them from the core beliefs. Amelia impressed upon me that the spirit world is always involved in our lives, as individuals and collectively.

I must also move on. I cannot immerse myself in our brief history, make it my life. I have no physical memories of Michael's touch, his smile, his voice. I have no photographs or shared experiences of this world. There is no living being with whom I can share memories of a man we both knew. I have only our letters and my private memories. I fight the urge to live in them. I cannot stay there.

Zachary once said, "Your spirit will endeavor to move your life forward, using your history only to facilitate your growth and encourage your strengths. Your spirit does not choose to dwell on past incidents from your life." Grief does not belong in the same category as dwelling on the past, and I know Mahalia has grieved with me, but she has a perspective on death that I do not, and she knows there are more lessons to be learned before we leave this life. It is time for me to move a few steps forward.

Three months have passed since Michael's death. I do not know what that means, if anything. It is a known quantity, a full season. In a few days I will go to where we would have met for the first time and there say another goodbye. It will not be the end of my grief, which will follow its own course through the next year, or more, of ordinary days, holidays, and the anniversaries that mark our time together. My trip may only signal a shift in its focus and intensity.

9/24

I walk out on the island in the late afternoon, past the shelter to the pond, where willow trees edge the path. A row of turtles sits on a half-submerged log catching the last heat of the sun. I count seven plunks as they drop, one by one, into the water. I tell them I mean them no harm; they could have stayed where they were. I pass by the inlet where a pair of Canadian geese has sheltered all summer, the female with a broken wing, the male at her side. I feel the bond of their devotion.

I continue on, at peace, aware of my surroundings, of my feet connecting to the earth. At the far end of the island, I sit on the bank of the river and meditate. As I reach a deeper level, it comes to me to meditate on love. Time passes. I sit in silence and listen: *Love comes, not from the desire to be loved, but from opening yourself to love, to that which flows from the Creator, and from extending that love to others.*

The slap of a beaver's tail upon the water alerts me: it is growing late. I make my way slowly through the meadow as the setting sun glances off the heads of prairie grasses and the last wildflowers of the season. I pass a doe, her coat turned to bronze, and two fawns, their white spots still faintly visible. I catch sight of a bald eagle just before it flies from its perch high up in a cottonwood tree. I stop and watch it soar.

I am past the meadow, drawing near to the pond, when I am aware of someone walking beside me—it is Michael. I stop, and feel not only his energy but his density, in the form of his physical self, along the entire length of my body. I say hello to him and then walk slowly on—he matches my every step.

I pause to look for the turtles on their log but now see only water bugs, darting on the surface. Opposite the pond, narrow reeds, now a golden brown, ripple in the slightest movement of air, their roots supporting the oozy, mucky ecosystem of the marsh. I hear music— three yellow-headed blackbirds trill their sweet song of nostalgia from the branch tips of a leafless tree.

Michael is still by my side. Overhead, the long, green and yellow fronds of the willow trees create a lacy canopy. The sun sinks to just below the horizon, leaving an aura of red and gold. The air is alive. The entire scene is infused with the ephemeral, mystical quality of twilight time, and then it turns to pure magic. We walk together down the aisle—through the hundreds of fireflies that dance and light our way.

30. Coda: that which completes and ends

MICHAEL'S PRESENCE IS STRONG FROM the time I leave home. The four-hour trip ends when I come to the lodge and turn in to face my first view of the lake. Seeing that it is crowded with people, I continue a few miles down the road to a cabin where I have stayed several times with Kenna and Callie. It has happy memories and a hot tub under the stars.

In the quiet of the evening, I return to the lake. I don't want to avoid this area, a place of spiritual renewal for me, but I need to first spend time here with Michael. This is a journey of intention and purpose before our paths diverge. I get out of my car, walk past the cabins, and am flooded with images of what Michael has described.

In that almost version of our life together, Michael makes our reservations, for a double cabin, and arrives first. He checks us in and comes outside to find me waiting in the spot we had set, a single wooden bench in a circle of pines. We do not run into each other's arms but slowly approach, reach out our hands and join them. We gaze at each other, speak softly, and hear the names that until now have been the whispers of our spirits.

Ordinary conversation is not possible. We embrace, we kiss, we reluctantly draw apart and sit down, embrace again. Our decision is made without any words; we get up and walk the short distance to the cabin. At the door, Michael is a bit formal and asks if I would prefer a room to myself. Of course I say no, and I lightly tease him, that he would think that I might. As we enter the cabin, I catch his eyes in the mirror, back the few steps to where he stands, turn, and rest my head on his chest as his arms enfold me and all formality is dropped.

Tonight, in this painfully real version of our lives, I walk alone around the lake, almost deserted now. Michael is beside me, walking with me—he is here after all.

9/26

I wake up early and drive to a secluded spot beside a murmuring mountain stream. A light mist imparts a mystical quality that is soon mirrored by the deep calm that descends on me as I sit in meditation on an old, weathered tree stump. With my eyes closed, I listen to the soothing water sounds and feel the first warm rays of the sun touch my face.

I have come seeking to be replenished for this journey. I draw energy from the earth, feel it rising up through my body, and then I draw energy from the sun. As these powerful forces converge, I reach out to the Creator and am enveloped by a white light. I am sustained.

This evening, as I make my way through the pines around the lake, Michael's presence is strong. Only one of my senses is aware of him—it is not any of the five that I want to be using.

At the far end of the lake, giant boulders frame the opening to the deep gorge below. A waterfall fills the enclosed space with the energy of millions of negative ions. I pause for a moment to breathe it in, then follow the path to where it opens out to layer upon layer of dark pine-covered slopes, lightly shrouded in an iridescent mist. A water-colorist has touched the reds and blues of the sky, washing them and inviting purple. I know that Michael is aware of the beauty before us. I talk to him. Whatever quality or vibration it is that tells us someone is near and listening, that quality is here. He shifts to the space just behind me. I lean slightly back and can feel his body supporting me, his arms around me.

9/27

Michael is witness to my personal triumph when I climb a mountain, a seven mile trail, more than a mile in elevation. I almost turn back when the path becomes very steep. My heart is pounding, my leg muscles are protesting, screaming at my sudden demands on them. I am afraid I can't do it, but it is easier to go on than to admit defeat. I need to stop every half minute and lean against a tree; if I were to sit down, I would not get up.

I rest for a minute and look with fascination at the bonsai-like junipers. Their stunted growth, gnarled branches, and wizened bark impart a look of the ancient; their roots reach through the smallest cracks in granite rock in search of sustenance. I gaze at them with respect and awe—a meditation.

I reach the peak, elated, the only one here to see the panoramic view of mountains, lakes, plains, and the specks of small towns. The beauty is an experience of my inner self, felt as much as seen. The whistling wind is cooler here, the sun a comforting warm. I am exhilarated, feel physically and mentally strong. I flash back to when it took all my effort to walk upright without falling down—the contrast leaves me feeling I can do anything now.

I find a spot in the sun, out of the wind, as exhilaration and joy mix with peace and contentment. From my backpack, I take some trail mix and a large orange. I share nuts and raisins with the chipmunks that scurry over the rocks, entice them to come closer. I feel the weight of the orange in my hand, its pebbled surface. I dig a finger into the soft peel and release its fragrant oils in a fine spray, apply some to my pulse points. As I savor each juicy section, my body calms and physical awareness is overtaken by spiritual. I sit in meditation, aware now that I am surrounded by gentle currents, so distinctive that I say their names—Michael is closest, then Zachary, Amelia, Jacob, and the strongest among them, Eli. They join in my celebration.

After almost an hour, I begin to make my way down the mountain. Into the stillness of my mind, come the words of an old hymn: "I Know That My Redeemer Lives." It is the closest, in my inner musical repertoire, to a song that speaks resoundingly of belief. I reach the gentler slopes and begin a walking meditation, repeating as my mantra the words I heard almost a year ago: "I am Mahalia. I return often, for the elements to be found here and for the children ... we will walk together."

9/28

I hike again this morning. I am pushing my limits with a second day of climbing, but I can't resist the pull of the mountains, the hit of adrenaline, the heady elixir of endorphins. A misty trail through ferny, shaded valleys changes to barren, rocky slopes; the last short leg to the summit is almost vertical. I make it—and discover a small pool in the embrace of pines and junipers. Michael by my side, I sit on a log to rest. Before I leave, I search for a small, smooth stone. I throw it with care, to gently land in the center of the pool. We watch as the ripples extend to the edge of the universe.

9/29

I will have spent five days and five nights here. Tomorrow, I will be ready to return home; any less time would not have been enough. I need to say a goodbye for every day we would have said hello, to inhabit a moment here for every one in which we would have re-enacted those glorious weeks we first reached out and found each other. Tonight, my walk with Michael is longer, full of conversation.

9/30

On my drive home, from mountains to prairies to river breaks, I am aware of Michael's constant presence. I listen to Wynton Marsalis' "The London Concert," a poignant reflection of our time together, a celebration of our love. Then I crest a hill and my peace is shattered—before me the river winds through miles of familiar landscape, ablaze with fall color. I picture us returning together, anxious to see the girls, still intoxicated with each other. Through my tears, I face reality—never will I return home with Michael.

My corner chair is waiting for me, and a fresh notepad, but I am ready to change the focus of my life. I will now let my grief exist in moments, as it will, sometimes longer, without recording it here. Even as I write those words, I am tempted to continue, to keep our relationship alive in this way, but it is time.

I search for some way to complete these entries, some few words to express all of the joy and sorrow of this past year, the agony and the ecstasy. It is this: for all of the pain and loss, there has been a greater joy. If I were to be told that my memories of Michael would be erased, that I could choose to live this last year over with the same outcome—I would not think twice. I would live it again.

Now I need to put my pencil down. I hesitate ... I do not want to let go ... I pick it up again ... and finally lay it down ....

Conversations with Michael

9/25

I can sense you walking by my side. I have an urge to explain that this is the lake I wrote of months ago—but you have already visited, in your ghostly way; you have seen our life that never was.

I can see us here, first totally absorbed in each other and then expanding our awareness to the beauty around us. I have to restrain myself as I imagine it. To picture it in too much detail would leave me curled up in a ball, still lying on my cabin bed being slowly eviscerated by the pain. I look from a distance and use a filter to mute the images.

Do you mind my tears? To know that you are here with me does not lessen my need for you. We will have five nights. One night, or two, would do little but open the wounds that had begun to heal. I knew they would be made raw and bleeding again, but I need to be here with you.

9/26

Michael, it is easier tonight, just a little. It is so real—my awareness of what we would have shared here—that the pain threatens to destroy me. It was at this point on the trail that I broke down last night. I need to get some control of myself before this couple comes closer; they aren't touching. I think we could not have stood any distance between us.

Do you hear the waterfalls? I stand close to immerse myself in the ion-charged air, the energy similar to what I feel when you are near. That clearing in the pines—is that where our wedding would have been? We would have needed no music besides that of the waterfalls—the largest one the melody, the many small ones a constantly changing harmony—a few notes in a minor key.

Here behind the boulders, where it opens to the valley below, I feel a quiet peace with you. We would have stood in this exact spot and watched the sun setting as it is now, perhaps on this very day. Michael, you astound me with the strength of your presence. You are just behind me now, so solid that, when I lean slightly back, I can feel your support.

It is growing dark. As I climb these steps, your weight is no longer obvious behind me. The serenity of knowing your spiritual presence is overtaken now by the pain of my physical reality. I will never walk with you here.

9/27

Were you with me on the mountain? I know that you were—you rejoiced with me in my triumph. You must have been aware of the others. I am blessed to have so much support from the world that is now yours.

I look across the valley to the distant slopes and wonder if your spiritual self is like the mist that engulfs them, as I feel you engulfing me. I see an image of your spirit blending with the mist, see it composed of the many spirits who have known this place and return to its peace and beauty, help to create it. Do you see how the setting sun tinges the mist with color and lights it from within?

9/28

My sweet Michael—we have tonight and then one more. Do you notice my tears? They are softer, not the deep, wrenching sobs of the last three nights. It is easier now to hold the memory of the life we shared, those eight months when you were yet in this world. In our first weeks of joyous discovery, our experience was its own proof. We did not question what it was; we were simply a part of it. Just as an infant cannot separate its sense of itself from the being of its mother, we could not identify or name all that encompassed us then.

9/29

Our final night here. I have come earlier to have more time with you. I feel at peace—or is it just that I am exhausted, emotionally and physically? No, it is more than that, a deep inner contentment.

Michael, it is here that we would have first known each other, would have found delight in each other. No, the delight would have come later, after we had satisfied our wilder passion, our need to consume and to be consumed by, to merge at some primal level. Then we would have savored a more gentle lovemaking—exploring, teasing, taking sheer delight in that we could see, hear, touch, smell, taste each other. Would we have compared it to our first weeks together? Then, our bodies merged completely, no boundaries to separate us—your touch made more evident by your absence. We knew a synchrony not possible within the limits of the physical body.

I remember vividly the night we were most aware of the presence of our spirits as they led us to another plane and directed our lovemaking. We were mystified at the extent of our response, at the realism of our experience. I long for a physical reenactment of that night—could we have matched it if we had met? I think we could have, Alexander and Mahalia our guides.

Michael, it feels entirely natural to speak to you this way, your presence so obvious at my side, no third party involved. We shared what amounts to a single moment out of all our lifetimes together. Will this one be the highlight? I smile to think it might be, considering we had no physical contact.

A final farewell must touch on the lives of our children. One of my fondest memories of Vince is of him walking into your room saying, "Bonsoir, Papa." I could see him clearly, could hear him in that moment. You said it would not have taken long for our girls to call you Dad, and they would have warmed to you immediately. I started to watch a movie last week, could not continue when I saw the main characters, a woman my age with a son like Vince. I miss him. I am in danger of turning this to tears.

Our experience of the Light—its warmth surrounded us, brought us comfort, strength, and its blessing. The light sent to me by Alexander, that star come to earth, was a message of hope and reassurance. These were experiences of a lifetime. My reaching out to you, our seismic connections and lingering aftershocks, was another. I heard Mahalia's voice, and I knew the presence of Eli, Amelia, and Zachary.

Michael, for all that I have railed at our circumstances, questioned if I could possibly be wrong, I have not once denied the fact of your existence. It would be a denial of my very self, of all that has made me who I am, of every moment that has contributed to how I sense the world about me, relate to others, arrive at my opinions and beliefs.

There are moments in which your truth, and the larger truth in which our love exists, coincide in a confirming synergy. Those singular moments when I meet the sweet innocence of a child, hear music that deeply stirs my soul, observe a client make a life changing self-discovery, when I am struck by the beauty of the world, of life itself.

Were you with me last week when I saw a documentary on the severe drought in Africa, as I watched the faces of the children and their parents? I saw their humanity starkly revealed and felt a connection that crossed the barriers of time and distance. I was aware of Mahalia feeling it with me and informing me—we are all one. In every such moment, I am aware of something greater than myself that enters into me and joins my spirit; it humbles me and connects me to the eternal universe. In every such moment, I am reminded of our love—it is of the same essence.

Michael mine, our brief sojourn here is almost at an end. I will think of you as sometimes out there in the mountain mist. I will see this deep lake as a reflection of the depth of our love. I will hear the waterfalls, the mingling of their voices an echo of our invisible choir. I will remember that mossy clearing under the pines, the last rays of the sun illuminating the wild flowers, and know that there we would have wed. I will remember the promise of our love and the promise of all that is yet to come for us. Together, we learned love's fullest meaning—we will take that knowledge to our next lifetimes. Our spirits will, for all eternity, be enriched by what we have entered into with them.

I am the only one here now in the dark, making my way to the giant boulder near the center of the lake. Are you holding my hand as I walk along the narrow ridge above the water? I will sit here with you and savor these last minutes...

Michael, do you hear the hooting of the owls? Do you see that the lake is a mirror, the slivers of reflected light, the dark shadows of the pines? The soft blanket of your presence envelops me in the stillness...that brightest star is a message for us...it is so quiet...we could be back in an earlier lifetime, alone in the forest, entranced by the mysteries of the night. I feel your spirit surrounding me, merging with mine... .

Epilogue

Sally

After September of 1996, Sally continued with weekly therapy until the full integration of the eight alter personalities. The once teenaged alters, who had matured to her age, bid farewell to their inner world and joined Sally in hers. A touching ceremony marked their transition as each alter stated what she would bring to the one, integrated personality of Sally. The three youngest alters also left that world and remain the inner children that are familiar to all of us— excited to play with kittens or fly a kite.

A short time after the final integration, when her husband had a job transfer to another state, Sally was quick to find new friends and employment. She sought advanced training and was cited in a national journal for her contribution to an innovative procedure. She became more assertive and spoke out as a community advocate.

Sally returned to the area every year or two, and we would sometimes have a chance to visit. Over the years, I have shared with her the information I was given. When I first began to tell my story to others, she signed a release giving me permission to include her involvement in it. Recently, she read my manuscript and said it furthered her acceptance of the part she played in making it possible.

Zachary and Amelia

When I have visited with Sally, Amelia has appeared a number of times and Zachary twice. They are aware of the content of this book, and Amelia said they are pleased with how I have presented their information. They have told me more about the spirit world and our purpose in taking a physical lifetime. It is too much to include in this book—another one is in the planning stages.

John

Two years after Michael's death, I was still frequently aware of his strong presence. Then I became aware of another spirit, one with qualities similar to the Michael I had first known. I was fascinated by how clear it was to me that it was the spirit of a living man. Over a period of several months, I was sometimes aware of a clashing of spiritual energies, a battle of sorts—each was striving for dominance. Michael was always the one to leave; the other one would stay near. I came to know his nature and to recognize his presence.

The next time I saw Amelia, I asked her if this was the spirit of the man who was to be my new destiny. I thought of John, the man I had felt compelled to make an appointment with fifteen years earlier and had seen only once since then, when we passed on the street. Amelia said she could neither confirm nor deny it. I was working on the first rough draft of this book, and she said my new destiny would not transpire until I had completed it. Two weeks after I did, my path crossed with John's at a community event and he asked me out.

A few months later, we began to talk of a future together, and I told him about Michael and how I had been approached. John knew I had been telling others and he was supportive, until he confided in his pastor, who said it could not be true. He then shared the story with one of his business partners, was met with further skepticism, and began to reconsider. He was concerned about the effect it could have on his reputation in the community and thus on his business. He understood that I could not give up the mission that had been entrusted to me, and I understood his dilemma. It was a difficult time for both of us. We grieved together as we took a week to say goodbye, and then another week, and finally made a clean break. Our paths have not crossed since, but his spirit would occasionally be close in the years that followed.

Some years later, Amelia confirmed that it was John who had been my destiny, and she told me of a secondary life. If Michael had lived, he would have met John first, soon after we married, and they would have become close friends, influenced by their past lifetimes as friends or brothers. When Michael was near death, he called John to his bedside, told him he was aware of his interest in me, and asked him to take care of me; eventually, we would have married. John's friendship with Michael would have changed his path, and he would have fully supported and joined in my mission.

Without that secondary life, our destinies took a different course. Amelia said it had been known by the Council that John would have difficulty committing to my purpose. Our relationship was meant to be a test for both of us. Would I choose this mission over John? Would he choose it over his reputation and his way of life? Our destiny did bring us together, in line with the desires of our spirits, but its primary purpose was for both of us to learn from the intersecting of our paths, to be put in a position in which we would each have to make a difficult choice. It was not an easy lesson.

Michael

Our goodbye in September of 1996 was not my last experience of Michael's presence. He was often close in the next two years and was with us at every holiday, a member of the family. He was present at graduations and weddings and was with me ten years ago when I first saw my oldest grandchild, Callie's son, whose middle name is

Michael. He was present recently when I first saw my second grand-child, Kenna's son, who shares the middle name of Michael.

Michael had said that he would watch over us from a distance, but he has often been an obvious, comforting presence. He was distant during the course of my relationship with John and then came close again to help me through the grief of that loss. When I took a wrong turn on a mountain path a few years ago, as darkness was closing in, it was Michael who showed me the way just as I was looking for a protected spot where I could spend the night. When I finally returned to my manuscript, after years of neglect, I was aware of the constant presence of both Michael and Mahalia—they were reliving it with me.

Why a Book Now?

Why not twenty years ago? I did send my first effort to a major pub-lisher, not realizing how rough a draft it was. Then the scope of my life changed and I set my manuscript aside, thinking I might be one of those approached who was meant to reach only a few.

The events of 9/11/2001 (the destruction of the World Trade Center twin towers and two other terrorist acts) were as shocking to me as they were to the rest of the country. I didn't know if they were the catastrophe Zachary had said was coming, but I thought it likely. A year later, he told me it had marked the beginning of the series of events of which he had spoken in 1995. The wars and natural disas-ters in the decade following were also in line with his predictions.

Events in the world have continued to support what I was told over twenty years ago. The effects of climate change, shifts in disease patterns, and some breaking discoveries in science, were all made known to me then. There has been continued unrest in the world and there are many who are searching for meaning. It is time to provide what answers I can by passing on the information that was given to me.

Mission

It took me a while to come to terms with the idea that I was embarking on a mission. I have simply been telling my story. But to recognize the gift of knowledge that has been given to me, and the greater purpose of which it is one part, is to accept that it is both an assignment and a calling.

I began to tell others in the year after Michael's death, starting with several colleagues, close friends, and family. I then contacted acquaintances, and some strangers, who I knew had an interest in spiritual topics, about one hundred people altogether. Reactions have been mixed. Some immediately accepted and wanted to know more about my experience; some were immediately skeptical or completely closed to the idea. The majority were somewhere in between. During most of these conversations, I was aware of the presence of one or several spirits lending their support. This was most apparent when I had a receptive audience—their spirits were drawn close.

I realized early on that my mission is to share what I know—it is not to convince others of its truth. My hope is that each will listen, or read, with an open mind and an open heart, and then consider what I was told in the light of their own beliefs and life experience.

As this book nears completion, I have had some regrets that I told so many in person. This account is more complete and the story builds and folds back on itself in a way that allows for a deeper understanding of it. Readers will have time for reflection, and to integrate their own experience, as they read it. Some will hear its truth and some will doubt. All are likely to question, to consider, and to reflect—in line with the intent of Zachary and Amelia, Eli, the Council, and the Creator.

Acknowledgements

My heart-felt appreciation goes to the many who have listened to my story over the years and to those who have read it. Cherlyn Leach-Valades, Beverly Smith, and Tammy McDaniel read my first draft and responded with encouragement and support. Nancy Sprynczynatyk, Linda Lueders, and Joanna Jones suggested some final refinements.

Twenty years of gratitude, and more, go to my daughters, who have brought their own wisdom to a journey in which we often walked side by side. My oldest grandson, I thank for his patience when he had to take second place to my writing, my youngest for bringing his newborn wonder to our lives.

Finally, my gratitude goes to Sally. To have known her, and each of the personalities who have contributed to the person she is, has enriched my life. She first gave of her time and later asked questions that reflected her own search for truth and aided mine.

Continue Your Journey

with

Answers to frequently asked questions
Blog posts on book content, and more
Excerpts from second book
Comments from readers
Local events and contact information
Questions for self-reflection or discussion
   in book clubs or other group settings

www.tessalynnebook.com

Made in the USA
Las Vegas, NV
14 April 2024

88680735R00164